Accelerated
Schools in
Action

Accelerated Schools in Action

Lessons from the field

Christine Finnan
Edward P. St. John
Jane McCarthy
Simeon P. Slovacek

CORWIN PRESS, INC.
A Sage Publications Company
Thousand Oaks, California

For information address:

Corwin Press, Inc.
A Sage Publications Company
2455 Teller Road
Thousand Oaks, California 91320
E-mail: order@corwin.sagepub.com

SAGE Publications Ltd.
6 Bonhill Street
London EC2A 4PU
United Kingdom

SAGE Publications India Pvt. Ltd.
M-32 Market
Greater Kailash I
New Delhi 110 048 India

Printed in the United States of America

Library of Congress Cataloging-in-Publication Data

Main entry under title:

Accelerated schools in action: Lessons from the field / edited by
   Christine Finnan . . . [et al.].
       p. cm.
   Includes bibliographical references (p.   ) and index.
   ISBN 0-8039-6242-8 (alk. paper). — ISBN 0-8039-6243-6 (pbk.:
alk. paper)
       1. Educational acceleration—United States—Evaluation. 2. Center
for Educational Research at Stanford. Accelerated Schools Project—
Evaluation. 3. School management and organization—United States.
4. School principals—United States. I. Finnan, Christine R.
LB1029.A22A2   1995
371'.04—dc20   95-22651

This book is printed on acid-free paper.

96 97 98 99 10 9 8 7 6 5 4 3 2 1 0

Corwin Press Production Editor: Gillian Dickens
Typesetter: Janelle LeMaster

Contents

PART II
Building Capacity

PART III
The Role of the Principal
in Accelerated Schools

PART IV
Powerful Learning Through Curriculum and Instruction

Preface

Accelerated Schools in Action: Lessons From the Field provides unique insights into one of the nation's largest and most comprehensive school restructuring movements, the Accelerated Schools Project. Since its inception in 1986, the focus of the movement has been on transforming schools with students at risk of dropping out into schools with high expectations of all students. The project is intended to transform school cultures that slow down learning through remediation into cultures that accelerate the learning of all students. This is accomplished, in part, through an internalization of three principles: unity of purpose, empowerment coupled with responsibility, and building on strengths. The project is implemented through a systematic school restructuring process.

This book includes chapters by researchers, Accelerated Schools facilitators, and teachers who have worked extensively in accelerated schools. It provides a voice for the founders of the movement, including Henry M. Levin and staff members at the National Center for the Accelerated Schools Project at Stanford University, as well as other researchers and practitioners from across the country. These multiple voices provide a unique window on restructuring, a window that provides illuminating glimpses for those interested in restructuring efforts in general and the Accelerated Schools Project in particular.

Genesis of *Accelerated Schools in Action*

To understand the origins of this book, consider the decision made in 1989 by the Chevron Corporation to support Professor Levin and a team at Stanford in the development of "satellite centers" (school-university partnerships) in four cities (San Francisco, Los Angeles,

Houston, and New Orleans). This was the first systematic expansion of the project into a national movement. In the spring of 1990, teams from four universities—California State University at Los Angeles, California State University at San Francisco, University of Houston, and University of New Orleans—were trained in the Accelerated Schools process and philosophy, and each soon began to facilitate the process in a pilot school. The four original satellite centers soon began expanding as a means of addressing growing local needs for restructuring, and new satellite centers were added. In response to growing interest in the project across the country and to gain a better understanding of the dynamics of school change, staff at the national center began to refine and develop new approaches to training.

This rapid expansion, coupled with the fact that the process itself was subject to change, made research and evaluation a challenge for all involved. Each of the original satellite center teams designated an individual to take responsibility for designing and conducting an evaluation of the 3-year project at the team's pilot school. A series of national meetings of satellite center teams was conducted so the members of these teams could share their experiences with staff from the national center at Stanford, representatives of the Chevron Corporation, and each other. At a meeting in New Orleans in the fall of 1991, a national evaluation and research cadre was formed as a forum for discussing approaches to research and evaluation.

The problems confronting this cadre were complex. Given the fact that the Accelerated Schools Project was intended to facilitate change, rather than to prescribe change, each satellite center had to develop its own approach to evaluation. Beyond considering test score data, which seemed implicit in the emphasis on accelerating the learning of students in at-risk situations, there was little basis for common approaches to evaluation. Each satellite center, and indeed each pilot school, had developed distinctive action plans based on the challenges they addressed. This led the teams at some of the satellite centers into qualitative and action-oriented approaches to research and evaluation, whereas teams at other centers used systematic approaches that included pretests and posttests with predetermined instruments. The problems confronting the members of the national evaluation and research cadre were varied—and complex. Those who used qualitative and action-research approaches gained insights into local problems, and indeed created valuable local knowledge, but this information was not necessarily in the concise form needed by the national center and

Chevron Corporation to rationalize continued funding. In contrast, those engaged in quantitative approaches found that the scales embedded in the instruments they chose did not always relate to the types of actions taken in the restructuring process at the pilot schools. In the Accelerated Schools Project, schools develop visions, take stock of where they are "here and now," and identify challenges, which become central to their local process of restructuring. The members of the national research and evaluation cadre discovered that different schools identified different challenges and that through the inquiry process, which was used by cadres in schools to address the challenge areas, the schools chose diverse strategies to pilot-test. This diversity made a common approach to establishing criteria for evaluation extremely difficult.

The spring 1992 meeting of the national evaluation and research cadre was held in San Francisco. In addition to developing an approach to responding to the reporting and information needs of the Chevron Corporation and the national center, the members of the cadre began to discuss the need for forums to discuss and share the results of their research and reflections on their experiences as facilitators and evaluators. As an outgrowth of the cadre's work, an American Educational Research Association (AERA) Special Interest Group (SIG) on accelerated schools was created, and an organizational meeting was held in Atlanta at AERA in 1993. Subsequent to the meeting, the SIG put out a national call for papers for the 1994 forum in New Orleans. After the organizing meeting, as the newly elected SIG chair, I wrote a letter to members of the network inviting them to submit proposals and papers for a "research handbook" on accelerated schools. The response to the call for materials was overwhelming. Researchers and practitioners from across the country had conducted studies and written reflective papers that could be used in such a publication. More than 40 papers and proposals were submitted, which not only meant that there was enough material for a book, but that editorial decisions needed to be made. Indeed, many high-quality pieces were eventually left out of this book.

Because of the range of topics proposed by prospective authors, and because the Accelerated Schools Project emphasizes collaborative decision making, I invited other researchers who had been involved in the Accelerated Schools Project to form an editorial team to review the proposals. The editorial team was expanded to include Jane McCarthy, Professor of Curriculum and Instruction at the University of Nevada-Las Vegas, who had been associate director of the Chevron Project;

Christine Finnan, an ethnographic researcher who had conducted a study of an accelerated middle school for the national center and started an Accelerated Schools center in South Carolina; and Simeon P. Slovacek, Professor of Foundations at California State University at Los Angeles who had served as an evaluator for that university's satellite center project. The editorial team met at the 1994 AERA meeting to review and discuss the papers and proposals that had been submitted.

In this editorial meeting, Christine Finnan communicated a clear vision of the book and its purpose. She spoke of the book as providing "voices from the field." This construct enabled members of the editorial team to make collective judgments about submissions. In particular, the editorial team began to focus on themes that emerged from their reviews of the submissions. Thus, by focusing on the "voices" from the field, the members of the editorial team identified a set of themes that guided the selection of papers and communication with publishers. To facilitate this process, Christine Finnan also took responsibility for contacting Corwin Press and organizing a book proposal. Given her crucial role in organizing and facilitating the process, Christine Finnan became the natural choice to be the lead person among the editors. Each member of the editorial team took responsibility for editing a part of the book.

Emergent Themes in the
Accelerated Schools Movement

Our subtitle, "Lessons From the Field," illustrates an important feature of the Accelerated Schools movement: The discourse within the movement about change processes involves an interaction among members of the national center, other Accelerated Schools facilitators, and practitioners. Beginning with early papers and conversations with graduate students, Professor Levin constructed a process that enabled issues others thought were important to emerge. Not only was this inquiry-based approach implicit in the early formulation of the Accelerated Schools Project, but it became an explicit component of the systematic process long before publication of *The Accelerated Schools Resource Guide* (Hopfenberg et al., 1993). This resource guide clearly advocates the use of an inquiry-based approach to restructuring—an approach that enables crucial challenges to emerge from within schools; these challenges then become the focus of action inquiry by cadres within the schools. Similarly, a set of themes emerged from the field in submissions for this book: themes that in a sense represent the challenges currently facing school practitioners and university researchers involved in the Accelerated Schools movement.

Our first theme, Inquiry Into Accelerated Schools, focuses on the crucial role inquiry has come to play in the movement. Although the Accelerated Schools Project provides a systematic process, which is described by Professor Levin in the first chapter, it is also an evolving process that is being modified at the National Center for the Accelerated Schools Project in collaboration with others from across the country who are involved in the movement. The chapters in the first part of the book not only describe the emergence of inquiry as an integral part of the organizational learning process in accelerated schools, but also illustrate how those who contributed to the development of the systematic approach—including Wendy Hopfenberg, Ilse Brunner, and Brenda LeTendre—have used inquiry and reflection in their own experiences as facilitators to develop and refine a strategy for systematic school restructuring. Thus, not only do the chapters in the first part speak to the importance of inquiry at all levels of the Accelerated Schools Project, but they also illustrate how the national center has used an inquiry process to pilot-test and refine its design for a systematic approach to school restructuring. In the concluding reflection, I focus on the role facilitation, inquiry, and reflection take in the Accelerated Schools movement as a whole, as well as in accelerated schools.

Our second theme, Building Capacity, focuses on the ways members of school communities make initial commitments to transform their schools and thus begin to embrace the process of using inquiry to change their schools. These issues are dealt with from three distinct vantages: James W. Kushman and Thomas G. Chenoweth examine the early stage of the process, characterizing it as a "courtship" process, a period when members of the school community discover the meaning of the process for themselves in their schools; Christine Finnan examines how the very notion of "change" held by members of a school community is transformed from being something done to you—that should perhaps be resisted—to something that is "a friend" and can be empowering; and a team of action researchers from the University of New Orleans reflects on how school communities learned the meaning of "unity of purpose" and began to act as "communities of inquiry" capable of fostering change. These chapters illuminate the ways members of school communities come to understand the value of using inquiry in the school transformation process. In her reflection on these chapters, Christine Finnan considers how the capacity-building process creates a climate in which members of a school community engage in inquiry and how the emergence of this capacity fosters the transformation of school culture.

Our third theme, The Role of the Principal in Accelerated Schools, focuses on the ways school leadership changes in the school restructuring process. *The Accelerated Schools Resource Guide* states, "While the principal is commissioned by the district or school board with the ultimate responsibility for the proper running of the school, he or she now *shares* this responsibility and works as a member of a school team" (Hopfenberg et al., 1993, p. 269). The chapters included in Part III investigate how the leadership role changes in schools engaged in the restructuring process. Thomas G. Chenoweth and James W. Kushman describe how the principal's role changes during the initial courtship stage. Betty M. Davidson and I examine how the leadership process changed in four new accelerated schools. The remaining chapters in this part are closely related. Both chapters are extensions of ground-breaking research by Sr. Georgia Christensen (1992) on the changing role of the principal in restructured schools. Christensen describes how principals' actions shape school change in Chapter 9, then Joan Sabrina Mims presents preliminary findings from a replication of Christensen's earlier work. In his concluding reflection, Simeon P. Slovacek discusses the importance of building a better understanding of the principal's role as facilitator of the Accelerated Schools restructuring process.

The final theme, Powerful Learning Through Curriculum and Instruction, focuses on the central aim of accelerated schools, which is to accelerate the learning of all students through the infusion of powerful learning techniques. The chapters in this part include a teacher's reflections on the first year of the process (by Cynthia J. Olivier), an examination of the consonance between the philosophies and processes in accelerated schools and the inclusion process now being used in special education (by Henry M. Levin and Jane McCarthy), the results of one cadre's efforts to improve reading instruction through the use of the inquiry process (by Vicky Gonzalez and Carolyn Tucher), and a study of classroom practices in accelerated schools (by Beth M. Keller and Pilar Soler). In the final reflection, Jane McCarthy focuses on the importance of teacher inquiry aimed at transforming curricular and instructional processes.

Thus, *Accelerated Schools in Action: Lessons From the Field* provides a view of the field through the eyes of facilitators, researchers, and practitioners in the Accelerated Schools movement. The co-editors have worked with the chapter authors to build an understanding of challenges facing practitioners involved in the Accelerated Schools movement. It is hoped that insights that emerge from these chapters will help those engaged in accelerated schools to reflect on their work, as well as provide background on the Accelerated Schools Project both as a systematic approach to school restructuring and as a process of building communities of inquiry within schools.

Edward P. St. John
New Orleans, Louisiana

About the Contributors

Leetta Allen-Haynes is Assistant Professor at Southern University at Baton Rouge. She received her doctorate from the University of New Orleans in 1994. She has done research into new models for school-university partnerships.

Ilse Brunner works with the Missouri Accelerated Schools Center at the University of Missouri at St. Louis. She received her PhD from Stanford University in 1991 in Sociology of Education. Her current professional interest is in organizational learning.

Thomas G. Chenoweth is Associate Professor at Portland State University. He received his doctorate from Stanford University in 1984. A former public school principal and teacher, he is interested in school change, instructional supervision, and problem-based learning.

Georgia Christensen, FSPA, is currently Team Leader of the Zimbabwe Catholic Education Staff Development Team. She received her PhD in education from Stanford University in 1995. Her research interests are in the area of staff development, with a specific concentration on the development of school administrators.

Betty M. Davidson is Research Associate and Site Trainer for the Louisiana Accelerated Schools Satellite Center and Adjunct Assistant Professor at the University of New Orleans. She received a PhD in educational administration from the University of New Orleans in 1992. She is interested in school restructuring and teachers as change agents.

Christine Finnan is the Director of the South Carolina Accelerated Schools Center located at the University/College of Charleston. She received her doctorate in education and anthropology from Stanford University in 1980. She is interested in studying the dynamics of school culture change.

Vicky Gonzalez is a primary school teacher in the Redwood City Elementary School District. She received her BA in anthropology from the University of California, Santa Barbara. She is interested in bilingual and multicultural education.

Wendy Hopfenberg is Associate Director of the National Center for the Accelerated Schools Project, Stanford University. She received a Master's in Public Policy from the John F. Kennedy School of Government, Harvard University, in 1987. Her recent professional interests are in school, district, and organizational change.

Beth M. Keller is Assistant Director of Communications for the National Center for the Accelerated Schools Project, Stanford University. She received a bachelor of arts in public policy/journalism from Duke University in 1986. Her primary research interest revolves around powerful learning—how much involvement with accelerated schools influences curriculum and instructional practices.

James W. Kushman is Research Associate at Northwest Regional Educational Laboratory in Portland, Oregon. He received a PhD in organizational behavior from Claremont Graduate School in 1990. He is interested in the change process and how students view their learning and school experience.

Brenda LeTendre is a consultant to the Missouri Accelerated Schools Project. She received an EdD from Stanford University in 1989. She is interested in strategies for building the capacity of school communities to solve problems.

Henry M. Levin is the David Jacks Professor of Higher Education and Economics at Stanford University. He is also Director of the Center for Educational Research at Stanford (CERAS). He received the PhD in economics from Rutgers University in 1966. Dr. Levin's recent work focuses on developing systems to better meet the educational needs of all children.

Jane McCarthy is Associate Professor of Education and Director of the Accelerated Schools Project at the University of Nevada-Las Vegas. She received an EdD from the University of Houston in 1978. She is interested in effective teaching strategies for at-risk children.

James Meza, Jr., is Associate Professor at the University of New Orleans and is Director of the Louisiana Accelerated Schools Satellite Center. He received a doctorate of education from the University of New Orleans in 1981. He is interested in school restructuring and statewide educational reform initiatives.

Joan Sabrina Mims is Director of the Los Angeles Accelerated Schools Project and is an Associate Professor in the School of Education at California State University, Los Angeles. Dr. Mims received a joint doctorate from Claremont Graduate School/San Diego State University in 1988. She is interested in bilingual and multicultural education.

Cynthia J. Olivier is a teacher at J. W. Faulk Elementary School in Lafayette, Louisiana. She received her Masters' of Education from the University of South Western Louisiana in 1992. She is pursuing a doctorate and is interested in the effects of socioeconomic status on education.

Simeon P. Slovacek is Professor and Chair of the Division of Educational Foundations and Interdivisional Studies at California State University, Los Angeles. He received a PhD in educational research and evaluation methodology from Cornell University in 1976. He is interested in evaluation of the Accelerated Schools Project and instructional technology.

Pilar Soler has been working with the Accelerated Schools project since its inception in 1986. Most recently she has been the Assistant Director of Training and Development at the National Center for the Accelerated Schools Project. She has a master's degree in public health. She is interested in training and the development of powerful learning experiences.

Edward P. St. John is Professor of Educational Leadership at the University of New Orleans. He received an EdD from the Harvard Graduate School of Education in 1978. His research has focused on higher education policy and finance. He is also interested in school-university partnerships and school restructuring.

Carolyn Tucher is Educational Consultant for the National Center for the Accelerated Schools Project working with the San Jose Unified School District initiative. She is a former president of the Palo Alto School Board. A graduate of the University of Colorado, she has done additional research at the Harvard Graduate School of Education.

Acknowledgments

We extend special thanks to the many dedicated people in accelerated schools across the country who are the reason the Accelerated Schools Project is making a difference for children. We want to thank all of the authors for capturing the voices of these people. The chapters provide a rich description of places and people that allow us to feel like we have gained an additional set of colleagues. Special thanks are also extended to Dr. Barnett Berry for his insightful and thought-provoking review of the book. We are also indebted to Dr. Henry Levin for his support of our work with the Accelerated Schools Project and his support for this book.

PART I

Inquiry Into
Accelerated Schools

INTRODUCTION
Edward P. St. John

The National Center for the Accelerated Schools Project, in conjunction with a national network of satellite centers, state networks, and trainers, has developed a systematic approach to school restructuring that is being used in hundreds of schools across the United States. The systematic approach has evolved over the past decade through the dynamic process of first, conceptualizing problems facing schools and envisioning practices that schools could use to address those problems; then, field-testing those ideas with a set of pilot schools; and finally, reflecting on these experiences to develop new facilitative practices to further enable school communities to engage in these transformational processes. Thus, the Accelerated Schools systematic approach has evolved through learning processes that have used action inquiry. In the process, the founders of the movement have come to discover for themselves the crucial roles facilitation, reflection, and inquiry play in the restructuring process. The chapters in Part I provide the readers with a window on this dynamic process.

In the first chapter, Henry M. Levin describes the Accelerated Schools philosophy and process, how the vision for the movement has evolved over its first decade, and the role his own research and inquiry has played in framing the movement. This chapter provides insight into how Professor Levin became interested in the school change process, as well as how his academic work on schools took a more activist turn in the 1980s.

In the second chapter, "Growth and Learning: Big Wheels and Little Wheels Interacting," Brunner and Hopfenberg examine their experience with pilot-testing the inquiry process in an accelerated middle school. They describe inquiry as a systematic process and show how as a result of working with teachers in a middle school on the inquiry process, they discovered that inquiry had spin-offs in the actions taken by teachers. As the result of this experience, they have conceptualized the inquiry process as "big wheels" (systematic inquiry) and "little wheels" (teacher action inquiry) interacting with each other in a dynamic process of school change. Thus, they provide the original conceptualization of inquiry in accelerated schools as a multilevel process.

In the third chapter, "Accelerated Schools as Learning Organizations: The Revitalization of Pioneer Schools," Brunner and LeTendre describe and reflect on their experiences introducing the inquiry process to some of the schools that began the Accelerated Schools process before the inquiry process was formulated. The authors document how a team with representation from the national center (Ilse Brunner), Illinois (Ann Heelen), and Missouri (Brenda LeTendre) collaborated on the design and implementation of a new training process. The chapter reflects the importance of revitalization to the Accelerated Schools movement. Given that the process will probably continue to evolve, there may be a growing need to revitalize schools in the future. Thus, Chapter 3 provides a further window on the dynamic nature of the Accelerated Schools movement.

In the reflection that concludes this part, the theme "Inquiry Into Accelerated Schools" is reexamined. On one level, this part documents the integration of the inquiry process into the systematic approach to restructuring used in accelerated schools. On another, the authors speak to the importance of facilitation, reflection, and inquiry at all levels of the Accelerated Schools process, from the actions of teachers who use inquiry to find better ways to empower their students, to the actions of those in the national center, satellite centers, and Accelerated Schools networks as they continue to experiment with new approaches to facilitating the Accelerated Schools restructuring process.

✍ 1

Accelerated Schools

The Background

HENRY M. LEVIN

A ccelerated schools are dedicated to bringing all students into the academic mainstream by providing highly enriched educational experiences for all children. This notion of viewing all children as deserving of and benefiting from the same approach that had been reserved exclusively for those who were labeled gifted and talented was certainly a strange perspective a decade ago when the Accelerated Schools Project was launched. At that time, the standard fare for children in at-risk situations was to immerse them in remedial experiences that emphasized basic skills and repetitive drills in a simplified curriculum. The result was that the longer they attended school, the farther they lagged behind the mainstream in their academic development. My colleagues and I suggested that these children, their parents, and the staffs of their schools had strengths that could be used to accelerate the educational progress of at-risk students to make them academically able at an early age.

Often I am asked how the ideas for the accelerated school arose. Usually, the questioner expects an inspired story about a moving experience or great event catalyzing this drastic replacement of conventional practices. The listener is usually disappointed to learn that the idea had a long and slow gestation. Indeed, after almost a decade of application, it is still evolving, growing, and developing, even as it has reached over 700 schools with almost 400,000 students in 37 states.

The purpose of this chapter is to provide a bit of the early background for the Accelerated Schools Project and link it to its present status. In the first part, I briefly set out some of the developments in my own career that led to the Accelerated Schools Project. In the second part, I provide a brief picture of the early features of the project and its evolution. In the final part, I suggest some future directions that are being explored and pursued.

Early Stirrings

I was trained as an economist, receiving my PhD in 1966. Prior to my graduate training, I had worked for a large specialty store as an executive trainee and section manager. I left this work in 1961 to become a student once again, inspired by the possibilities and dreams of John F. Kennedy's social revolution of the sixties. While working on my thesis in the area of government finance, I served as an instructor of economics for a year at Rutgers University and for an additional year on the research staff of the Mayor's (Robert Wagner) Temporary Commission on New York City's Finances estimating the economic impact of New York City's sales tax. With a freshly minted PhD, I arrived in June 1966 at the Brookings Institution in Washington, D.C., as a research associate in economic studies to work in a new area called social economics, which involved education, health, public assistance, and training. This was the Washington, D.C., of the Great Society in which Lyndon Johnson and an activist administration had promised an end to poverty through government action. Although the ugly war in Southeast Asia had suddenly become visible with the Gulf of Tonkin resolution some months before, the war in Vietnam was receiving only a distant, second billing in the shadow of the more prominent war on poverty. I am sad to say it would not be long before the two were reversed in importance.

At Brookings, I chose to work in a new field called the economics of education. To learn more about the field, I took a job as a long-term substitute in a Black, inner-city, junior high school teaching social studies for half of the day. The other half day was spent reading documents, interviewing experts, and trying to formulate a research project. Fortunately, the Coleman report (Coleman et al., 1966) had just been published when I arrived in Washington, so this gave me a point of departure as well as an enormous data set to work with. My 2 years at Brookings were active ones in which Sam Bowles (then in the Department of Economics at Harvard) and I published the first serious critique of the Coleman report (Bowles & Levin, 1968a, 1968b) and in which I used Coleman data to study the quality and supply of teachers in urban areas (Levin, 1968b). My work on the Coleman report also linked me to a number of relatively young and dynamic researchers and social commentators at the Harvard Seminar on Equality of Educational Opportunity, including Marshall (Mike) Smith, Barbara Heyns, Herb Gintis, Sandy Jencks, Pat Moynihan, Ted Sizer, Nate Glazer, David Cohen, and Eric Hanushek. I also managed to get involved in the movement to turn over control of urban schools to their communities, a movement launched in the frustration with the glacial pace of desegregation a decade after the Supreme Court decision in *Brown v. Board of Education* (1954). Ken Haskins of the Adams-Morgan Community School in Washington served as my mentor. This work ultimately led to a Brookings conference on the subject and the publication of a book on *Community Control of Schools* (Levin, 1970a).

But by 1967, the war of destruction in Asia had begun to preoccupy Washington and its institutions, with rising divisiveness and a diversion of funds from the domestic to the military agenda. In late 1967, my work on the Coleman report and some new analyses of the data had generated sufficient notoriety that I began to receive offers from distinguished universities. At the same time, I had joined the opposition to the war in Southeast Asia, a commitment that was not received warmly at Brookings or inside the Beltway. The pull of academia on top of the push of a bellicose Washington was too much. By the end of 1967, I had decided to join the School of Education faculty at Stanford University with a joint appointment in economics to begin in the summer of 1968.

My arrival at Stanford was tumultuous. The antiwar movement and antidraft movement had just taken hold there, and mounting student and faculty protests at Stanford's involvement in the war were soon to be joined by indiscriminate bombardments of tear gas to quell the crowds, attacking participants and observers alike. With three children and a failing marriage, I was preoccupied with a combination of domestic and academic tasks and had little time for protests. At Stanford, I was expected to teach classes in educational finance and the economics of education and to continue my research on teacher markets, cost-effectiveness analysis (1970b), educational effectiveness (1970c), community control of schools (1970a), and educational vouchers (1968b). With the Nixon administration obsessed more with victory in Vietnam than with the inner cities and Appalachia, the action in education shifted to the states. Of particular importance was the legal challenge that states were violating their constitutions and those of the federal government by basing school financing on local property tax wealth so that richer communities often had lower tax rates even as they provided their children with higher expenditure schools than poorer communities (Coons, Clune, & Sugarman, 1970). I had the opportunity to get involved in the first research supporting these challenges, ultimately resulting in the publication of a book on the subject (Guthrie, Kleindorfer, Levin, & Stout, 1971). In addition, I was able to get involved in the Mission Coalition, an attempt by academics and community organizations in the Latino district of San Francisco to overcome poverty in that neighborhood. My first marriage had failed, and I met my present wife at this time. As a Latina, she sharpened my sensitivities to the challenges of the Latino community and a new culture into which my two youngest children were born.

Along with my colleague Martin Carnoy, who had also come from Brookings, and others (e.g., Bowles & Gintis, 1976), I began to focus on the difficulties of getting successful school reforms, particularly for children from poor and minority families. To the degree that schools prepared students for authoritarian and hierarchical workplaces, we argued that the schools must also be hierarchical and authoritarian and reproduce the inequalities of the workplace (Carnoy & Levin, 1976). Logically, then, we should explore the forms of and strategies for attaining workplace democracy if we are to achieve democratic schools, a quest that led to a study of democratic workplaces. Some 20 years before the current rage for the topic, my colleagues and I were studying the use of work teams, self-managed workplaces, and worker cooperatives (Jackall & Levin, 1984; Levin, 1974, 1976) and a new perspective on the possibility of democratic schools (Carnoy & Levin, 1985).

In the latter book, we placed the school within a democratic and capitalist state in which two dynamics struggled for control of public institutions. The democratic dynamic pushed for expansion of citizen rights and benefits through legislation, courts, and popular movements; the capitalist dynamic pushed for expansion of capital and the rights of property, including the reproduction of labor in appropriate quantities and with appropriate skills and attitudes for the capitalist workplace. In this respect, schools had characteristics of both the democratic and the capitalist dynamic and were viewed as a site of ongoing struggle between the two forces. Thus, schools are authoritarian, hierarchical, and unequal in their treatment of students, mirroring some of the same conditions that adults face in the workplace. But students and teachers have more rights than workers in capitalist institutions, and the inequalities are considerably less.

Although females and males are roughly equal in school attainments—with differences in participation going in both directions—women do far more poorly in the workplace than do men. The fact is that in the struggle between the capitalist and the democratic dynamic, schools are more democratic in participation and more equitable in outcomes than workplaces even though they share patterns of inequality with the workplace. Carnoy and I (1985) found that the major democratic gains in schooling came about through social movements that extended far beyond the school, such as the women's movement. Accordingly, we concluded that broad social movements more generally are also the best strategies to gain educational participation and rights for the poor and minorities in the schools (Carnoy & Levin, 1985). This was a lesson that still holds prospects for the extension and broadening of accelerated school ideals to all children.

Origins of Accelerated Schools

During the 1978-1984 period, I became deeply immersed in issues of educational finance, law, organizations, and governance as the director of a nationally funded R&D center at Stanford, the Institute for Research on Educational Finance and Governance. Although I continued to do work on cost-effectiveness analysis, educational vouchers, and educational finance, my concerns turned once again to the needs of disadvantaged students. I was struck by the absence of mention of these students in the rash of reports in the early eighties that called for national school reforms. Most of these reports, such as *A Nation at Risk* (National Commission on Excellence in Education, 1983), addressed the educational status of secondary school students in academic tracks, particularly the decline in their test scores over the previous two decades and their poor test scores compared with those of students in other countries (National Commission on Excellence in Education, 1983). Although these reports called for more required courses and more demanding courses in high school, they said nothing about students who dropped out because they found the present regimen too difficult or simply opted for a nonacademic course of study.

Two hypotheses came to mind. One possibility was that we had won the war on poverty, but no one had noticed. The other possibility was that we had accepted a clandestine truce in that war. My curiosity won out, and I decided to turn my attentions once again to the so-called educationally disadvantaged student to find out what had happened. I began by studying issues of definition and demography and proceeded to educational practices and outcomes for these students and their continuation into adult life. In short, I found that (a) by almost any definition, the numbers of educationally disadvantaged students had risen because of rising poverty rates among children, increasing minorities and immigrants, and rising numbers of children in families under stress; (b) these students enter school without many of the developmental skills and behaviors that schools value, they get farther and farther behind academically the longer they are in school, and they have a better than 50% chance of dropping out; and (c) their poor educational foundation leads to low productivity, poor employment prospects, costly involvement in the systems of criminal justice and welfare, and the spawning of another generation of disadvantaged. By 1984, I completed the first of several reports on this subject that were published subsequently (Levin, 1985, 1986), but by this time I had also become curious about solutions.

Why hadn't we made more progress over the 20 years of Title I and Chapter I and all of the other categorical programs? What about the exemplary programs diffused by the National Diffusion Network, under sponsorship of the U.S. Department of Education because they had been "shown" to demonstrate success? What did recent research say about school effectiveness for educationally disadvantaged or at-risk students? How did teachers, other school staff, parents, and students view their schools? And for a naive outsider (myself), what does one observe in these schools that leads to success or failure? During the 1985-1986 academic year I was obsessed with finding answers to these questions. I read considerable research; pursued sites of projects of the National Diffusion Network; visited and observed numerous schools and classrooms; and interviewed school staff, students, and parents at sites around the country.

There were many surprises. First, many of the usual criticisms of the schools seemed patently absurd. I saw few teachers who did not arrive early and leave late carrying an armful work to complete at home. Many school staff members attended meetings in the evenings and weekends to prepare for major school events. The pace of work was continuous and challenging, with many external disruptions and the need to respond to the diverse needs of students from many different cultures and backgrounds. Interviews with teachers confirmed to me their obvious insights and great desires to succeed, as well as their frustrations with the failures of conventional school practices. Most of the classrooms were stifling in the obsession with low-level basic skills and repetitious drill and practice. Calls to projects of the National Diffusion Network brought additional, discouraging insights. Many that had been listed only a few years before no longer existed at their original sites. Even those that continued in operation were unable to provide longitudinal evaluations of their effectiveness. Some of the projects seemed promising, but they were piecemeal at best, focusing on a particular subject or instructional technique rather than on schoolwide reform.

Worst of all was the notion of remediation. *Webster's New Collegiate Dictionary* (1979) offers as one definition for the adjective *remedial*: "concerned with the correction of faulty study habits and the raising of a pupil's general competence" (p. 970). Interestingly, there is no verb *remediate*, even though the term is commonly used in the educational literature as a transitive verb. The *Webster's New Collegiate Dictionary* (1979) describes *remediation* as the "act or process of remedying" where *remedy* is defined as "treatment that relieves or cures a disease" or "something that corrects or counteracts an evil" (p. 970). Presumably, children who are put into remedial programs are children who arrive at school with "defects" in their development that require repair of their educational diseases, evils, or faults. But the school repair shop is peculiar because children are never repaired. Rather, they remain in the repair shop for their entire education, whether it is labeled as Chapter I, LD (learning disability), or any of the many categorical labels. This, in itself, convinced me that programs that slow down the pacing of the curriculum and reduce its depth, emphasize drill and practice, proscribe meaningful applications and problem solving, and ignore or derogate the experiences and culture of the child will have a predictable effect in stunting the educational development of that child. Although educational remediation was designed with the best of intentions, one must judge it by its results. Once in the repair shop, children are treated as permanently damaged goods and view themselves in that way for the rest of their educational careers.

The obvious solution seemed to be to do the opposite. If children arrive at school without the skills that schools expect, slowing down their development through remediation will get them farther behind. If all the young are ultimately to enter successfully the academic mainstream, we must accelerate their growth and development, not retard it. This notion was further reinforced by the fact that the only educational stimulation and excitement that I saw in schools with high concentrations of at-risk students was in the few classrooms characterized as "gifted and talented" or "enrichment." In these classes, students were identified according to their strengths and provided with educational activities and projects that built on those strengths. Instead of being stigmatized with labels such as "slow learner," they were celebrated for their talents. And learning was palpable in those classrooms, as these highly valued and stimulated students were continually motivated and challenged to think, reflect, create, and master.

By the late spring of 1986, I had written a 6-page, single-spaced memo calling for accelerated schools for at-risk students, which was adapted as a short article in *Educational Leadership* in March 1987 (Levin, 1987b). The idea was to create a school that would accelerate the development of all of its students by building on their strengths rather than searching for and "remediating" their weaknesses. However, the ideas in themselves would not carry the day, being opposed to the conventional wisdom and practices on the subject of educating at-risk students. To succeed, we would have to transform profoundly the culture of the school, a task that some (e.g., Sarason, 1982) thought was not possible. I asked my colleague Larry Cuban to assist me during the summer of 1986 to find pilot schools in two San Francisco Bay Area school districts that might work with us to implement the ideas, schools with high concentrations of children in at-risk situations. At the same time, I gathered a group of interested graduate students to help search out sources on accelerated education and to prepare to work with these schools.

By the fall of 1986, we had located two schools that had been nominated by their school superintendents for consideration as accelerated schools. In both schools, more than 80% of the students qualified for free or subsidized lunches, an indicator of poverty. But there the schools departed considerably in their characteristics. The smaller school, which I will call Alpha, had only about 350 students comprising about 30% Hispanic; 27% African American; 24% Chinese American; and about 19% Other, including those of Filipino and Pacific Island backgrounds, Native Americans, and Anglos (less than 10%). About one third of the students were drawn from the local neighborhood, and two thirds were bused to achieve racial balance in compliance with a districtwide court mandate. Many of the students from the local neighborhood lived in a public housing project that had a notorious reputation for drugs and violence.

The other school (I will call it Beta) was about twice as large, with Hispanics accounting for over 90% of its enrollment, mostly children of recent Mexican immigrants from rural villages. Both schools shared high student turnover and very low student achievement, whether assessed by standardized test scores or direct evaluation of written work and discourse both inside and outside of the classroom. Neither school had much evidence of parent participation, and even teacher conferences and major school events attracted relatively sparse attendance. Disruptive incidents were frequent in both schools, with a constant stream of students headed to the school office for discipline.

Each school was assigned a team of three or four doctoral students from Stanford who spent 1 or 2 days a week at the school observing classrooms and school events and interviewing teachers, support staff, parents, and students. Within a few weeks, our teams were viewed as part of the schools, with many invitations given to team members to observe lessons and visit classes. During this period, we provided written accounts of the ideas underlying accelerated schools to all staff and made short presentations at staff meetings. We made it clear that we would not move forward unless the school voted to make a 5-year commitment to the project. That commitment came in February 1987 for Alpha and at the end of the school year for Beta; both staffs voted unanimously to adopt the accelerated schools philosophy and practices.

We then initiated a process in the two schools that was a crude precursor of our present approach. We did extensive work on vision and then chose priorities to receive initial attention. These priorities became the basis for establishing cadres and a steering committee, which included representatives of the cadres as well as members-at-large from support staff and parents. By this time, our three principles of unity of purpose, empowerment with responsibility, and building on strengths had been developed, so we worked these into the process (Levin, 1987c). At each school, the process was somewhat different. For example, under the guidance of Brenda LeTendre, Alpha worked heavily on group process and meeting management to avoid some of the disruptive problems of the past. Under the guidance of Bob Polkinghorn and John Rogers, Beta worked at using a Deweyan-inspired process of inquiry to address its challenges. In both schools, cadres addressed parental involvement, student behavior, school organization, and student learning, with an emphasis on language at Beta.

At this point, we had not developed either the extensive taking stock or the powerful learning components of the project. Progress was slow initially. Both schools had a range of teachers, from highly talented ones using constructivist approaches to large numbers who used more traditional teacher-centered lessons buttressed by a heavy emphasis on classroom discipline and drill exercises. But as they began to work together, we saw discussions leading to the creation of thematic units both within and among grades that combined all of the subjects and extended them into field trips and school events. With strong principal support, parents came in increasing numbers to Alpha as parent volunteers and participants in all school events. Beta's parental involvement revolved primarily around major school events rather than parent volunteers, with greater diffidence about working in the school shown by parents who had gone to rural schools in Mexico. Disciplinary problems plummeted as both schools adopted a more consistent approach using praise, role modeling, and a uniform set of values as well as developing a more supportive school climate. Most teachers, but not all, began to look for strengths in all students and to share their successes in the informal conversations at lunchtime, yard duty, and prior to meetings. Student attendance began to improve, and teacher morale rose considerably. The quality of student work began to rise, slowly at first as reflected in student projects and writing. Because of the well-known limitations in the standardized test scores, they were not the prime focus for assessment. Nevertheless, as a by-product of the process, test scores began to rise by the third year.

By this time, Beta's principal had been transferred to another position and replaced with a new principal who lacked background in and insights into accelerated schools. Unfortunately, the new principal refused to participate in training workshops. (Since then, we have been confronted with other districts that have not taken the specific nature of accelerated schools into consideration in assigning principals, a factor that has been instrumental in generating our recent work on transforming entire school districts rather than just individual schools. This situation has also generated an extensive effort on our part in trying to understand the roles and requirements of effective principals for accelerated schools; see Christensen, 1994.)

For every hour spent in the schools by the Stanford teams, there were many hours devoted to trouble shooting, problem solving, development of training exercises, and meetings on strategy. The two teams met regularly to share both results and challenges and to solve new problems that had arisen. Although staff members at both schools were enthusiastic about the ideas behind accelerated schools, they resisted changes in their daily practices in the initial stages. In many cases, excellent decision processes and wonderful solutions lost out to the comforts of tradition and a preference for cosmetic changes. All of these experiences in the two school settings honed (and sometimes dulled) our own skills, but also inspired us with possibilities as we saw children formerly relegated to remedial classes taking on advanced work and enrichment activities and prospering academically. We learned that real change is not smooth and continuous, but proceeds in fits and starts and must necessarily address tension and conflict rather than avoiding them. Teaming, mutual support, and solidarity can only succeed when past conflicts, divisiveness, and isolation are overcome. As time went by in the two schools, more and more of the learning experiences drew upon the cultures and experiences of the students and engaged them in real-world activities, projects, and research endeavors.

By 1988, publicity on the project through publications (Levin 1987b, 1987c, 1988b, 1988d) and word of mouth had generated interest in other states and school districts. With our assistance, the state of Missouri launched five accelerated schools in the autumn of 1988. The state of Illinois received a grant and launched some 25 accelerated schools in 1989. We recommended beginning with only a few schools and building a strong training and support component, but Illinois officials plunged in with much larger numbers and without the provisions for training and support, a situation that took almost 5 years to remedy. By 1989, we had begun to establish systematic plans for expansion that included extension of the project to middle schools, planning and initiation of regional satellite centers, and the development of a training model that incorporated all that we had learned. And in 1990 we launched our first middle school, the first four satellite centers, and the first systematic training workshops for school coaches and teams incorporating the complete philosophical approach, principles, and process of accelerated schools including governance, inquiry, and powerful learning.

Present Status

The Accelerated Schools Project is a 30-year experiment in creating a learning community. It is not a completed work, but a project that is always coming into being through continuous trial and error, theory and practice, inspiration and hard work. Acceleration necessitates the remaking of the school in order to advance the academic and social development of *all* children, including those in at-risk situations. This has meant creating a school in which all children are viewed as capable of benefiting from a rich instructional experience rather than relegating some to a watered-down one. It means a school that creates powerful learning situations for all children, integrating curriculum, instructional strategies, and context (climate and organization) rather than providing piecemeal changes limited to periodic changes in textbooks, training, and instructional packages. It means a school whose culture is transformed internally (Finnan, 1994) to encompass the needs of all students through creating stimulating educational experiences that build on their identities and strengths.

Such transformation is neither simple nor swift. Schools are provided with training and follow-up as part of a systematic process (Hopfenberg et al., 1993). The training and follow-up activities require the participation of the full school staff, parents, and students (*Accelerated Schools Newsletter,* 1994), who are empowered to make informed decisions through the Accelerated Schools governance and inquiry process to transform the school. A coach is trained to work with the school using constructivist activities that engage the members of the school community in problem-solving experiences that lead to a sequence of major activities that the school undertakes over subsequent months. The focus is on the school internalizing the Accelerated Schools philosophy and values through constructivist activities and school processes that lead to school change and the transformation of school culture (Finnan, 1994). Ultimately, these emerge in a school governance and decision-making process that focuses on the creation of powerful learning situations for all children. The details can be found in *The Accelerated Schools Resource Guide* (Hopfenberg et al., 1993). Through a particular governance structure and an inquiry approach to decision making, the school addresses its major problem areas in a way that creates powerful learning throughout the school.

Over the 8½ years since the initiation of the two pilot schools, the Accelerated Schools Project has expanded considerably in the number of schools, coaches, and regional centers and in the depth and sophistication of the transformation process. In 1994-1995, the project encompassed over 700 elementary and middle schools in 37 states. Some 200 coaches have been trained and are being mentored by the national center through communication, site visits, and retreats. In addition, 10 regional centers have been established to work with schools and co-train coaches with the national center. The project includes an active research and development initiative to explore the restructuring of school districts so that they can more fully support the Accelerated Schools philosophy and practices. Over the years, we have found that the typical cost of Accelerated Schools transformation has been about $30 to $40 per student, less than 1% of the per-student budget in the initial years, and declining in subsequent years as the coach is no longer needed on a weekly basis.

Evaluations of accelerated schools have shown substantial gains in student achievement and attendance, full inclusion of special needs children in the mainstream, increased parental participation, and growing numbers of students meeting traditional gifted and talented criteria (see, e.g., the summary in Wong, 1994). These evaluations have also shown reductions in the numbers of students repeating grades, student suspensions, and school vandalism (see, e.g., Chase & Levin, 1994; English, 1992; Knight & Stallings, 1994; McCarthy & Still, 1993). The evaluations include multiyear assessments comparing accelerated schools with control schools (Knight & Stallings, 1994; McCarthy & Still, 1993).

Accelerated Schools Principles and Values

The Accelerated Schools Project is not just a collection of programs or an attempt to put together a school through piecemeal accumulation of different policies and practices. It is a set of practices based upon a coherent philosophy and principles. The goal is to bring all students into a meaningful educational mainstream, to create for all children the dream school we would want for our own children. This is the guiding sentiment for the transformation of an accelerated school, one that is embodied in its three central principles: (a) unity of purpose, (b) empowerment with responsibility, and (c) building on strengths.

Unity of Purpose. Unity of purpose refers to the common purpose and practices of the school on behalf of all pupils. Traditional schools separate children according to abilities, learning challenges, and other distinctions; staff are divided according to narrow teaching, support, or administrative functions; and parents are usually relegated to marginal roles in the education of their children. Accelerated schools forge a unity of purpose around the education of all students and all members of the school community, a living vision and culture of working

together on behalf of all of the children. Strict separation of either teaching or learning roles works against this unity and results in different
expectations for different groups of children. Accelerated schools formulate and work toward high expectations for all children through
daily practice, not slogans, and children internalize these high expectations for themselves.

Empowerment With Responsibility. Empowerment with responsibility refers to who makes the educational decisions and takes responsibility for their consequences. Traditional schools rely on higher
authorities at school district and state levels, as well as textbooks and
instructional packages formulated by publishers far removed from
schools. Staff at the school site have little discretionary power over curriculum and instructional practices, and students and parents have almost no meaningful input into school decisions. This powerlessness
leads to a feeling of exclusion from any ability to influence the major
dimensions of school life.

In an accelerated school, school staff, parents, and students take
responsibility for the major decisions that determine educational
outcomes—all constituents participate in school life. The school is no
longer a place in which roles, responsibilities, practices, and curriculum
content are determined by forces beyond the control of its members. In
its daily operations, the school community hones its unity of purpose
through making and implementing the decisions that determine its destiny. At the same time, the school takes responsibility for the consequences of its decisions through continuous assessment and accountability, holding as its ultimate purpose its vision of what the school will
become. This result is accomplished through a parsimonious, but highly
effective, system of governance and problem solving that ensures participation of students, staff, and parents in the daily life of the school.

Building on Strengths. Traditionally, schools have been far more assiduous about identifying the weaknesses of their students than looking
for their strengths. A focus on weakness or deficiencies leads naturally
to organizational and instructional practices in which children are
tracked according to common deficiencies. The logic is that "lower"
groups cannot keep up with a curricular pace appropriate for "higher"
groups. Accelerated schools begin by identifying strengths of participants and building on those strengths to overcome areas of weakness.

In this respect, all students are treated as gifted and talented students, because the gifts and talents of each child are sought out and recognized. Such strengths are used as a basis for providing enrichment and acceleration. As soon as one recognizes that all students have strengths and weaknesses, a simple stratification of students no longer makes sense. Strengths include not only the various areas of intelligence identified by Gardner (1983), but also areas of interest, curiosity, motivation, and knowledge that grow out of the culture, experiences, and personalities of all children. Learning themes can be chosen in which children show interest and curiosity and in which reciprocal teaching, cooperative learning, peer and cross-age tutoring, and individual and group projects can highlight the unique talents of each child in classroom and school activities. These group processes and the use of specialized staff enable recognition and building on the particular strengths and contributions of each child with assistance provided in areas of need within the context of meaningful academic work.

Accelerated schools evoke the participation of all children in the activities of the school, validating the children's strengths and addressing their areas of special need. This is accomplished by employing classroom and schoolwide curricular approaches based on inclusion of every child in the central life of the school. This can be done by multiability grouping and multi-age grouping, and by recognizing that all children have different profiles of strengths that can be used to complement each other and create strong teams that provide internal reinforcement among students. The process of building on strengths is not limited to students. Accelerated schools build on the strengths of parents, teachers, other school staff, and the community. Parents can be powerful allies if they are placed in productive roles and provided with the skills to work with their own children. Teachers bring gifts of insight, intuition, and organizational acumen to the instructional process that often go untapped by the mechanical curricula typical of remedial programs. Through acknowledgment of the strengths found among participants within the entire school community, all of the participants can be expected to contribute to success.

Values and Learning

Accelerated schools acknowledge a set of values that permeates relationships and activities. These include the school as a center of expertise, equity, community, risk taking, experimentation, reflection, participation, trust, and communication. The focus is on the inner power, vision, capabilities, and solidarity of the school community. Especially important are such values as equity—the view that the school has an obligation to all children to create for them the dream school that any of us would want for our own children. Such a school must treat children equitably and must address equitable participation and outcomes. The school is viewed as an overall community rather than as a building with many separate communities represented, although the cultures and experiences of different students are acknowledged and incorporated into the school experience. Addressing the needs of all children requires experimentation, risk taking, reflection, trust, and communication. The concept of unity of purpose is a linchpin for all of the values and practices of the school.

The three principles and nine values of Accelerated Schools are all embedded in a process of change and school practices that lead to the creation of powerful learning situations (Hopfenberg et al., 1993, chaps. 6-9). A powerful learning situation is one that incorporates changes in school organization, climate, curriculum, and instructional strategies to build on the strengths of students, staff, and community to create optimal learning results. What is unique about this approach is that changes are not piecemeal, but integrated around all aspects of the learning situation. This contrasts sharply with the usual attempts to transform schools through idiosyncratic reforms involving the ad hoc adoption of different curriculum packages, instructional practices, or organizational changes to address each perceived problem that the school faces. Over time, some of these are pruned and others are added, without any attempt to integrate them into an overall philosophy and vision of the school. Powerful learning builds on the strengths of all community members and empowers them to be proactive learners by developing skills through intrinsically challenging activities that require both group work and individual endeavor.

Accelerated schools also emphasize the connections between the big wheels of the school and the little ones. "Big wheels" are the overall school philosophy and change process that are shared collaboratively by all members of the school community. "Little wheels" are the informal innovations that grow out of participation by individuals or small groups in embracing the school's philosophy and change process. These little wheels result from the internalization of the school philosophy and change process in the belief system of school members, resulting in changes in their individual decisions and commitments in classrooms and in individual and group interactions (see Chapters 2 and 14). The three guiding principles of the Accelerated Schools Project, the underlying values, the focus on powerful learning, and the links between big wheels and little wheels provide an integrative setting in which all activities are connected.

Getting There

Accelerated schools are created through working together under the guidance of a coach who is trained and mentored at the National Center for the Accelerated Schools Project or one of the regional centers. Coaches are drawn from school districts, state education agencies, and universities and participate in periodic retreats to share what they have learned and to work on new challenges. All teaching and learning is cast within a constructivist framework in which case studies and real-world situations are posed as problems to solve. By exploring the nooks and crannies of those situations and posing the problem in different ways, testing hypotheses on why the problem exists, brainstorming on alternative solutions, and simulating and testing solutions, the participants—coaches, teachers, other school staff, students, and parents—experience an understanding that builds knowledge and creativity. Coaches work with their schools at least one day a week during the first year or so, and less frequently in subsequent years as school community members internalize Accelerated Schools processes and values.

The accelerated school is largely a self-governing community that has established a system of governance that enables decision making over its own destiny. The process that is used requires intense scrutiny of both practices and results, problem solving, and the sharing of information with the larger community. All staff members, parent representatives, and student representatives are expected to participate in decisions. The school community initiates its empowerment by taking stock of its resources, activities, teaching and learning processes, students, community, and other dimensions (Hopfenberg et al., 1993, pp. 60-73). All members of the school community are involved in taking stock, from identifying which dimensions of the school to investigate to setting out the questions that must be answered and the methods for answering them. Data are gathered using these methods and analyzed by taking stock committees devoted to particular school dimensions. Analysis of the data and reflection provide the ingredients of a schoolwide report to which everyone contributes. Especially central is the search for school and community strengths and resources as well as challenges. The school ultimately builds on these strengths to overcome its challenges.

When the taking stock process is completed, the school has developed a baseline of information and brought the school community together around a common understanding and enhanced familiarity through working together. This is followed by establishing a vision for the future that the school will be dedicated to (Hopfenberg et al., 1993, pp. 74-81). All participants work in groups to design a dream school that would be worthy of their own children, a learning community with a high level of professional development for staff and active engagement of parents. Students are asked to participate in the design of their dream school, incorporating the concepts in academic work through essays, interviews, artistic renderings, comparisons of different perspectives, and so on. Although the vision may be summarized by a vision statement, it is the system of goals, beliefs, and shared practices that arise from the months of working together that truly constitute the vision. The words of the vision statement are only a reminder. This hard work and its resulting inspiration and excitement are celebrated with a community-wide vision celebration that launches the next stage.

At this point, the school compares its baseline data from taking stock and its vision and compiles a list of differences between the two. To get from baseline to vision requires substantial changes in the school. These necessary challenges are listed and clustered according to major areas. Through extensive discourse, the school community chooses a few priority challenges to begin to work on initially (Hopfenberg et al., 1993, pp. 82-85). Given the salience of these priorities, there is no difficulty in obtaining participation from all staff, parent, and student representatives to choose one of the areas to work on. These self-selected groups are called cadres and are responsible for carrying out the most intensive analysis in their particular priority areas. Typically, there are three to five cadres per school, depending upon the size of the school community. Cadres may focus on priorities from school organization and resources to parental involvement to curriculum areas.

In addition to cadres, there are two other levels in the governance structure of the school (Hopfenberg et al., 1993, pp. 86-94). A steering committee comprises representatives from each cadre along with the principal and at-large representatives from teachers, support staff, parents, teachers, and the larger school community. The steering committee is responsible for coordination of activities, distribution of information, monitoring the progress of cadres, and refining the recommendations of the cadre for submission to the school as a whole (SAW). The SAW is the primary decision-making body and includes all staff, parents, and student representatives as well as other members of the school community. Cadres are expected to meet weekly, the steering committee meets biweekly, and the SAW on an as-needed basis. Announcements of minutes and agendas are provided in advance for the entire school, and minutes are made available in a timely fashion to enhance discussion and communication.

The entire school is trained in both group dynamics and meeting management (Hopfenberg et al., 1993, chap. 5) as well as in group problem solving (Hopfenberg et al., 1993, chap. 4). Problem solving follows an inquiry method in which cadres and committees take sufficient time to define and understand the challenges that they are addressing, followed by generating hypotheses on the causes of the problem. Hypotheses are tested by gathering information through surveys, interviews, school records, and observations—that is, the cadres learn how to do research and continually hone their research skills. Those hypotheses that are confirmed are used as a basis for brainstorming for solutions, with a search for solutions both within the school community from those with expertise and successful experience and outside the community to find what others have done. The cadre formulates an action plan that is pilot-tested, revised if necessary, and submitted for approval to the steering committee and the SAW. The plan includes the details and logistical requirements for implementation as well as an assessment framework; the plan must include answers to the question of how the school will know if it has succeeded in solving the challenge, and thus, an assessment plan must be set out in advance. Based on the assessment results, the school community may wish to modify the intervention or continue it intact while undertaking a new challenge.

When schools have adopted this process, they use it to create powerful learning situations for all students and across the entire school. It is common to enter an accelerated school and see students engaged in research projects, artistic endeavors, schoolwide themes that build on all areas of learning, and community activities. The walls are covered with student work in many forms, including essays, poetry, artwork, and ingenious solutions for the "problem of the week." Many rooms are alive with musical performances and theater, and monolingual students are becoming bilingual, just as bilingual students are practicing both languages in conversation, writing, and reading. Parents are in evidence everywhere, tutoring individual students, assisting teachers in preparing materials for a new activity, leading students in song, and meeting together to assist school staff in launching a new special event. Cadres of teachers, school staff, parents, students, and community representatives work together on how to solve the problem of inadequate resources. A room is being prepared for in-service training of all staff on how to help students generate and test hypotheses. A bulletin board displays minutes of recent cadre and steering committee meetings and agendas of upcoming meetings. It also displays the recommendations of the steering committee that will be presented at the next meeting of the school as a whole. Another part of the bulletin board shows the names of students who were "caught in the act" of doing something good for the school, such as tutoring, helping staff, assisting at cleanup, sharing ideas or supplies, raising funds for school activities, volunteering to participate in visits to the local convalescent hospital, collecting items for a food drive for the homeless, excellent attendance, and so on. Although only 3 months of the school year have elapsed, over half of the students are already represented, and almost one third have multiple citations. Accelerated schools are busy places, truly learning communities.

And this is our vision for the future—that *all* children have the opportunities to participate in schools like these whether they are called accelerated schools or not. In fact, our greatest success will be if this approach becomes so highly accepted in U.S. education that it does not need a label, but is the standard approach to educating children. In the meantime, we are pushing for a movement that recognizes the gifts and talents in all children, indeed, in all parents and school staff, and enlists these to enrich the educational experiences of the young. To do this, we must continue to improve our understanding and practices for getting school change and the public policies that provide the resources and climate to support such changes.

A main source of growth for the entire Accelerated Schools movement is the knowledge gained at local sites, by coaches, and by satellite center staff. This knowledge needs to be shared and reflected upon widely for its implications, usefulness, and applicability to school transformation. That direction is a major goal of this volume. What have we learned about buying in, about the interactions between big wheels and little wheels, about school change, about inquiry, about innovative practices, about teacher perspectives, about principals' roles, and so on? How can these lessons be used to stimulate insights into our own practices and new lessons that can be shared with others? We see this as a continuous process of learning, reflection, application, and improvement, a never-ending cycle. In this spirit, we see these lessons as markers on a longer journey, ones that others may find helpful as they follow the accelerated path, but that also stimulate new departures, to be documented in future publications.

℘2

Growth and Learning

Big Wheels and Little Wheels Interacting

ILSE BRUNNER
WENDY HOPFENBERG

The most exhilarating part of our work in the Accelerated Schools Project is our active collaboration at school sites. It is inspiring to see how previously isolated stakeholders in a school come together to form a community of learners by taking ownership of their school's situation through the Accelerated Schools process. As we work intensively in the schools, we have become intrigued by our observations of the transformation process coming to life. By observing this process closely, we have abstracted a growth and learning pattern that we labeled "big wheels and little wheels interacting." Using this concept, we have carefully analyzed several experiences over time to illustrate the interaction of individual and large-group change processes that produce learning and long-term changes within the whole school community. After sharing this concept with others, we have found that it helped all participants in the Accelerated Schools movement make sense of the tremendous magnitude of simultaneous, interactive, and long-term

AUTHORS' NOTE: Another version of this chapter was presented under the name "The Interactive Production of Knowledge in Accelerated Schools" as part of the symposium Collaborative Change in Accelerated Schools: Big Wheels and Little Wheels Interacting, at the annual meeting of the American Educational Research Association, San Francisco, California, April 21-24, 1992. The initial paper includes two full case studies (the Family Involvement and the Instruction cadres).

changes occurring at accelerated school sites. We also find this concept helpful in explaining the interactive nature between design and implementation—how we incorporate our collaborative learning experiences back into the model.

In this chapter, we analyze the pattern of "big wheels" and "little wheels" interacting in particular case settings. We begin by briefly describing the evolution of the Accelerated Schools model and defining big wheels and little wheels. The concept of big wheels and little wheels applies to each and every part of the Accelerated Schools philosophy and process. It applies to the philosophy in general as well as each specific part of the process—taking stock, forging a vision, setting priorities, forming governance structures, and using the inquiry process. Although it applies to all parts of the model equally, we have chosen to use the inquiry process to exemplify this interaction. We conclude by analyzing the interaction of big wheels and little wheels and showing how a school's use of the accelerated schools process can influence the overall Accelerated Schools model.

The Growth Pattern of Big Wheels
and Little Wheels Interacting

The Accelerated Schools Project began in 1986 as a philosophy about creating accelerated schools (Levin, 1987b). Since then, our collective experience working in partnership with a variety of schools across the country has contributed to the constant evolution of our model—from a philosophy of acceleration to the full philosophy *and* process described in Chapter 1.

As the model has evolved, we have also refined our strategies for transmitting it to schools. At first, we shared the model implicitly, through modeling and working together with schools, even offering solutions in the areas of curriculum and instruction. Now we are very explicit in the way we *initially* share the model with school communities. After initial training, we provide systematic follow-up at each school site, using a Socratic questioning approach to build the capacity of the school community to internalize the Accelerated Schools philosophy and process and become self-sufficient and *self-renewing* organizations.

As more schools have joined the movement, the Accelerated Schools model has continued to evolve. This evolution is driven by an interactive learning process involving the Accelerated Schools Project staff,[1] who develop, refine, and transmit the model, and the practitioners,[2] who actually use the model to transform their school communities. The collaborative ongoing experience of the Accelerated Schools Project staff with school communities implementing the model creates a natural and ongoing set of experiences for continued learning and growth. Instead of telling schools what to do and how they should operate, the Accelerated Schools Project staff have taken a set of ideas about how to transform schools and collaboratively worked to implement them at school sites. These interactive experiences merge the model and its implementation so that the developers/transmitters of the model immerse themselves in its practice and the practitioners contribute to its design.

Over years of working in partnership with schools to implement the model, we have observed an interaction and growth pattern at school sites. We have noticed that there seem to be "big wheels" and "little wheels" interacting that push a school's transformation process forward. We define big wheels as the formal, explicit components of the state-of-the-art Accelerated Schools model that are collaboratively bought into by all participants. The big wheels encompass the Accelerated Schools philosophy and process. In terms of our philosophy, the big wheel components include our overall goal of creating for all children the kinds of schools we would want for our own children; the three principles of unity of purpose, empowerment coupled with responsibility, and building on strengths; and a theory about what creates powerful learning. In terms of the process, the big wheel components include taking stock, forging a shared vision, setting priorities, creating governance structures, and using the inquiry process.

For school communities, the big wheels involve collaboratively engaging in bringing the model to life—transforming their school communities using the Accelerated Schools philosophy and process. The engagement in the big wheel components brings about long-term change in schools. For example, a school's cadre, or working group, created to understand and address the priority challenge area of family involvement will eventually develop and institutionalize strategies that allow families to be partners in the education of their children. The outcomes of these big wheel efforts will be long term in nature and unique for each accelerated school site.

Little wheels are the informal innovations initiated by individuals or small groups as a result of participating in the big wheel experiences. Little wheels are the spin-offs of the public and collaborative big wheel activities. We have observed that when individuals are immersed in the big wheel components, they are inspired to take risks to try something they believe will bring their learning community nearer to its vision.

In the school communities, little wheels occur as small, creative experiments by teachers, parents, students, support staff, and administrators. For example, in one school a teacher became so inspired by the all-inclusive process of creating an ambitious vision for the school community that he reconsidered his teaching approach with his so-called remedial students and decided to use the same stimulating and sophisticated techniques and materials he used with his "higher" classes in his "remedial" class as well. Within a few weeks, he reported excellent results and his own personal growth at a school as a whole (SAW) meeting.

Little wheel innovations are crucial to the Accelerated Schools model for at least four reasons. First, because big wheel processes take time and produce institutionalized changes over the long run, little wheel innovations give participants an outlet for making some immediate changes, thereby meeting the natural inclination we all share for wanting to see change happen quickly. This benefits the individual(s) making the change as well as the students and others involved. Second, little wheel innovations give all members of the school community an opportunity to take responsibility for making improvements and changes in their daily activities. It is important for everyone involved in the Accelerated Schools movement to search continuously for ways to reach a shared vision as part of everyday activities. Third, at times pressing situations occur in schools that require immediate action. Finally, sometimes little wheel activities are so effective and powerful that they interact with and influence the big wheels. In an accelerated school, this interaction plays out as a schoolwide change supported by everyone.

There are many examples of big wheels and little wheels interacting to produce long-term change. In the example of the teacher above, his own risk taking (along with that of others and a look at the research) gave the school the impetus to totally eliminate tracking. This example of big wheels and little wheels interacting is easy to understand. However, the overall interaction between big wheels and little wheels is quite complex, embracing public and private transformations, large and long-term processes and small innovations, the radical transformation of entrenched structures and behaviors, and invisible changes in the thinking and feeling of individuals. It also involves formal and informal communication between the producers/transmitters of the model and members of the school communities who implement the model, bringing it to life in different concrete situations. Finally, the interaction is played out in the cross-fertilization between the model and its implementation, and the concepts and the experiences it creates.

This multilayered interaction may best be illustrated through a case study that shows how different actors in the Accelerated Schools movement come together as a community of learners and collaboratively produce knowledge that brings them nearer to a shared vision of the *best* schools they can create for children.

Big Wheels and Little Wheels Interact— Sparking Excitement, Innovation, and Knowledge Production: A Case Study

In their first year, all accelerated schools go through a transformation process that consists of an initial launch training on the philosophy and process, taking stock, forging a schoolwide vision, setting priorities, forming governance structures, and beginning to use the inquiry process. Little wheels can spin off of every part of the Accelerated Schools process, but we have chosen to illustrate this interaction through the example of the inquiry process because this process is ongoing in schools and continuously produces systematic changes over the years. Further, inquiry explicitly builds on the creativity and experience of the school community, providing a fertile ground for both whole-school changes and individual initiatives.

The case is drawn from an inner-city middle school in California with a predominantly poor, minority population.[3] At the time of the case study, the school was in its third year in the program. The school had completed the processes of taking stock, forging a vision, setting priorities, and creating governance structures. Five cadres had been created to address the priority challenge areas: Curriculum, Culture, Family Involvement, School Interactions, and Instruction. Each of these cadres, made up of teachers, parents, staff, and student members, used the inquiry process to problem-solve and find lasting solutions to their challenges. The version of the inquiry process used at the time is shown in Figure 2.1.

The case documents an Instruction Cadre's inquiry into an extremely broad challenge area. Using the inquiry process (a big wheel), the cadre collaboratively researches, experiments, and self-assesses

The Inquiry Process

1. Focus in on the Challenge Area

- explore the problem informally
- hypothesize why challenge area exists
- test your hypotheses
- interpret results of testing and come up with a focus area

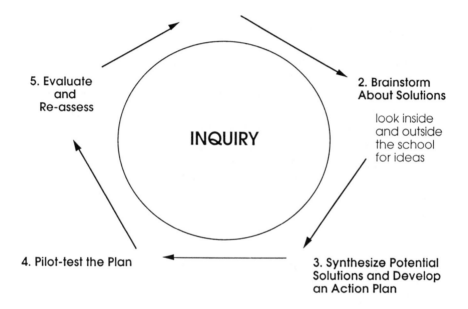

5. Evaluate and Re-assess

INQUIRY

2. Brainstorm About Solutions

look inside and outside the school for ideas

4. Pilot-test the Plan

3. Synthesize Potential Solutions and Develop an Action Plan

Figure 2.1. The Inquiry Process Used at the Time of the Case Study

their work. In this way, the cadre members create schoolwide changes bringing the school closer to its vision. As a result of participating in the big wheel practice of inquiry, individuals and small groups spin off little wheels producing innovations and change on a smaller scale.

In setting priorities at this inner-city school, the school community decided to establish a cadre for instruction/achievement because of the gap between taking stock findings and the vision for the future. In taking stock, the staff found that students entered the school scoring below the district average on standardized tests and left the school scoring even lower. Although most of the cadre members who were teachers felt satisfied about their own teaching, they also realized (through the taking stock reports) that lectures and worksheets were the most frequently used instructional techniques at the school at the time. All of these findings were far from the school vision of success for all students through active and meaningful learning experiences. Therefore, the Instruction Cadre began to address the long-term challenge of improving instruction. The case is told from the point of view of one of the cadre members.

Stage 1. Focusing in on the Challenge Area

Step a. Exploring the challenge area informally and Step b. Hypothesizing why the challenge area exists. Because we chose to tackle the entire area of "instruction," rather than a single aspect of it, our cadre had a difficult time focusing in on the challenge. After some discussion, we began with a general analysis of the taking stock report with respect to achievement. Our first reaction to the low test scores was to blame the students. Some members said: "After all, they come to us from elementary schools with their study habits already established. They don't come to school prepared. They don't bring their binders. They don't bring pencils. Most of them don't do homework. They don't care about learning. They don't have respect for each other. And they do not respect the teachers." For all of these situations, we found immediate solutions: detention, a stricter homework policy, calls to parents and bringing them in to see how their children act, not allowing students into the building if they do not come prepared, and many more in that same vein. Finally, one of our members pointed at the inquiry chart on the wall and reminded us that we were jumping to solutions before we had even defined the problem. She suggested that we try to think in a less negative way as well.

After some discussion, we all agreed that if children had fun learning or felt some intrinsic satisfaction when they learned something, they would come prepared and they would actively participate. We had an excellent example for this at our school: The music teacher had an amazing jazz band and jazz choir. Students who participated in these groups came to school early on their own, many lugging their instruments because they had been practicing at night. These kids were not our "best" students. In fact, some of our more problematic students were in the jazz band and the jazz choir. And yet, here they came prepared, they practiced innumerable hours, repeating the same pieces over and over until they were satisfied with their performance; they learned to improvise and be creative. Why couldn't this commitment and dedication to learning carry over into the other classrooms?

Based on our collective experience as teachers and learners (students were members at several of our cadre meetings), we developed a broad hypothesis about powerful learning. Because we chose such a broad challenge area, our hypothesis was also broad. The steering committee tried to get us to make a list of hypotheses for one aspect of instruction, but we all felt that we wanted to tackle the whole thing under the umbrella of powerful learning. Our umbrella hypothesis was that learning can only occur when students are interested in the subject or topic, when what they learn is somehow relevant to their lives, and when they can use all their abilities building on their strengths.

Some of us felt that we had jumped from an implicit understanding of our problematic situation ("Our students do not want to learn") to a conclusion about what powerful learning is. Some urged the rest of us to make the logical connection between the two statements explicit: "Our students do not want to learn, *because the school does not provide enough powerful learning experiences." This was indeed a more appropriate hypothesis.*[4]

Step c. Test your hypotheses. To confirm or disprove our hypothesis, we decided to ask our students what powerful learning was to them. We developed a survey instrument and used it as an assignment in all of our classes. We felt that this was a good research design because our cadre membership represented each grade level and subject area. Each of the teachers in our group asked their students to answer the questions in the web shown in Figure 2.2.

In some classes, the students helped to summarize the data and to calculate percentages, in others the teacher prepared the summary. In our next cadre meeting, we analyzed the data from each teacher. Table 2.1 shows the results that emerged as characteristics of powerful learning.

Most teachers felt that we had not learned anything that we did not already know deep inside, but that it was good to obtain these confirming results from our students and to make our students aware that we as teachers and support staff are concerned with their learning and want to satisfy their learning needs. A member of the cadre also pointed out that it was important to actively acknowledge what *really* works in teaching.

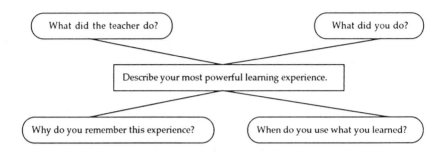

Figure 2.2. Web Used by Students to Analyze Powerful Learning
Experiences

*Step d. Interpret the results of your testing and come up with a clear
understanding of the challenge area.* After we finished tallying the survey,
our first school year as an accelerated school came to an end. We had
not yet introduced any schoolwide changes, but we felt that we had a
clearer understanding of our problem: When students do not want to
learn, we must motivate them rather than punish them. We agreed that
students need to be actively involved if learning is to reach its greatest
potential. And we thought that a way to help students learn would be
to build on our findings from the student survey above. Our focus areas
were to make learning relevant and interesting, and to build on students' experiences and their best ways of learning.

We shared our findings with the school as a whole and others
seemed impressed with what we had done. Their interest in the findings
and eagerness for us to link them to a plan of action contributed toward
our impetus to move forward.

Stage 2: Brainstorming About Solutions
(Looking Inside and Outside the School for Ideas)

As we began our second year as an accelerated school, we had a
47% rise in student population, which greatly increased class size—a
challenge that was exacerbated by the unusually small classrooms in
our school. All of us were desperate for effective instructional and classroom management strategies. Rather than ignoring these immediate

TABLE 2.1 Results of Inquiry Into Students' Powerful Learning Experiences

STUDENT ACTIVITIES

Individual	Group	Group/Individuals
role-playing	hands-on activities	hands-on activities
written and oral	active learning	active learning
repetition	dramatizations	computer use
	role playing	research activities
	games	projects
	competitions	
	debate	
	field trips	

TEACHER ACTIONS AND ATTITUDES

high expectations and belief in students
supportive and motivating and insistent
(i.e., "The teacher made me do it.")
caring for each individual student and for the group
individual help
demonstration of expected behaviors
modeling of learning processes
being a facilitator of learning
giving rewards

CHARACTERISTICS OF THE LESSONS

fun
novel, different
clear relationship to the outside world
important to current student concerns
involve students actively
interesting
useful
challenging and difficult, but within the reach of all students
dramatic/shocking
related to rewards

concerns and continuing with our focus from the previous spring, we asked the entire staff to share areas of greatest concern so that we could plan relevant staff development. We found that most people were concerned with discipline. Several members of the cadre, who were certified trainers of a classroom management approach by "Fred Jones," offered that as a solution and volunteered to train the rest of us.

Once this training had begun, we returned to our exploration of powerful learning strategies to address the results of the student survey. We began searching for solutions and strategies to bring teaching more in line with our findings from our powerful learning survey. Throughout the late fall, we looked at the most recent educational literature. We read and shared articles from professional journals about innovative instructional techniques and discussed their merit.

In searching for solutions, we also explored a number of instructional strategies with accompanying training. One that we were particularly interested in was called the Program for Complex Instruction, a cooperative learning approach by Elizabeth Cohen at Stanford University. A few of us attended an orientation session to explore the program. We were so impressed that we organized an orientation for our entire staff at our own school site. After the orientation, people broke off into cadres and discussed whether we should pursue the program. There was definite interest. Our cadre followed up on the interest by visiting schools that already were using Complex Instruction. We kept the school community in touch with our continued findings in this area.

In our continuing search for solutions, we sometimes found ideas when we weren't even looking. The seeds for many of our favorite ideas came to us as we reflected on our retreat at the beginning of our second year as an accelerated school. At that time, we had participated in a building on strengths exercise, where all members of the our school community interviewed each other in pairs, writing out our strengths, our interests, and what we would like to share with others in the school. Members of our cadre remembered liking this exercise and introduced the ideas into our cadre meetings. We knew it was important to keep looking outside the school, but we thought that there were a multitude of strengths *inside* the school that we could tap. Many of these strengths would address our list of powerful learning elements. For example, one of our support staff members has her own cake-decorating business— she could come into the home economics classes and help do a special unit on cake decorating for the holidays.

Stage 3: Synthesize Potential Solutions
and Develop an Action Plan

As I said, the classroom management situation was most pressing for all of us during the fall, and we focused first on implementing Fred Jones's approach. The cadre presented the Fred Jones positive approach to discipline at a school as a whole meeting and received approval to begin voluntary classes for interested staff, presented by our own certified trainers.

The broader work of our cadre stemmed from the results of the student survey about powerful learning, the teacher needs survey we conducted at the beginning of the second year, our interest in the Program for Complex Instruction, and the idea we liked about accessing our own strengths inside the school. We synthesized these ideas into a series of action plans. We were able to flesh out and move forward with the first two components of our plan:

- Publish a periodic teacher newsletter with "pearls of wisdom," or teachers' advice on specific successful teaching experiences that relate to our study of powerful learning. We arranged how to collect these "pearls," who would be responsible for their collection and dissemination, what they should consist of, how to present them on a regular basis to the rest of the school community, how to keep track of them, and how to assess their influence.
- *Move forward with the program for complex instruction.* For this, our cadre arranged a visit to a nearby middle school utilizing Complex Instruction. Teachers from other cadres and our student representatives came with us to explore further the program and report back to the school as a whole. We were most impressed with the cooperation and collaboration, individual accountability, thematic approach to studies, emphasis on self-esteem, critical thinking skills, incorporation of ESL students, and strategies for evaluation. We felt that these issues were all relevant to our cadre's focus area, our powerful learning survey results, and most important, our school vision. We identified partial funding and participants from each subject area to participate in formal training so that the program would have the potential for school-wide implementation in the future.

We did not get to flesh out the other components of our action plan. When we returned the following year, we planned to:

- Organize short sample lessons for our monthly school as a whole meetings.
- Set up a master calendar and get substitute teachers, so that teachers can visit each other and develop peer coaching relationships.
- Catalog strengths through a survey of all staff members, asking about their interests, their strengths, what they do best in the classroom, what instructional strategies they would like to share, and in which areas they would like to grow. Using the Hypercard program on a Macintosh, we will develop a catalog to increase access to our in-school resources.
- Organize a group of students to videotape teachers when requested. Staff can use these tapes either privately for self-assessment or for exemplary lessons that will be kept on file in the media center for everyone to check out.

Stage 4: Pilot-Test and/or Implement the Plan

In response to the staff concern with student discipline, the Fred Jones seminars have taken place weekly, with both an afternoon and a morning class due to great interest. Teachers walked around with Fred Jones videotapes discussing successful and failed implementation efforts.

We also piloted the pearls of wisdom in the school's daily news sheet for the last 4 weeks of school. We divided responsibility for ensuring that at least one pearl appears each day. The pearls came from personal conversations and interviews with our colleagues in each cluster of the school.

We also moved forward with the Program for Complex Instruction. After approval by the school as a whole, the cadre prepared a grant request to obtain funding and finalized arrangements with staff members who would attend the training during the upcoming summer months.

Stage 5: Evaluate and Reassess

Through the Fred Jones training, discipline problems have diminished in the school. Staff feel that the Fred Jones approach is useful and want a half-day refresher course in September.

In our assessment of the pearls of wisdom, we found that concrete suggestions of activities and organizational ideas were more useful than some of the quotes and anecdotes that were submitted. We came up with the idea for thematic pearls of wisdom that would be most appropriate for the full implementation at the beginning of the school year. We are planning to save the pearls of wisdom on a database, compile them in a notebook in the media center, and post them on bulletin boards around the school as well.

To assess other components of our plans, we decided to include an assessment procedure for each of our pilot plans, so that we can see which parts of each plan get effective use and which parts make a difference in student learning and achievement.

The instructional issues uncovered by this cadre are ones faced by the entire school community. Realizing their responsibility to the school as a whole, the cadre takes time to adequately explore the challenge and craft solutions that will positively affect everyone in the school. At the same time, this case illustrates how the inquiry process must accommodate immediate, pressing concerns at the school. The dramatic increase in class size affected instruction and classroom management—that could not be ignored by the cadre. Once the immediate need was assuaged, we saw how the big wheels of an accelerated school continued to turn, more slowly than the little wheels, but in a more structured way that addressed the underlying causes of the challenge area in a way that will eventually lead to systematically improved instruction across the school community.

Little Wheels Spinning Off
From the Cadre's Inquiry Process

As discussed above, little wheels are important because they give school community members an outlet for immediate action—both in fulfilling their wish to take responsibility for improving their current situation and in meeting our natural inclination to see change happen immediately. Some of these little wheels address parts of the challenge area that the cadre is working on. However, the overall inquiry process has inspired cadre members to initiate other innovative actions in areas that do not relate directly to the cadre's challenge. We highlight several of the little wheels that stemmed from the Instruction Cadre's work:

• At the beginning of the first year of the Accelerated Schools process, many of the teachers favored traditional instructional strategies, such as lecturing and using the textbook and ditto sheets, a fact confirmed by the taking stock survey results. One such teacher on the Instruction Cadre was so influenced by the cadre's inquiry into powerful learning, and especially, the results of the student survey, that she totally transformed her style of teaching during the summer between the first and second years of the Accelerated Schools process. After years of lecture and seatwork, this teacher began experimenting with vastly different strategies to make learning relevant and interesting and build on students' strengths and their various ways of learning. For example, one day the teacher brought in a bag of trash from her own home. Like archaeologists at a dig, students were to analyze each piece of trash and come up with a hypothesis as to the characteristics and makeup of her household. This exercise was a precursor to a unit on comparing civilizations and culminated with a cooperative learning project centered on building a time capsule characterizing U.S. society. Students in this teacher's classroom are excited, motivated, and deeply engaged in their work.

- Another member of the Instruction Cadre coordinates the work of the student council. She has totally embraced the inquiry process and has trained the student council members to use it in their work. For example, when the school experienced the 47% increase in student population, the school lunch period became chaotic with many students left unserved during the time provided for lunch and therefore late for classes. Using the inquiry process, the student council came up with an idea for a pilot test. They organized a staggered release system for lunch period. The system worked well on the very first day it was implemented and the students experienced a valuable lesson in empowerment.

- When the discipline problems accompanying the 47% increase in student population overwhelmed the staff, the cadre acted quickly to meet staff needs, building on existing staff strengths through the Fred Jones training. Although the cadre believed that better instructional methods would eventually address the discipline problems, they wanted to help staff solve an immediate concern.

Little Wheel Discoveries Influence the Model

The interaction of big wheels and little wheels at accelerated schools helps push each school community's transformation process forward. As we have shown above, different types of little wheels spin off of the big wheel practice of inquiry, some of which are so powerful that they produce some whole-school changes (i.e., untracking, staggered lunch breaks).

At the Accelerated Schools Project level, we have observed a similar interaction of big wheels and little wheels. For the Accelerated Schools Project, the big wheels are our continual development and refinement of the model, and the little wheels are the informal experiences we have on a daily basis through collaborating with those "living" the model at participating schools. For example, by working and talking with teachers in cadre meetings and other school processes, we gain experiences that we may then transform into new training ideas and exercises. This interaction influences how we perceive the formal model (big wheels) and allows us to transform it as well.

For example, our participation on cadres has led to our own little wheel discoveries that have produced refinements in the inquiry process and how we transmit it. Below, we describe what we have learned by participating on the cadres in this particular school and how these lessons have affected our model. We focus primarily on our experience with the Instruction Cadre, but we also share lessons from the Family Involvement Cadre in the same school. The Family Involvement Cadre used the inquiry process in a very different way, and the comparison of the two cadres' experiences have led us to some important conclusions that have influenced our model. To best explain our conclusions, we felt it was necessary to draw on both experiences.

The Iterative Nature of the Inquiry Process

When we initially conceptualized and shared the inquiry process with schools, we viewed it as a cyclical process with five stages that cadres would pass through consecutively. Our experience with these cadres illustrates that these five stages are extremely interrelated and the process is much more iterative than linear.

Interrelatedness of the four substages of Stage 1 of the Inquiry Process. Within the first stage of inquiry, we set out four substages—explore problem informally, hypothesize why challenge area exists, test hypotheses, and interpret results of testing and come up with a focus area. As coaches to the cadres, we assumed that the cadres would need to complete each substage before proceeding to the next. We discovered, however, that problem exploration, hypothesis generation, and "final" problem definition were interrelated. Moreover, in order to create an initial understanding of the challenge area, cadres needed to interpret the part of the vision that their challenge area fell short of. (Cadres are formed by the priority "gaps" between the school's taking stock data and the vision statement.)

For instance, in the beginning the Instruction Cadre focused on the low test scores and the lack of preparedness of students. The cadre members informally hypothesized why students were not successful and emphasized student deficits: Students did not respect themselves and others and they did not care about learning. Only when the cadre looked to the school vision that all students should develop a love of learning did it come up with examples where students were successful. This led the cadre to a broader hypothesis that did not put the blame on the students, but characterized the problem as a mismatch that could be changed by the school.

The Family Involvement Cadre could not begin to hypothesize about why parents were not involved until they had discussed what family involvement meant to them. Once they had defined family involvement, they transformed it into an explicit goal related to their unique vision—active support of students both in the school and at home. Once the Family Involvement Cadre had defined its goal, the members began hypothesizing among themselves, which was followed by an informal exploration of the challenge with others who were not on the cadre. These informal explorations with other members of the school community led to the generation of more hypotheses as well as an informal testing of the hypotheses they had initially generated.

This cadre chose to test its hypotheses formally through a focus group of parents. This testing exercise led to the confirmation of 3 of the 25 hypotheses and to solutions appropriate to the 3 confirmed hypotheses. Given that the two solutions they eventually pilot-tested had different levels of success, the cadre members discovered that they needed to return to their list of 25 hypotheses to see if there were others that might be additional explanations for their challenge area. They also felt that they needed input from a larger group of parents to validate their hypotheses (and even come up with more).

These and other experiences have led us to revise the first stage of inquiry to include the following substages: initially define challenge area, explore challenge informally and hypothesize why challenge exists, test hypotheses, and interpret the results of the testing and come up with a clear understanding of the challenge area. These stages portray how the definition of a problem changes over time from an initial definition related to a goal to a working definition that can be used to search for solutions.

In our writings and training, we now stress the iterative nature of these substages and the inquiry process as a whole. We also encourage cadres to clarify their goals by referring to the vision.

Interrelatedness of All Stages of the Inquiry Process. Most of the solutions the Instruction Cadre proposed during the first year were geared to improving the learning experiences for students. The cadre developed awareness activities for teachers and proposed observations of exciting classroom activities. It promoted a new discipline program and a cooperative learning model called Complex Instruction. It also developed activities involving students and teachers to document powerful learning and proposed a catalog of strengths for the whole school. As the cadre evaluates the implementation and the results of each of these solutions, members will gain important information about the best *vehicles* to motivate students to learn. This effort can then feed into a new inquiry process that will suggest new hypotheses to the Instruction Cadre that will relate the vehicle of powerful learning with the outcome of student achievement. In this way, the entire inquiry process is iterative.

Balance of Reflecting and Doing Something Concrete

Earlier in this chapter, we described several reasons why little wheels are crucial to the Accelerated Schools transformation process. By participating in the cadres, we learned firsthand why maintaining a balance is so important. One example occurred in the Instruction Cadre with the member who totally changed her teaching style based on her cadre's inquiry. Her changes in her teaching style exemplify taking individual responsibility. The results of her little wheel initiative were fed back into the cadre's inquiry. The cadre also took immediate action when they provided the Fred Jones training in response to the school's pressing discipline problems. The natural inclination to see immediate change can also be exemplified in the Family Involvement Cadre by a teacher who became impatient with the slow nature of the long-term inquiry process and decided to make positive phone calls to parents as a "solution." She was able to balance the long-term work in the cadre with some concrete action of her own.

Broad Versus Specific Challenge Areas in the Two Cadres

Despite our expectations for a more uniform application of the inquiry process, we found that individual cadres interpret the inquiry process uniquely depending on the nature of their challenge area, how they interpret their challenge, the group personality, and the school vision. We also learned that when the problem definition is broad, the cadre has more trouble moving through Stage 1 of the inquiry process and articulating specific solutions. Alternatively, when problems are specifically defined, the cadre members need to take care to keep an eye on the broader vision so that the solutions do not become piecemeal projects unrelated to the big picture.

The Instruction Cadre took on a broad challenge area. The members' initial understanding of their challenge was, "Learning can only occur when students are interested in the subject or topic, when what they learn is somehow relevant to their lives, and when they can use all their abilities building on their strengths." They then took this problem definition and transformed it into one broad, overall hypothesis on which they chose to focus: "Students have difficulty achieving because the school does not offer enough powerful learning experiences." The Family Involvement Cadre, on the other hand, developed a list of 25 specific hypotheses as to why family involvement was a challenge for this school.

One of the related lessons we have learned with regard to the breadth or specificity of cadres' challenge areas is that cadres need direction from their colleagues as to where to begin their inquiry. No matter the challenge area, we observed cadre members beginning the inquiry process with difficulty over sorting out which of the subchallenge areas to focus on. Our colleagues at other schools found similar situations with their cadres. To address the challenge, the Accelerated Schools Project has refined the setting priorities process so that school communities go beyond setting broad priority areas to setting subpriority areas for cadres to explore. These subpriorities are created by the most important differences between the taking stock and the vision, and provide more direction to cadres.

Method of Conceptualizing Hypotheses

The inquiry process in general and the word *hypothesis* specifically present a challenge to schools. Given the many years schools have operated under conditions where problems typically were solved outside the school building, this challenge should be no surprise. We tried to overcome it by helping schools conceptualize the causes of their challenges as hypotheses by asking themselves questions about their challenge area. By working with these cadres over time, we have collaboratively constructed new ways of helping schools develop hypotheses. We now encourage schools to develop hypotheses statements in response specifically to *why* the challenge exists. For example, "I think _____ is a challenge because x, y, z." We are also using synonyms for hypotheses, such as exploring the underlying causes of challenges. Having a variety of ways to describe the meaning of hypotheses helps cadres with both broad and specific challenge areas in moving through the first stage of inquiry.

Membership in Cadres

In the earlier accelerated schools, cadres were constituted of teachers, some support staff, and some administrators. At the school where the case studies took place, we encouraged the school to form cadres that were fully representative of their school community. In both case studies, cadre membership included teachers, support staff, administrators, parents, and students. We discovered that the different perspectives these diverse members brought to the problem definition and analysis enriched the work of all the cadres and the school. The diversity clearly prevented the school from overlooking important realities that had been consistently ignored in schools without such a diversity of cadre membership. For example, in the Instruction Cadre the presence of students was crucial to the understanding of the relationship between powerful learning and powerful teaching strategies. In the Family Involvement Cadre, a parent member brought up one of the most cogent hypotheses that cadre examined—parents feel treated like second-class citizens at the school. This statement made the school take responsibility for the lack of family involvement and shifted attention away from looking only at shortcomings in the families as reasons for their lack of involvement.

Role of the Accelerated Schools Project Coach

Although we conduct a full day of initial inquiry training, we have learned that school communities in fact grasp the inquiry process only over time by applying it in the cadres. For this reason, we initially participated regularly in the cadres as members and capacity builders. As capacity builders, we do not offer solutions or even hypotheses to the cadres; rather, we ask questions to help cadres discover their own way. By participating so intensively as members in the cadres, we were able to gain the legitimacy to ask questions in a capacity-building manner. This participation also allowed us to informally address issues with cadre members outside of the cadre meetings as the need arose, which was another form of building individual capacity. Finally, the legitimacy we gained through our initial intensive involvement has allowed us to remove ourselves gradually from the school while maintaining an ability to give input to the school and cadres on a more intermittent basis.

Some Final Thoughts

We would like to end this chapter with two additional thoughts: (a) All components of the Accelerated Schools model have the potential to spin off little wheel innovations, and (b) design and implementation —the model and the school experiences—are necessarily integrated.

In this chapter, we have analyzed a growth pattern we have observed in both the schools and the Accelerated Schools Project, which we have labeled big wheels and little wheels interacting. Although we have illustrated the little wheels that have spun off from the inquiry process, we want to stress that little wheels can spin off from every component of the Accelerated Schools philosophy and process.

For example, the big wheel of the entire Accelerated Schools philosophy can spark a wide variety of innovations. In the school of our case study, one teacher initiated an activity that he felt embodied the philosophy of Accelerated Schools. Using concepts from applied math, physics, and engineering, students were to design and build contraptions that kept eggs intact when dropped from a rooftop. Almost every child in the school entered the "egg drop contest," many as part of a team. Members of the school community became actively involved, business leaders served as judges, and community businesses and organizations donated prizes and materials. The egg drop contest was so successful that it has snowballed into an annual schoolwide event.

In the Accelerated Schools Project context, an example of a little wheel spinning off from the vision process occurred when we were building schools' capacity to develop their shared vision. Our staff used to ask school staff members to describe the best possible school they could think of for at-risk students. This question certainly produced some wonderful vision statements for early accelerated schools. However, during a training session a few years ago, one of our team members experimented by asking one group to describe the best possible school for at-risk students and another group to describe the kind of school they would want for their *own* children. The Accelerated Schools Project staff member and both groups noted a dramatic difference in the types of visions they produced. This little wheel experiment was so powerful that it has changed the way we transmit the big wheel of forging a vision to new schools.

As we have mentioned and as we can see from this last example, big wheels and little wheels build bridges between the model and individual schools. Experiences in schools lead to improvements in the model, which in turn allows schools to be more effective in their own transformation: Design becomes implementation.

Recognizing the importance of little wheels in the transformation process of schools, we have explored ways of more formally weaving little wheels into our training process. For example, we encourage powerful learning little wheels during training by asking school staff members to design lessons for their students that would help them understand and apply the Accelerated Schools philosophy.

After training schools in the philosophy of powerful learning, we conduct a thorough debriefing so that the participants understand that *both* big wheels and little wheels are the strategies that produce powerful learning. This type of debriefing helps participants understand that powerful learning does not occur either solely through the group processes of Accelerated Schools or totally through individual initiative. By collaboratively focusing on the larger challenges and concerns of the school community, a social infrastructure emerges that is supportive of powerful learning and spurs little wheel innovations.

Because little wheels are so crucial to keeping the momentum of the 6-year Accelerated Schools transformation process going, the challenge is not only to promote little wheel innovations, but also to detect them when they occur, make them public, assess them, and continually feed them into the larger school change effort. This chapter represents an initial effort to document our observations of the way accelerated schools and our project continue to learn and evolve. Over time, we hope to document and analyze a broader range of big wheel and little wheel interactions at many school sites. By finding ways to incorporate these growth patterns in the model, we will then be able to abstract from the individual school community learning experiences and share the pattern with all schools that are part of the Accelerated Schools movement.

Notes

1. Accelerated Schools Project refers to the staff at the National Center for the Accelerated Schools Project at Stanford University and satellite centers and coaches in various districts throughout the country.

2. Practitioners are those members of school communities who are actively engaged in using the Accelerated Schools model to transform their schools—teachers, parents, students, administrators, support staff, local community members, and others.

3. This case study is drawn from Hopfenberg, Levin, and Associates (1993) "The *How* of Powerful Learning: Instructional Innovations and Rediscoveries." *The Accelerated Schools Resource Guide* (pp. 211-223). Copyright 1993 by Jossey-Bass Inc.; reprinted with permission. For more examples of big wheels and little wheels throughout the Accelerated Schools model, refer to this source.

4. Because the Instruction Cadre chose such a broad challenge area, its members had trouble following the first stage of the inquiry process systematically. With an area as broad as "instruction," developing a list of 15 or more hypotheses using the phrase "I think _____ is a challenge because . . ." became difficult. You can see how the cadre tried to stay true to the problem-solving purpose of the inquiry process by embarking upon a research project with the students to define this challenge area.

✍ 3

Accelerated Schools as Learning Organizations

The Revitalization of Pioneer Schools

ILSE BRUNNER
BRENDA LeTENDRE

In contrast to earlier educational reform efforts, current school re-formers emphasize systemic change, considering schools as parts of a larger, nationwide educational system. These reformers stress that schools, neighborhoods, districts, local communities, state departments of education, the federal government, and society at large must become more and more involved in shaping the teaching and learning that is going on in the classroom (Barrett, 1991; Conley, 1992; Lunenburg, 1992; Mitchell, 1992; Norris & Reigeluth, 1991; Prager, 1992; M. S. Smith et al., 1992). To make the involvement of so many different organizations and agencies meaningful and productive, these social actors have to become stakeholders and interactive parts of the educational system. A precondition for a fruitful collaboration between the different organizations is their capacity to interactively change their organizational cultures and the attitudes and behaviors of their mem-

AUTHORS' NOTE: The first version of this chapter was written by Ilse Brunner, Ann Heelen, and Brenda LeTendre, and was presented at the annual meeting of the American Educational Research Association, New Orleans, April 4-8, 1994. In this initial paper, Ann Heelen was responsible for the description of the Accelerated Schools Center in Illinois and the revitalization process of its schools. We want to thank Ann for her collaboration and for her important contributions to this chapter.

bers, so that they become capable of mutual flexible adaptation and constant internal renewal (Bonstingl, 1992; Fullan & Stiegelbauer, 1991; Sashkin et al., 1992; Senge, 1990; Villa et al., 1992).

Schools prepare our children for a future that is being created by the current activities and interactions of the social forces of our society. This future is uncertain, difficult to imagine, and impossible to foresee. Schools and the agencies that serve them need to direct their attention to the future and become learning organizations, constantly in the process of self-renewal. Peter Senge (1990), in his book *The Fifth Discipline* defines a learning organization as one "that is continually expanding its capacity to create its future" (p. 14). Learning organizations need to acquire skills and competencies in a lifelong learning process. Senge identified five areas in which development is necessary for true learning organizations. These areas, which he calls *disciplines*, are systems thinking, personal mastery, mental models, shared vision, and team learning. Each one of these disciplines is "a body of theory and technique that must be studied and mastered to be put into practice" (p. 10).

When educational reformers want to involve school personnel in rethinking their practices and reshaping their organization, their curriculum, and their instructional strategies to prepare our students for the 21st century, they need to build the schools' capacity to learn. The Accelerated Schools Project (Hopfenberg et al., 1993; Hopfenberg, Levin, Meister, & Rogers, 1990; Levin, 1986, 1993a, 1993b) provides a good example of how organizational learning is needed for a decentralized educational movement in which participants continuously learn from their own experiences. In 1986-1987, Henry M. Levin and his staff at Stanford University in conjunction with the staff of two San Francisco Bay Area elementary schools launched the first two accelerated schools. After 8 years, at the beginning of the 1994-1995 school year, the National Center for the Accelerated Schools Project, with the help of coaching teams and satellite centers, was working with over 700 schools in 37 states.

Analogous to Senge's (1990) five disciplines, the Accelerated Schools Project has developed a philosophy and process that helps schools become learning organizations. The three principles—unity of purpose, empowerment with responsibility, and building on strengths —the Accelerated Schools values, and the concept of powerful learning provide schools with a body of theory that guides their practice. Further, the first-year transformation process—taking stock, visioning, setting priorities, and developing a democratic governance structure—allows school community members to develop personal mastery and a shared dream of their ideal school. Finally, the inquiry process enables schools to find systemic solutions to the challenges they face. Thus the Accelerated Schools philosophy and process teaches schools the skills and competencies necessary to prepare children for the future.

Schools that joined the movement in the early years were true pioneer schools—schools that had to develop their own path. Members of the school communityrallied around the philosophy of Accelerated Schools, but they lacked the benefits of a systematic process to embed the philosophy into their daily life. The pioneer schools based their change process on the three guiding principles and the Accelerated Schools values. They transformed their schools in response to the belief that all children are gifted and talented and that all children can learn. They were committed to the idea that a school is only good for all children if it is good enough for their *own* children. But the path toward their vision lacked the guideposts provided by the process that came into being after their initial launch. Through their effort to make the Accelerated Schools philosophy a school reality, they helped the project develop a systematic process that now is used by all other accelerated schools that have joined the movement in later years. In this way, the philosophy and process of the Accelerated Schools movement has been evolving over the past 6 years.

To provide the pioneer schools with the latest developments in the philosophy and process and bring them into the mainstream of the Accelerated Schools movement, the project team at the national center found that one more component was necessary: a process for periodic self-renewal that (a) would allow pioneer schools to partake in the later developments of the evolving school reform model, and (b) would provide all accelerated schools with a mechanism to periodically assess the progress they have made and reaffirm their commitment to continue to enhance their capacity to live up to their highest aspirations.

Accelerated schools need to revisit periodically the Accelerated Schools philosophy and process. In this way, all Accelerated Schools become learning organizations that constantly incorporate the latest developments of the evolving Accelerated Schools movement. This periodical revitalization process also permits the school communities to reexamine where they are headed and to see how far their school has come. Further, it allows new members (new students and their families and new staff) to be brought on board so that their visions of a dream school can be incorporated and the school vision continues to represent the dreams of all members of the school community. Many accelerated schools across the nation that are in their fourth or fifth year of implementation are currently involved in this cyclical self-renewal or revitalization process. Two major efforts of self-renewal have been developed by the Illinois Accelerated Schools Satellite Center and the Missouri Accelerated Schools Project.

In this chapter, we examine the revitalization process of the pioneer schools in Missouri and Illinois as an example of how schools can become learning organizations and remain at the cutting edge by involving themselves periodically in a self-renewal cycle. We describe the self-renewal cycle and the factors that prompted the revitalization efforts in both states. After an analysis of the response of the Missouri and Illinois schools, we identify conditions that facilitate or hinder the revitalization process and develop a list of recommendations to help guide self-renewal efforts at other accelerated schools.

The Need for Revitalization

Two years after the first two Accelerated Schools were launched by the National Center for the Accelerated Schools Project at Stanford University, training teams from the Missouri State Department of Elementary and Secondary Education (DESE) and the Illinois State Board of Education (ISBE) launched their own Accelerated Schools. When these schools began their transformation process, the Accelerated Schools philosophy was in place but the process was only just being developed.

The training these pioneer schools received differed substantially from the training new accelerated schools receive currently. During the training sessions, the presenters from Stanford spoke at length about the three guiding principles, but the systematic process that accelerated schools now use in their first year of transformation had not yet been developed. The inquiry process so crucial to finding solutions to challenges within an accelerated school was simply a one-page draft description of a six-step process that one of the pilot elementary schools was using to grapple with its challenges.

In 1988-1989 when the pioneer schools began in Missouri and Illinois, there was very little written documentation about Accelerated Schools other than Henry Levin's initial paper written in 1986 for the National Education Association, *Educational Reform for Disadvantaged Students: An Emerging Crisis.* In this paper, Levin laid out the framework for a new type of school—an accelerated school. In 1988, Levin and his colleagues had not yet published any articles on how schools might in practice actually transform their schools into accelerated schools. The first draft of *The Accelerated Schools Resource Guide* (Hopfenberg et al., 1993) was still several years away.

After their initial training, these pioneer schools were mentored and coached by training teams who charted their own course with only periodic consultations with the national center staff. From 1992 on, the collaboration between the training teams in Missouri and Illinois and the national center intensified. Through systematic interactions and a continuous dialogue with the national center, both state teams concluded that their initial groups of schools needed a revitalization process in order to benefit from the latest developments in the Accelerated Schools process. The revitalization process they developed, based on the model of a self-renewal cycle, was implemented by 8 schools in Missouri and 22 schools in Illinois. Table 3.1 gives an overview of these revitalization efforts in both states.

The Accelerated Schools Self-Renewal Cycle

The self-renewal cycle that served to revitalize the Missouri and Illinois pioneer schools was developed by Brenda LeTendre (1993a, 1993b) in collaboration with staff at the Missouri and Illinois State Departments. It was designed to rekindle the initial excitement and enthusiasm of the schools and to bring them into the mainstream of the Accelerated Schools movement. However, the self-renewal cycle is not limited to use with pioneer schools. It is a revitalization model that can be used by all accelerated schools in need of revitalizing their change efforts and renewing their commitment toward reaching a shared vision of excellence. The self-renewal cycle helps schools periodically and systematically review their goals, reflect on their progress, and make sure that all stakeholders continue to be involved in meaningful ways in a permanent effort to provide quality education to all children.

The self-renewal cycle helps nurture the three guiding principles of Accelerated Schools. Going through the cycle every 3 to 4 years allows school communities to maintain their unity of purpose, reestablish their commitment to shared decision making and quality implementation, and continue to build on their strengths and accomplishments. It allows them also to incorporate the latest developments in the Accelerated Schools model, which is continuously evolving and being refined based on the lessons learned from the implementation processes at many schools.

TABLE 3.1 Overview of Revitalization Efforts for Illinois and Missouri Pioneer Accelerated Schools

	Illinois	Missouri
Factors that prompted revitalization efforts	1. Recognition that the state steering committee meetings and two annual professional developmental institutes were not enough to sustain momentum within the schools 2. State-mandated school recognition process for all Illinois schools 3. Impending evaluation study of the effectiveness of Illinois Accelerated Schools	1. Loss of momentum over the years 2. Launching of 16 new accelerated schools
Revitalization process	State board staff and Stanford-sponsored consultant conducted up to 16 hours of on-site training in 22 schools to guide schools through the stages of the self-renewal cycle: a. revisiting the school's vision b. taking stock c. setting priorities d. reorganizing governance structure e. embedding inquiry in the school	All eight pioneer schools received up to 16 hours on-site training and guidance to work through the five-stage self-renewal cycle: a. revisiting the school's vision b. taking stock c. setting priorities d. reorganizing governance structure e. embedding inquiry in the school

The training focused on the above five stages and also included the following topics: a. Embedding the philosophy and beliefs of Accelerated Schools b. Powerful learning c. Skills for collaboration d. Meshing the self-renewal cycle with the Illinois accreditation process	Teams from all eight schools attended the 1994 June retreat. Teams from three schools attended the 1993 summer coaches' training designed to help them "relaunch" their schools. Teams from three schools attended eight monthly coaches' meetings throughout the 1993-1994 school year. Teams from five schools attended three coaches' workshops during the 1993-1994 school year.
Factors that hindered revitalization 1. Pressure in preparing for the Illinois school accreditation process 2. Staff, especially principal, turnover	1. Enthusiasm hit the brick wall of reality 2. Staff turnover 3. Lack of well-established culture of reflection 4. Principal or teacher leadership not focused on renewal
Factors that promoted revitalization 1. Emphasis on progress made 2. Recognition of the schools through visits 3. Participation in the Illinois Network of Accelerated Schools	1. Impending visit of evaluators connected with the state-mandated accreditation process 2. Imminent statewide evaluation to gauge how well Missouri accelerated schools have embraced the philosophy and processes of Accelerated Schools 3. Financial support for rejuvenation 4. Availability of staff development time

As with other Accelerated Schools processes, the self-renewal cycle involves the entire school community. Teachers, support staff, students and their families, administrators, district personnel, and interested community members all work together to take stock of their school's progress, revisit their vision, reset priorities, and reexamine their governance structure. Following its renewed commitment to Accelerated Schools, the school community uses the inquiry process at all levels of the school context to find lasting solutions to problems and bring the school nearer to its vision.

The Accelerated Schools self-renewal cycle parallels the processes that newly launched Accelerated Schools follow, but is flexible enough to be adaptable to the specific needs of each individual school. The cycle includes the following:

1. Revisiting the school vision
2. Taking stock of the current situation of the school
3. Identifying priority challenge areas for action
4. Reorganizing the school governance structure
5. Embedding the inquiry process for problem solving in the life of the school

Figure 3.1 gives a graphic representation of the Accelerated Schools self-renewal cycle.

All pioneer schools in Missouri and Illinois participated in an intensive training that prepared them for the revitalization process. At each step of the process, the whole school community came together to reflect upon the need for that step and to recall or to learn the skills required to complete the step successfully. The complete training consisted of eight workshops covering the Accelerated Schools philosophy, powerful learning, skills for collaboration, visioning, taking stock, setting priorities, the inquiry process, and revisiting the governance structure.

The training started with a session on how to embed the philosophy and the beliefs of the Accelerated Schools Project in the day-to-day activities of the school. It continued with a workshop in which school community members developed a shared understanding of the necessary changes in curriculum, instruction, and school organization to promote and nurture powerful learning. A third workshop helped the participating schools to reflect on issues of meeting management, group dynamics, consensus building, and conflict management.

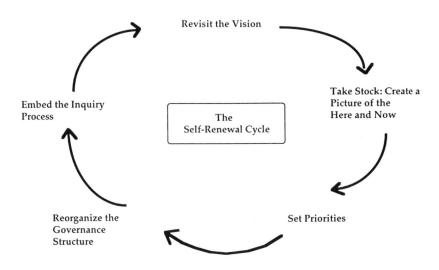

Figure 3.1. Accelerated Schools Self-Renewal Cycle

To revisit their vision, training participants started with an organizing workshop that helped them in developing strategies to involve all stakeholders in the revisiting process. After gathering input from all members of the school community, the whole school participated in a workshop on how to organize the information and how to write a vision statement that reflects the school's philosophy and the enthusiasm and commitment the school has with respect to its vision.

Most schools took several months to take stock, as they had not taken stock in the past. They initiated the taking stock process with a workshop in which the members of the school community completed the first five steps of the process, leading up to the formation of Taking Stock committees responsible for developing the taking stock questions and the instruments for the gathering of information. This workshop included exercises in developing appropriate questions and in data analysis.

After the pioneer schools had developed their vision and analyzed their taking stock data, they participated in another whole-school workshop, in which they compared the taking stock information to their vision and reset their priorities. The workshop ended with the reorganization of their cadres with a balanced representation from all members of the school community. These new cadres were to address the challenge areas the schools had identified as their priorities.

Both the Missouri team and the Illinois team put special emphasis on the inquiry process as a problem-solving strategy that can be used at every level of the school organization—for personal problem solving, for classroom issues, for the solution of problems that involve school-wide changes and affect the entire school community. The teams gave an introductory workshop at each school on the inquiry process, using a schoolwide simulation to teach the process. Then they worked with each cadre separately, using the challenge areas of the cadres to teach the inquiry process once more, step by step, to ensure that it would become embedded into the everyday life of the schools.

The last part of the training was dedicated to the governance structure of the schools. School communities identified their current governance structure and compared it to the three-level structure of an accelerated school—cadres, steering committee, and school as a whole. Based on this analysis, they determined how the different committees, task forces, and advisory groups currently working in their schools could be incorporated into or absorbed by the new governance structure.

Impulses for the Revitalization of the Missouri and Illinois Pioneer Accelerated Schools

Just 2 years after the launch of the first pilot Accelerated Schools in California, five Missouri elementary schools began the journey of transformation into places where all students accelerate their learning. Teams of 5 to 15 people from each school attended a 5-day summer academy sponsored by the Missouri Department of Elementary and Secondary Education (DESE). At the summer academy, these school teams received training provided by staff from Stanford University. The Missouri teams then returned to their schools and began the work of embedding the Accelerated Schools philosophy within their schools. By 1990, three other elementary schools had joined the family of Missouri Accelerated Schools.

As the pioneer schools moved into their third, fourth, and fifth years of acceleration, the excitement of the initial thrust of beginning the transformation dissipated. School community members moved beyond the small, quick changes (we now call these the little wheels of acceleration) to the more persistent and seemingly intractable challenges within their schools. That is where teachers and principals grew weary as they struggled to find workable solutions to the tough problems of low student achievement, high mobility of students and staff, and the lack of parent involvement in the education of children. The realities of limited resources, entrenched bureaucratic structures, and dysfunctional politics took their toll on staff members working to transform their visions into reality.

Many pioneers schools also suffered the negative effects of staff turnover. Three of the eight schools had lost their principals. Indeed, one school had three new principals in 3 years. Since beginning their journey toward acceleration, all the pioneer schools had experienced teacher turnover. In one school, only 50% of the original staff that launched the Accelerated Schools ideas remained in the 1993-1994 school year.

The DESE team worked for 3 years with the first generation of schools and in consecutive years started a second and a third generation of schools. With the most recent developments in the Accelerated Schools model came new requirements for training. Now, the training included the systematic process of taking stock, forging a vision, setting priorities, creating a governance structure, and embedding the inquiry process within the life of the school. It also incorporated the newly defined concepts of powerful learning and interactions between big wheels and little wheels changes (Brunner & Hopfenberg, 1992).

To meld the pioneer schools into a single network with the second- and third-generation schools in Missouri, it was necessary for the schools to share a common vocabulary and understanding. The Missouri team realized that teachers and principals of the pioneer schools needed training to incorporate the changes made to the philosophy and process of Accelerated Schools. A systematic plan for rejuvenating the pioneer accelerated schools would serve to make sure that the statewide family of Missouri Accelerated Schools maintained a unity of purpose.

In Illinois, in 1989, teams from 24 schools that shared the common characteristic of high enrollments of students in at-risk situations (as identified in Chapter 1 of *The Accelerated Schools Resource Guide*, Hopfenberg et al., 1993) were brought together to participate in a joint venture with the Illinois State Board of Education (ISBE) to transform into accelerated schools. After a 2-day orientation session, these teams returned to their schools and began to find ways to embed the three guiding principles of Accelerated Schools into the day-to-day activities of their schools. Using the three principles as their parameters, the schools developed vision and mission statements and set up a new governance structure of cadres, a steering committee, and the school as a whole. They started to build on the internal and external strengths of their school community, focusing on student and teacher/staff capabilities and talents, increasing parental involvement, and forming business partnerships. The Illinois initiative was rooted in the three principles but lacked as yet a systematic process of implementation. The initiative was strengthened through a network of the participating schools via electronic communications.

In 1992, all Illinois schools of the first generation were experiencing a need for revitalization to sustain the momentum of their change effort and to receive new information and the most recent training provided by the national center. The state steering committee meetings and the two annual professional development institutes provided opportunities for networking and sharing of experiences for representatives from each school, but each school as a whole needed training to build the internal capacity for embedding the Accelerated Schools principles and process.

During the summer of 1992, the state board Accelerated Schools staff and a consultant trained at the national center made a first attempt at revitalization. They began by training four- or five-person teams from 8 of the 24 Illinois Accelerated Schools. The intent was to build the capacity of these eight teams not only to train their own school community but to co-train and mentor the remaining 16 Accelerated Schools. This approach proved ineffective. The school teams were unable to commit the time to work in all schools. Team members also felt that they did not have the skills and expertise needed to train the staff of other schools. The training was then revamped to apply to all 24 Illinois schools. It was also revised to be more interactive and constructivist, so that the participants were able to construct their own meaning. To increase the service capacity, ISBE staff recruited and trained 20 persons as coaches for their Accelerated Schools. These new coaches have started to co-train with an ISBE staff person and provide on-site support as the pioneer schools revitalize and implement the process.

Another impetus for the revitalization in Illinois was the mandated school recognition process. Illinois had passed major educational reform legislation in 1985 and in 1990 was changing the way in which the

State Board of Education monitored schools. A financial watch list for schools had been a part of traditional monitoring as well as the by-the-book review of items such as safety codes, staff certification, and building maintenance. The new school accreditation system focused on academics, that is, state goals for learning, equity, and student outcomes. Fortunately, the Illinois School Accreditation System and the Accelerated Schools philosophy and process—both aimed toward school improvement—are compatible.

The need for revitalization came also from an impending evaluation study of the Illinois Accelerated Schools. Each year, the State Board of Education selects four programs for an external, independent evaluation. For 1993-1994, one of those programs was the Accelerated Schools. To promote the feeling that evaluation was being done *with* the schools and not *to* the schools, the ISBE staff kept school personnel informed about the evaluation through the state steering committee meetings and a subgroup of that committee that provided the ISBE staff with the schools' perspectives.

The Revitalization Process in the Missouri and Illinois Schools

In Missouri, during the spring of 1993, the DESE team mapped out a plan for systematically rejuvenating the eight pioneer schools. Using the model of the self-renewal cycle (see Figure 3.1), the team conceived of an approach that connected the different generations of Accelerated Schools in the state. During the 1993-1994 school year, all eight pioneer schools received up to 16 hours of on-site training and consulting designed to help the school community implement the five steps of the self-renewal cycle. At the end of the year, representatives met with personnel from the new schools at the 2-day Missouri Accelerated Schools summer retreat.

In addition, several pioneer schools sent coaching teams to the 1993 Missouri Summer Coaches' Training. This 4-day training session focused on giving school teams from schools new to the Missouri Accelerated Schools Project the background and skills they needed to launch the third generation of Missouri Accelerated Schools. For the pioneer school educators, the summer coaches' training served to reinforce prior knowledge about Accelerated Schools and to introduce the newest thinking on powerful learning, the systematic first-year transformation, and the inquiry process. It also provided them with skills and knowledge for nurturing the revitalization efforts within their schools. Throughout the 1993-1994 school year, these coaches continued to join the third-generation coaches in their training sessions. Other pioneer school teams joined the coaches from the second-generation schools at three daylong training sessions.

Revitalization has continued into the 1994-1995 school year. Three training centers have been established recently in St. Louis, Kansas City, and Springfield with staff to coordinate and assist the revitalization efforts of the pioneer schools. Center staff will launch new accelerated schools and review the self-renewal cycle with all schools every 3 to 4 years.

In Illinois in 1993, the ISBE staff, with consultant services provided by the national center at Stanford, began whole-school trainings (teachers, ancillary staff, support staff, parents), affording everyone the same opportunity to hear the same message and to interact as a total group. Each school scheduled blocks of time to complete the training. All but 2 of the initial 24 schools had completed the training components (at least through taking stock) by December 1993.

The revitalization efforts in Illinois focused on helping the Illinois Accelerated Schools complete the steps of the self-renewal cycle. Because the Illinois accelerated schools already had many components of the process in place prior to the more formalized training being developed at the national center, these schools needed to *revitalize* rather than *launch* the process. The intention was to renew the school community's commitment to being an accelerated school, reinforce beliefs and values, reflect on (and revise) the vision, refine the governance structure, review and expand taking stock information, and reestablish priorities.

Building on the strengths of what each school had already managed to implement, each training session was geared differently. For instance, schools that had major personnel changes needed more time on the commitment phase, reviewing beliefs and values. A school that was scheduled for a state recognition visit needed more emphasis on the taking stock phase, that is, getting a picture of the "here and now" to develop Part I of their School Improvement Plan.

As part of the revitalization process, the ISBE developed an affiliation agreement with each accelerated school and Rising to the Challenge school. These agreements were modeled on the affiliation agreement with the national center and the scoring rubric of the state recognition system. ISBE staff visited each school during the fall of 1993 to discuss the purpose of the affiliation agreement, its components, and its implementation. From information gleaned at these meetings and a follow-up report submitted by the school, ISBE staff drafted an affiliation agreement plan for each school, which the school reviewed, revised, and resubmitted. The affiliation agreement plan is written documentation of the support needed by the school and the intended expenditures of the ISBE grant money.

Response of the Pioneer Schools to the Revitalization Efforts

Principals and teachers in all pioneer schools readily recognized the need for rejuvenating their schools. They found the self-renewal cycle logical and easy to comprehend, as it was modeled after the latest innovations in the transformation process of Accelerated Schools. However, none of the pioneer schools followed the self-renewal cycle precisely as spelled out for them. They all adapted the cycle to the needs of their particular context.

For example, one school community elected to begin with the taking stock step because it was in the midst of the self-study required by the Missouri School Improvement Process (MSIP). Nine study groups were formed around the major categories for the MSIP self-study. These study groups examined the following areas using the state-defined standards as a guide: curriculum, instruction, differential instruction and supplemental programs (including parent and community involvement), instructional climate, guidance and counseling, professional development, governance and administration, facilities and safety, and achievement. Taking stock has taken most of the 1993-1994 school year to complete at this school. At the same time, the school community also revisited its vision, making sure that staff, families, students, and other community members have a part in the reflection.

Some pioneer schools had just recently revisited their vision, selected new priorities, and reorganized their cadres based on the new priorities. These schools were reluctant to put their new priorities on hold while they moved through the taking stock process as specified by the self-renewal cycle. They decided instead to accomplish the taking stock within their cadres as a prerequisite to the inquiry process.

Two schools in particular welcomed the revitalization. One pioneer school had experienced tremendous success in its early years, and with this success came much recognition. The principal and teachers often spoke at conferences both inside and outside of Missouri. However, as the years passed, more staff members from second-generation schools were being asked to tell the Accelerated Schools story. The staff of the pioneer school began feeling like second-class citizens as they realized that they did not know the newest Accelerated Schools vocabulary and processes. They saw the revitalization training as a chance to get back up to speed.

School community members at another pioneer school located geographically distant from all other pioneer schools developed a sense of isolation and a concomitant uneasiness about whether or not they were truly on the accelerated path. The revitalization training helped to affirm for them that they were indeed on the right track.

Revisiting the Accelerated Schools philosophy was an important step in the revitalization process. The principle of unity of purpose gave the participants many ideas on ways to promote the philosophy of "Accelerate, don't remediate" and "All children can learn." In many cases, schools that joined the Accelerated Schools Project in both states were the lowest-ranking schools in their districts and the publicity gained from affiliation with a statewide network was a long-awaited morale booster. Schools capitalized on the renewed interest in what they were doing by answering the phone as "XYZ Accelerated School" and using the phrase and the logo on stationery, student handbooks, T-shirts, caps, and other items. Media coverage became more common for the Accelerated Schools with a focus on the "good things" that were happening at the schools.

Related to the principle of shared decision making with responsibility, many schools have shown in their revitalization process that teachers are willing and able to make schoolwide decisions and to implement them. At one school, the principal moved out of state midyear and the empowered staff kept the school going for the rest of the school year with the assistant superintendent filling in for administrative authority as necessary. Another school was saddled with an ineffective, ready-to-retire principal, but the building steering committee provided leadership to sustain the school until a new principal was hired the next year. Early retirement incentives in Illinois have increased the turnover for new principals and teachers in many accelerated schools. Staff are now asking for and being included in the interview process for hiring new principals, teachers, and even custodians.

The self-renewal was strongly supported by the principle of building on strengths. To identify once more the strengths of the staff, teachers, students, parents, and community was an important step to sustain present resources as well as locating new resources. Resourceful school personnel became successful grant writers for state and local funding sources, financial wizards who reallocated district or school funds for cost-effectiveness, and shrewd partners with local businesses and civic groups (e.g., fast-food restaurants, banks, chambers of commerce). Accelerated schools brought parents into the school to share in decisions, participate in their children's learning, and make a stronger connection between home and school.

Participants at many pioneer schools understood the purpose and function of the steering committee, but the cadre idea was unclear. Through the revitalization training, they learned to differentiate between cadres that find solutions to schoolwide challenges using the inquiry process and committees that address more focused school issues. In addition, many schools in Illinois have a well-functioning social committee to boost morale and sustain the momentum.

With revitalization, many pioneer schools systematically used the Accelerated Schools governance structure as the umbrella for committees and decision-making bodies. Especially in Chicago, where each school is governed by a local school council (LSC) and has strong union representation, the steering committee structure usually includes an LSC member and a union representative. In some cases, the steering committee and the program planning action committee (PPAC) have the same membership to avoid excessive meetings and cross-purposes.

Factors That Hindered Revitalization

Not enough time to meet and plan was the Number 1 complaint of most schools. Most time was given by dedicated teachers who spent more than the contract day at the school. However, schools have been innovative in capturing school time to receive revitalization training and to meet as cadres. For instance, some schools use using "rotating substitutes" once a month. That allows the Discipline Cadre to meet for $1\frac{1}{2}$ hours while substitutes cover members' classrooms. Then those substitutes rotate to the classrooms of the Inclusion Cadre members while they meet for another $1\frac{1}{2}$ hours, and finally to the Curriculum Cadre members' classrooms during their $1\frac{1}{2}$-hour meeting time. The steering committee meets (with representatives from cadres, principal, support staff, parents, and community) for an hour after school for a status report on each cadre's progress during the day and for any immediate decisions that the cadres need from the steering committee prior to their next session. Minutes from each cadre and the steering committee are also routed to the whole school.

Another creative use of time is "banking" time by adding minutes on 4 days of the school week and dismissing early on the fifth day for weekly cadre meetings. Accelerated schools have also requested and received permission to be excused from districtwide or county in-service sessions for building-level planning instead. When staff at another school in the district complained about favoritism, the superintendent responded that only the staff at the accelerated school had ever made such a request. Because no one else had ever asked, everyone assumed the status quo was inflexible. Taking a risk can pay off if the case is properly stated.

Just as some factors within the context of the pioneer schools prompted and propelled the revitalization efforts, several circumstances tended to impede rejuvenation. Some pioneer schools experienced difficult early years as participants' enthusiasm hit the brick wall of reality. Some schools struggled against limited resources, entrenched bureaucratic structures, and dysfunctional politics. School community members saw their innovative suggestions ignored or rejected. For some, these false starts at acceleration left a sour taste. They felt hopeless and felt that putting time and energy toward the activities outlined in the self-renewal cycle would be a waste.

Another deterrent to self-renewal was the extent of staff and, especially, principal turnover. Although the shared-decision-making structure of an accelerated school changes the principal's role from sole leader to facilitator, the principal is key to the process. An effective leader in the shared-decision-making process knows when to step back and when to step forward. With the early retirement option in Illinois in 1993-1994, several schools have new principals. These principals needed nurturing and guidance in the Accelerated Schools philosophy and process beyond that provided during the state steering committee meetings or the institutes. One accelerated school has had such extensive turnover each year due to budget cuts that the principal feels each beginning year is a launching rather than a renewal. Without a doubt, continuity of staff helps to sustain the Accelerated Schools process.

All of the pioneer schools experienced a wane in commitment as veteran teachers and principals left. Unfortunately, new staff members were not systematically inducted into the knowledge of the Accelerated Schools philosophy and processes. Veteran staff members simply assumed that new staff would gain understanding and commitment through osmosis. As the years passed, fewer and fewer people in the school community shared a common understanding and language about Accelerated Schools. Within some pioneer schools, faculty members began expressing doubts as to whether or not they should continue their Accelerated Schools journey.

Few of the pioneer schools had a well-established culture of reflection. All schools included at least a few staff members who valued and practiced continual reflection, but most staff members preferred to focus on the future rather than reflect about the past or the here and now. They were more inclined to action than reflection. To many, the self-renewal cycle represented just more talk and no action.

In some pioneer schools, revitalization efforts lagged because the principal or teacher leadership (e.g., the steering committee) was not focused on self-renewal. The crises of the day or conflicting demands of the district distracted them from rejuvenation. Initially, a main hindrance to self-renewal in Illinois has been the pressure on schools that are preparing for the new state school accreditation system. After many years of traditional state visits, the schools were asked to prepare much more documentation about their demographics and emphasis on learner outcomes and assessment. The fear of the unknown was ominous in most schools, and panic prevailed instead of the daily routine of teaching and learning. The state accreditation visit took priority over the recommitment and revitalization as an accelerated school. Accelerated Schools are voluntary and without funding, but state recognition is mandated, tied to school funding, and publicized within the community. When participants finally made the connection between Accelerated Schools and the school accreditation system as complementary improvement processes, they used the self-renewal cycle to collect the data for the accreditation process.

Factors That Promoted Revitalization

Although the loss of momentum and the launching of new Accelerated Schools with improved training strategies prompted the efforts to revitalize the pioneer schools, other factors helped to propel the rejuvenation. For some pioneer schools, an impending visit of state evaluators hastened revitalization efforts. Recently, the Missouri Department of Elementary and Secondary Education established a new process, the Missouri School Improvement Process (MSIP), to ensure the quality of Missouri's schools. This new accreditation scheme parallels in many ways the language, philosophy, and processes of Accelerated Schools. Staff in three pioneer accelerated schools recognized that the requirements of the Missouri School Improvement Process meshed nicely with revisiting the vision and taking stock steps of the self-renewal cycle.

For many pioneer schools, an imminent statewide evaluation of Missouri's accelerated schools was an incentive to initiate the rejuvenation efforts. This evaluation represents the first of a two-stage evaluation to answer the question: Do the Accelerated Schools philosophy and process result in increased achievement for students? This first stage of evaluation gauges how well each school has embraced the philosophy and process of Accelerated Schools. The rubric of indicators has proved a good tool for giving members of the pioneer schools a clear picture of the current expectations for Accelerated Schools, particularly regarding the vision forging, taking stock, and setting priorities steps of the systematic process for change. The rubric has prompted the pioneer schools to begin embedding the inquiry process in the work of the cadres as well as the life of the school as a whole.

Financial support was also important. Funds from the Danforth Foundation and Smart Family Foundation proved crucial in sustaining self-renewal within the pioneer schools. Finally, the availability of staff development time within the school calendar facilitated revitalization. All pioneer schools conducted some of their self-renewal training and activities on staff development days normally built into the district's calendar. However, no school had enough designated staff development time to complete the activities. All found ways to capture time to free up cadres and groups during normal school days so that they could receive additional training and complete various self-renewal activities.

One major factor in the self-renewal process was to emphasize the current progress of the school and not to insult participants' efforts or insinuate that no progress has been made. Changes do not occur quickly, and any setbacks can be discouraging. Therefore, encouragement was a very strong factor in self-renewal. The coaching teams reminded all participants that many activities can support and promote the school, such as the following:

- The school vision developed by the whole school community, which unites and inspires the community

- Strategies for continuous quality improvement developed and implemented by the whole school community
- A start-of-school parade that gets bigger each year
- Visits to the school by dignitaries (local, state, national)
- Letters of appreciation from dignitaries, alumnae, or others
- A videotape about the school that can be shown at local civic group meetings, the local school board, parent night, or other gatherings

Recognition as an accelerated school is definitely a source of pride for the schools. The Accelerated Schools flag over the school in Illinois; the Accelerated Schools logo in Missouri; the professional development opportunities; the adaptation of innovative programs; the communication between schools; and a personal, ongoing relationship with the statewide project staff have increased the visibility of these schools within their communities and the state. Being in the public eye made many aware that they had to continue to improve and that the self-renewal cycle was an excellent vehicle for doing so.

Another factor that promoted self-renewal in each state is the statewide network to which all accelerated schools belong. Personnel from accelerated schools have bonded in a very special way through the state steering committee meetings, the professional development institutes, the summer academies, and other training sessions. Teachers comment that for all the changes going on in their districts, contact with other schools throughout the state has remained a constant source of support. This feeling of being part of a family was also evident in the examples of a daughter of a teacher in a northern Illinois accelerated school doing her student teaching in a central Illinois accelerated school, and an accelerated school assistant principal who moved on to become the principal at another accelerated school.

Recommendations and Lessons Learned

Our experiences in revitalizing the pioneer schools in Illinois and Missouri have taught us lessons that can help guide educators working with both existing and newly launched Accelerated Schools. We offer the following recommendations to satellite center staff and coaches guiding self-renewal efforts in existing Accelerated Schools:

Be sure to honor the past. Teachers, principals, and parents struggled, often in the face of overwhelming odds, to transform their schools. Coaches guiding the revitalization process must never imply that the prior efforts of the school community members were misguided because they did not follow the current systematic process of Accelerated Schools. In Missouri, the team found the following analogy helpful in assuaging doubts:

> Your school is a pioneer. You are like the early pioneers who sat in their wagons in Independence ready to head west. They had a vision—they wanted a better life in Oregon. They knew they needed to head west, but they really did not know what lay before them. The Oregon Trail was not yet marked. They did not know where the pitfalls lay, where they could cross the raging rivers, where they could safely scale the mountains. They discovered these the hard way, through trial and error. Like the early pioneers, you have a vision. You want to transform your school into a place where all students accelerate their learning. You had three guiding principles, but you knew little about how to make your accelerated school happen. You found your way through trial and error. Now others, second- and third-generation schools, are following your trail. These schools are benefiting from your hard-won knowledge. Because of your experiences, they know where to ford the rivers, where to head south to avoid the deserts, where and how to scale the mountains. Thanks to your perseverance, creativity, and commitment, those who follow you are accelerating.

- *Always gauge the prior understanding participants possess about Accelerated Schools before beginning to introduce new knowledge.* Do not assume that everyone understands what an accelerated school is. The passage of time can fade and distort understanding. Schools often have experienced some turnover, often without bringing new staff into the process. Conversely, do not insinuate that the pioneer school participants do not know anything. They have a deep and personal understanding of the philosophy of Accelerated Schools. They often understand the concepts of powerful learning, problem solving using the inquiry process, and steps within the systematic process. They just do not yet have the labels for these concepts.

- *Honor the accomplishments and successes of the school.* When the coaches in Missouri and Illinois first introduced the self-renewal cycle, school community members frequently felt that they had done something wrong. Focusing on the school's accomplishments can help diminish this nagging self-doubt. Pioneer participants have often grown weary, forgetting just how much they have accomplished. The taking stock step of the self-renewal cycle can serve to celebrate these successes.

- *Find a "hook" to show the pioneer school community members how the systematic self-renewal process will help them.* We have found it helpful to take a seemingly unsolvable challenge within the school and show how the systematic process of Accelerated Schools, and particularly the inquiry process, provides fresh thinking. For example, in one of the Missouri pioneer schools, school community members continued after many years to struggle with dysfunctional student behaviors in the classroom. The cadre had generated numerous solutions, but none seemed to work over the long haul. Once the cadre members began examining the challenge using the steps of Stage 1 of the inquiry process, they immediately saw some underlying causes they had never before considered. This examination gave them a renewed sense that they could solve the problem, and they continued to work their way through the steps within the inquiry process.

- *Allow schools flexibility in how they carry out the various self-renewal activities.* Emphasize self-renewal rather than a slavish adherence to a predetermined recipe for the process of self-renewal. The self-renewal cycle offers an idealized model of how revitalization activities might play out in a school. However, each school's context often dictates some adaptation. Indeed, one hallmark of successful reform efforts is how amenable they are to local circumstances. For example, some participants were reluctant to stop the work of their cadres to do the taking stock process as prescribed for the self-renewal cycle. Instead, they took stock within the context of cadre work, particularly as a prerequisite to the inquiry process. However, adaptation must be tempered with a commitment to standards. This is not a situation of anything goes. Rather, make sure that the spirit of the law is maintained, while still allowing for adaptation to local school needs and context.

- *Formalize the renewal of "vows," making sure that the pioneer school community wishes to continue its journey as an accelerated school.* As the years pass, commitment of the school community members may diminish. Before beginning any of the activities outlined in the self-renewal cycle, school communities should first come to consensus about whether or not they wish to continue as an accelerated school. The full commitment, in word and deed, of the principal is especially crucial to the success of renewal. If a school community lacks sufficient will to continue, it may wish to drop out of the network or take a "sabbatical." The Illinois affiliation agreement between the schools and the Illinois State Board of Education offers a workable example of documenting a school community's renewal of "vows."

- *Make sure that the pioneer schools establish formal methods for inducting new staff members into the accelerated school community.* This includes providing them with the knowledge about the Accelerated Schools philosophy and process, building their personal commitment to the philosophy, and getting them immediately involved in cadre work.

- *Explicitly identify how the self-renewal activities mesh with state and district-mandated accountability processes.* School community members are always looking for ways to work smarter by combining activities. In both Illinois and Missouri, school communities were keenly aware of the high stakes attached to the state-mandated accountability systems. By showing them that they could easily incorporate the state-mandated activities within the context of the self-renewal cycle, the coaching teams alleviated much tension and bolstered commitment to the rejuvenation activities.

- *As state education department or university personnel design formal evaluations of the efficacy of Accelerated Schools in their regions, they should explicitly interweave self-renewal activities within the framework of the evaluations.* For example, the indicators of the Philosophy and Process Rubric that Missouri Accelerated Schools are using to gauge how well they have embraced the philosophy and process of Accelerated Schools tightly meshes with the activities of the self-renewal cycle.

- *Let participants know up-front the amount of time needed for them to do the various activities of the self-renewal cycle.* No school can accomplish the self-renewal activities by relying solely on regularly scheduled staff development days normally built within a school's calendar. Participants will need to find ways to "capture" time throughout the school year to ensure successful renewal.

The Missouri and Illinois experiences in rejuvenating pioneer schools also leads us to offer two recommendations to coaches working in newly launched accelerated schools. First, school community members within a newly launched accelerated school should understand that they will go through a formal self-renewal cycle every 3 to 4 years. Several members of Missouri's accelerated schools were surprised to learn that forging a vision and thoroughly taking stock were not once-in-a-lifetime endeavors.

Second, school community members in newly launched accelerated schools must build their school's capacity to anticipate and deal with the inevitable frictions that will slow down momentum as they work to transform their school into an accelerated school. All schools face staff turnover, failures, "brick walls," and a tendency to feel that nothing has changed. Knowing that these pitfalls exist is the first step to finding ways to minimizing their ill effects.

Conclusion

Pioneer schools of the Accelerated Schools movement that participated in the Accelerated Schools revitalization process in Illinois and Missouri have renewed their commitment to the Accelerated Schools philosophy and incorporated the latest developments in the Accelerated Schools process. By going through the processes of taking stock and revisiting their vision, school community members were able to strengthen their ties and to affirm their promise to become a community of learners. Revitalization helped school communities to look critically at organizational structures and capacities to solve problems with a systemic approach. This allowed participants to focus on those structures that help sustain the disciplines of a learning organization—systemic thinking, self-reflection, a constant dialogue among stakeholders, a shared sense of mission, and the will to improve oneself individually in order to make the shared dream of excellence a reality.

The self-renewal cycle has proven to be a powerful learning strategy for schools that are committed to lifelong learning. It has helped school community members to embrace the future and look for new ways to prepare the students of today to become productive, critical, creative, and caring citizens for tomorrow.

Reflection

Learning to Facilitate, Reflect, and Inquire

EDWARD P. ST. JOHN

The Accelerated Schools movement is a dynamic, evolving school restructuring practice that has attracted commitments from hundreds of schools. It is attractive because it offers members of school communities a guiding philosophy that makes sense to most educators —that all children, especially those in at-risk situations, benefit from the enriched, challenging curriculum and instruction usually reserved for gifted children. The process used to carry out this mission has evolved as a group of committed facilitators worked with an early generation of school communities to transform their schools. Refinements in the process, ongoing today, occur because of a commitment on everyone's part to facilitate change, reflect on current practices, and inquire into additional improvements. Through this process of facilitation, reflection, and inquiry, the Accelerated Schools inquiry process has developed into an integral component of the Accelerated Schools movement. I focus here on these three processes —facilitation, reflection, and inquiry.

Learning to Facilitate

The chapters in this part include the reflections of some of the leaders of the Accelerated Schools movement about how they came to understand the role of inquiry as integral to their efforts to restructure schools. As a result of their efforts to facilitate change in a few schools, they began to reflect on their methods. In the process, they learned that inquiry played a vital role in the change process. To build an understanding of the vital role of inquiry in the restructuring process, it is appropriate first to focus on what these reflective chapters tell us about the lessons learned from the initial efforts to facilitate school transformation.

The Accelerated Schools process began with a vision, a vision that has evolved over nearly a decade. In the first chapter, Henry M. Levin describes how his vision for accelerated schools grew out of his reflection on his own academic work, juxtaposed with conditions of schools and school reform efforts. The Accelerated Schools model, Levin tells us, began with the efforts of a small cadre of students and faculty at Stanford University. The focus of the initial efforts was on transforming schools that served at-risk students into better places for those students. In the process, the early participants learned not only about the change process as they had initially envisioned that it might be but also about ways the process could be improved upon.

In the second chapter, Brunner and Hopfenberg provide a window on the method the National Center for the Accelerated Schools Project has used to learn to facilitate school restructuring. To understand the insights embedded in this chapter, the reader should reflect on the fact that Brunner and Hopfenberg were part of a team from the national center that field-tested changes in the Accelerated Schools process— changes that formalized the inquiry process as a basis for all cadre decision making—and they observed something they had not expected. As a part of their efforts, they discovered that cadre-based inquiry had spin-offs, and that people engaging in a collective process of inquiry (through involvement in cadres) also began to use it in their own lives as a means of experimenting with new approaches in their classrooms. This insight was used to refine the Accelerated Schools process and was integrated into *The Accelerated Schools Resource Guide* (Hopfenberg et al., 1993). This chapter illustrates that through learning to facilitate, the founders of the Accelerated Schools movement have also refined and adapted their methods.

In the third chapter, Brunner and LeTendre provide insight into the way the national center and local Accelerated Schools facilitators join together to facilitate transformation in agencies that govern schools. Because the "pioneer" accelerated schools in Missouri and Illinois were trained prior to refinements in the Accelerated Schools process, they were not formally introduced to the inquiry process. The authors describe how the national center staff and representatives from the two states collaborated on the design and implementation of a strategy designed to revitalize these pioneer schools. In the process, they provide insight into the ways the national center and state agencies are working together to develop new facilitative methods at the state level.

Learning to Reflect

Reflection, the introspective process of examining the lessons learned in one's own experience, is not yet an explicit part of the Accelerated Schools process. Yet the chapters in this part provide insight into the crucial role individual reflections have played in the development of the Accelerated Schools Project, as well as in the continued evolution of the methods used in this movement.

All three of the chapters describe a dynamic process of developing designs for school change based on a shared appreciation of problems, using facilitating processes to test these designs, and reflecting on the results to modify and enhance the designs. The importance of reflection as a link in this learning process should not be overlooked, for it provides a key insight into the learning processes of the founders of this movement. The fact that they have used their reflections on their experiences as facilitators to modify their methodology indicates that double-loop learning is integral to their process. If the founders had been using a single-loop learning model, then they would have used their experiences in the initial process simply to confirm or disconfirm their model. Instead, they were open to the possibility that they might not know the best approach in advance, and they reflected on their experience with the facilitation process to make major adaptations to their facilitative model, including the integration of inquiry in the Accelerated Schools process.

For practitioners who are involved in Accelerated Schools or other restructuring efforts, these examples of the use of reflection as a means of assessing the results of pilot tests illuminate the inner workings of action inquiry. If the Accelerated Schools Project founders had been content to validate their initial claims that a schoolwide process—taking stock, developing a vision, and changing school practice—could transform learning, they probably would not have discovered that the inquiry process could help cadres in schools to address the challenges they identified. Similarly, practitioners in schools who are engaged in the pilot-testing of their initial designs for changing their practices need to reflect on the results of their pilot tests to see if their designs can be enhanced, modified, or transformed to better address the challenges they face.

Learning to Inquire

In my experience, the inquiry process is the most difficult aspect of the Accelerated Schools process for school practitioners to learn. The three principles of accelerated schools—unity of purpose, empowerment coupled with responsibility, and building on strengths—are easy for most teachers to accept, at least at an espoused level, because they are consonant with the values that led many of them into education in the first place. Further, the processes embedded in the Accelerated Schools start-up process—taking stock, developing a vision, and identifying challenges—are similar to the methods for school improvement used by states and accrediting agencies. Thus, it is possible for teachers to engage in these processes without changing their practices, given that many of them have used similar methods and can treat them as routine. And, indeed, these processes may even be experienced as a burden unless practitioners realize that the Accelerated Schools process provides them with an opportunity to break out of the constraints placed on them by a myriad of state and district mandates. The three chapters in Part I illustrate the important role inquiry plays at many levels of the Accelerated Schools movement.

First, these chapters illustrate that the founders of the Accelerated Schools movement have used inquiry to develop the process. They not only describe a process of developing and field-testing designs (the primary loop of the learning process) but also illustrate the process they have used to reflect on their experiences, which has enabled them to refine their methods (the secondary loop of the learning process).[1] Thus, the capacity to reflect on experience seems to be a crucial in transforming a single-loop learning process into a double-loop process, a quality reflected in the work of the national center.

Second, trainers who facilitate the Accelerated Schools transformation process also need to use inquiry to facilitate the emergence of meaningful inquiry. Brunner and Hopfenberg's chapter illustrates the double-loop inquiry process integral to the facilitation process when they describe how their discovery of "little wheels" led them to reconstruct the inquiry model. And Brunner and LeTendre describe how they used their reflections on their experiences with first- and second-generation accelerated schools to design and field-test a revitalization process. It can be hypothesized from these chapters that those who work in the Accelerated Schools facilitating centers that have been created in universities, school districts, and state agencies need to evolve a capacity to reflect on their experiences with the facilitation process to envision ways of refining their practices. Through such a process, the Accelerated Schools facilitating organizations—and there is a growing number of them—can better use inquiry to facilitate the process.

Third, the integration of inquiry into the Accelerated Schools process has given schools a systematic way of empowering school community members to address critical challenges. However, to use inquiry as a double-loop process means that cadres do not simply implement their designs, but that members also reflect on their experiences with the implementation process to build a shared understanding of whether the strategies they have chosen to pilot-test actually address the challenges that have been identified, how these strategies might be modified to better address these challenges, and whether they need to refine or change their definition of the challenges they face. In other words, practitioners engaged in the inquiry process need to reflect on the results of their action experiments and make adaptations that fit, and indeed build, their school cultures. Unless this capacity develops, these cadres may be exercising choices about which strategies to implement, but they may not be transcending their historic role of teachers as implementors. The discovery of little wheels may be a vital link in the integration of inquiry into accelerated schools, because teachers may need first-hand experience with inquiry in action—and especially in the process of reflecting on results of their efforts to improve their personal practice—if they are to participate as contributing members of a cadre.

Finally, the discovery of the little wheels of inquiry represents an important step in the evolution of the Accelerated Schools process, from a process that focuses on the school as a whole, to a process that includes a focus on cadre-level inquiry within schools, and finally to a process that also focuses on practitioner inquiry. This all leads to a crucial insight: The process of reflecting on experience may be essential to the Accelerated Schools process—and to successful school restructuring. The development of a better understanding of how practitioners learn to reflect on their actions represents a challenge for those of us who are involved as facilitators in the Accelerated Schools movement. Further, the process of gaining a primary—or personal—experience with the use of inquiry and reflection in our professional practice may represent the essential challenge for all of the practitioners in the Accelerated Schools movement. The remainder of this book provides further insights into the nature of this challenge.

Note

1. This construct of single- and double-loop learning is adapted from the work on reflective practice and action science by Argyris and Schön (1973; Argyris, 1993; Schön, 1983, 1987, 1991).

PART II

Building Capacity

INTRODUCTION
Christine Finnan

As the chapters in this part illustrate, early capacity building is a major factor in successful long-term implementation of any change initiative. The part provides three illustrations of the interweaving of the implementation of the first stages of the Accelerated Schools process and the context surrounding implementation. This part should be of particular interest to readers considering implementing a restructuring initiative like the Accelerated Schools Project. It will also provide an opportunity for reflection for those already engaged in the process, as well as thought-provoking analyses for readers interested more generally in restructuring and program implementation.

In Chapter 1, Henry M. Levin describes the Accelerated Schools Project philosophy and process. He stresses the importance of the early stages of the process, from initial buy-in to creating a vision and taking stock and finally to setting priorities and learning to use the inquiry process. I view this phase of the project as the capacity-building phase because during it, school communities build the capacity to change themselves. Although capacity building continues throughout all phases of project implementation, it is the defining activity of the first year of implementation. By the second year, most schools are in the implementation phase of the project; participants have internalized the philosophy, have established a democratic governance structure, and are ready to implement some of their plans.

We often equate a capacity-building phase with the first year of implementation, but, as Kushman and Chenoweth illustrate in Chapter

4, school communities begin to build capacity prior to project implementation as they explore the possibility of implementing the Accelerated Schools Project. Chapter 4 documents the "courtship" phase of the project when members of a school community explore the fit between their school and the Accelerated Schools model. Kushman and Chenoweth illustrate the importance of participant buy-in during the courtship process and the importance of allowing all members of the school community to investigate the project thoroughly before buying into it.

During this extended capacity-building phase, there is a flurry of activity—school community members explore the feasibility of joining the project; they receive training in the philosophy and process; they engage in research into their current situation; and they develop a vision. These are the formal steps of the Accelerated Schools process. There are also many other changes that occur as participants begin to internalize the philosophy and carry out the steps of the process. Finnan (Chapter 5) describes how a school's culture begins to change during this phase of the project. The school's existing culture is made more explicit during the taking stock process, and it begins to change as the Accelerated Schools philosophy is internalized and people work together to create a shared vision. St. John, Meza, Allen-Haynes, and Davidson (Chapter 6) emphasize how, even in this early phase of the project, people begin to let inquiry and reflection guide their actions. School communities become communities of inquiry in which reflection and systematic research into problems become the norm.

The three chapters in this part share many similarities. The authors report on research conducted in the first year of project implementation and work from studies using qualitative data collection methods. They share a deep commitment to the Accelerated Schools Project and have been actively involved in refining and implementing the model. James W. Kushman and Thomas G. Chenoweth "courted" the Accelerated Schools Project as a possible restructuring model for their local school district. They both serve as coaches to project schools in addition to their other obligations at Portland State University. I am currently Director of the South Carolina Accelerated Schools Center, located at the College of Charleston, Charleston, South Carolina. I conducted the study described in Chapter 5 as a freelance researcher in California. After completing the research, I moved to South Carolina and established the South Carolina Accelerated Schools Center, which has grown into a statewide network. Edward P. St. John, James Meza, Jr., Leetta Allen-Haynes, and Betty M. Davidson have all been associated with the Louisiana Accelerated Schools Center at the University of New Orleans. In their chapter, they report findings from a comprehensive qualitative study of first-year implementation issues. The depth of their analysis reflects the varied relations they had with the project at the time as project director, external researcher, and doctoral students.

4

Building Shared Meaning and Commitment During the Courtship Phase

JAMES W. KUSHMAN
THOMAS G. CHENOWETH

In this chapter, we examine the "courtship" phase in the Accelerated Schools process and how it can become a vehicle for building shared meaning and commitment to school change. In the typical Accelerated Schools adoption process, the school staff is asked to vote on adopting the model after spending a period of time learning about its principles and processes, observing other accelerated schools, and discussing the model's strengths and shortcomings. It is this preadoption period that we call courtship. It is a time when the change initiators (state or district leaders, a school principal, outside facilitators, or all of the above) engage school communities in a discussion of the need for change and attempt to garner the initial commitment and support needed to embark upon a major school restructuring.

Courtship may be viewed cynically as a time of "wooing" or "selling" a particular change model, but we view it positively as a critical opportunity to begin building the shared meaning and commitment that will be needed for a long-term restructuring process. In our view, the goal of courtship is not to force-fit a model of change. Rather, it is an opportunity for both the change leaders and change followers to consider whether or not the Accelerated Schools model represents the right fit for students, community, and staff. Courtship is also a time to begin understanding the starting point for change, particularly initial understandings, values, and beliefs that reflect the existing school culture. If adopting the Accelerated Schools model means long-term cultural change, then understanding this starting point is essential to success.

Compelled by powerful ideas and pressed to make school change happen quickly, change agents frequently ignore or underestimate the importance of building shared meaning and commitment during the early stages of a change project. For a process like Accelerated Schools to take hold, people at all levels (teachers, parents, students, principals, district administrators) must assimilate the model into their own constructions of reality and their own belief and value systems. A major challenge is to integrate many individual subjective meanings of key stakeholders into a *shared* meaning, and over time, a shared school culture (Fullan, 1982; Fullan & Stiegelbauer, 1991; Sarason, 1971, 1990). This challenge begins as early as the courtship phase because although the initiators of the change may have a clear vision of what *they* want to accomplish via Accelerated Schools, unwitting teachers, parents, and others coming into the process may lack a clear sense of what an accelerated school really is and how it will help students. Different individuals and groups may also have vastly different views about what is best for the school at a particular point in time.

Change agents who ignore the personal meaning of change from the various stakeholder perspectives do so at their own peril because concerns, issues, and differing points of view left unaddressed will result at best in confusion and a slowing down of the process, or at worst in a loss of commitment and even sabotage among key people. Michael Fullan (Fullan & Stiegelbauer, 1991) has noted how different stakeholder groups focus on different facets of a change effort as they struggle to construct their own personal meaning. For example, teachers tend to adopt a "practicality ethic" by being concerned with how the change will affect their everyday work and students whereas the principal, as the classic line manager, evaluates change both in terms of district pressures from above and staff complaints from below. In an extended courtship process involving the whole school, change agents can identify how personal meanings initially differ, and more specifically, what conflicting viewpoints and pockets of resistance will eventually have to be dealt with.

In this chapter and Chapter 7, we present a qualitative study of the courtship process in three accelerated schools located in an urban district in the northwestern United States. It is somewhat unusual to study the preimplementation activities of a change effort, but our hope is that this research will provide insights into two important areas. The first area (covered in this chapter) is how different stakeholder groups (teachers, principals, and central office administrators) view accelerated schools at the end of a courtship process and what these different viewpoints imply for building shared meaning and commitment as the implementation proceeds. Of concern here are the dynamics of building shared meaning out of the many personal and role-bound meanings that individuals bring to a change project. The second area of interest (covered in Chapter 7) is the role of leadership in building understanding and commitment during the courtship and early implementation. In our study, principals emerged as being central to building staff commitment to school change.

In essence, these two companion chapters address the larger question: What does it take to build the kind of early commitment to a school change project that will keep staff energized and involved through a long-term restructuring? Although the focus of our study was on school staffs, it is recognized so that the commitment of the entire school community is essential. This study will be of most interest to Accelerated Schools change initiators and leaders, but we also believe that the results apply to similar whole-school change models that require the long-term commitment of different stakeholder groups.

The Setting and Courtship

The three elementary schools involved in this study—which are given the pseudonyms of Bridgeport, Clark, and Seaside—are among the lowest-achieving elementary schools in their region. Despite a number of effective teachers and many classroom curricular/instructional improvement projects over the years, these schools have remained "stuck" with the lowest 5% of district students in third-grade achievement in mathematics and reading. A socioeconomic ranking of area elementary schools, based on attendance, student mobility, and parent education and income levels, reveals that the schools are located in the one of the city's most disadvantaged areas. Further, within this school attendance area lies the largest concentration of public housing in the region. These housing projects have traditionally been racially segregated and pose numerous sociological problems to the schools and the community.

The three schools are "sister schools" located within several miles of each other and embarked together on the implementation of the Accelerated Schools Project under the guidance of a leadership team composed of the three school principals; a teacher representative from each school; the district administrator with direct line authority over the three schools and his instructional specialist; a curriculum department administrator; and the two of us, who served as university facilitators. This leadership team designed and led the schools through a 3-month planned courtship before the final staff vote was taken to implement the Accelerated Schools model.

The purpose of this courtship was to give the staff at the three schools enough information and time to learn about the model, discuss the model among themselves, surface different points of view, and observe the model in action through school visits and personal contacts. The actual courtship activities included (a) attendance by the leadership team at a 1-week Accelerated Schools summer academy conducted by the National Center for Accelerated Schools Project at Stanford University, (b) dissemination of written materials and videotapes about the Accelerated Schools Project to staff at each school, (c) presentations and short interactive workshops meant to introduce Accelerated Schools concepts and provide the staff with time to work with the ideas and discuss the strengths and shortcomings of the model, (d) a visit by Henry M. Levin to observe the three schools and make a joint presentation to staff at all three schools, and (e) visits and one long-distance conference call by teachers to operating accelerated schools in the region. These courtship activities extended for a period of approximately 3 months. At the end of these activities, the three school staffs were asked to vote on the model and all three voted (with virtually 100% agreement within each school) to begin the process of becoming an accelerated school.

Overview of the Chapter

Following this introductory section is a section on the conceptual framework for change used in our study. Key results are then presented in two sections. The first presents rich descriptions of how different stakeholders in different schools view the Accelerated Schools process —their beliefs, hopes, fears, and expectations. The following results section is more interpretive and explores two larger themes about the dynamics of shared meaning. We conclude with lessons learned about building shared meaning and commitment to school change. The research methodology employed is that of a qualitative case study. The study was conducted in the tradition of participant observation in that both of us, acting as university facilitators, were involved in helping to design and carry out the courtship and implementation activities that they were at the same time studying. For further discussion of methodology, see the chapter appendix.

Framework for School Change

The Accelerated Schools Project is one of several prominent national restructuring models for schools serving at-risk students (see Levin, 1987b). It is a model for creating a school in which problem solving and continuous improvement become the means to accelerated student learning. Like all models of restructuring, it is based on a particular point of view about what needs to be changed most and what the focal point of the restructuring should be. Using Elmore's (1990) typology of school restructuring models, Levin's Accelerated Schools Project is perhaps best described as *reforming the occupational conditions of teaching*, by creating a school organization in which teachers assume greater responsibility for identifying and solving the school's problems and for cultivating their own teaching practice as well as the practice of their peers. In accelerated schools, building teacher capacity is the key to accelerating the learning of all students. The model also includes elements of what Elmore (1990) calls *reforming relationships between schools and their clients* in that it stresses creating an inclusive school community that engages parents and other community members as partners in education.

The present research on the courtship process is part of a longer-term study of the implementation of the Accelerated Schools model in the three sites. In conceptualizing this research, we have developed a four-phase change model to describe the successful implementation of an accelerated school. The hypothesized four phases of successful implementation are the following:

- Courtship
- Training and development
- Changing school structure and culture
- Changing classroom practices

In the courtship phase, initiators of the change (in this case, district and building administrators and university facilitators) engage the school staff and interested parents in a discussion of the need for change and a model for change, and in the end garner the initial commitment and support needed to embark on a major school transformation. The goal of the courtship phase is to begin building a shared meaning and commitment around a particular reform model and to achieve a critical mass of staff support so that efforts to restructure the school can begin. In our study sites, an extended process of courtship (approximately 3 months) was deliberately built into the project.

In the training and development phase, school staff members receive training in the skills, knowledge, and attitudes that are required for the model to succeed. In accelerated schools, the requisite skills and knowledge include working in teacher teams, group process and meeting skills, using an inquiry process to identify and solve school problems, and knowledge of instructional and curricular practices that create powerful learning experiences for all children. Part of the training and development is to instill in teachers the work norms of collegiality and continuous improvement.

In the third, or structural and cultural phase, real changes in school structure and culture are introduced, experimented with, and refined for a particular school site. Changing school structure and culture are placed together because they must be integrated and must support each other. In the Accelerated Schools model, changes in school structure and culture include implementation of a new governance structure and decision-making/leadership roles for teachers and principal, creation of a collaborative and team-oriented work culture, increased parent and community involvement, and a continual focus on a vision and goals that are developed by the entire school community.

Finally, the last and most critical phase for student learning is the classroom practices phase in which structural and cultural changes pass into the classroom and lead to real changes in the curriculum and teachers' instruction and practice. It is only when this last phase is in place that widespread improvements in student learning can be expected to occur (Murphy, 1991).

This four-phase implementation process corresponds roughly to what Rosenblum and Louis (1981) have called the rational model of school change, whereby change is viewed as a logical, sequential process of readiness, initiation, implementation, and continuation (a framework originally developed by Berman & McLaughlin, 1976). We propose our four-phase model only as a heuristic device for understanding some essential steps in successfully implementing the Accelerated Schools Project. The actual change process is hardly as linear and sequential as this framework suggests. For example, training and development is really an ongoing activity, and cultural change, we would argue, can begin as early as the courtship when new ideas are introduced, discussed, and assimilated among staff members. We also believe that change is best viewed within a systems framework, recognizing that planned change is embedded within an existing school structure, culture, and environment that can either support or impede the school's transformation (see Rosenblum & Louis, 1981). Nonrational processes as well as rational planning are part of the change process, most notably the politics and personalities of schools and school districts that impinge upon the change process.

The central premise of our research is that in the press to make school reform happen quickly, school community members tend to pay insufficient attention to the early foundational phases (i.e., courtship, training and development, and laying the groundwork for changing the school's culture) and move quickly into changing organizational structures and classroom practices. This is a tempting approach because it is these latter changes (particularly those in the classroom) that are most directly tied to student improvement. Yet the research on school change has pointed to the folly of beginning with an insufficient foundation. School change efforts tend to fail when they are purely top down or centrally designed with little consideration given to building teacher commitment, ownership, and personal meaning; when they fail to provide needed training and professional development; and when they ignore school culture and history (Berman & McLaughlin, 1976; Fullan, 1982; Fullan & Stiegelbauer, 1991; Hall & Hord, 1987; Rosenblum & Louis, 1981; Sarason, 1971, 1990).

A recent example is provided in a study by Wehlage, Smith, and Lipman (1992) of the educational component of the Casey Foundation's New Futures program. The study involved a Year 3 midcourse assessment of a 5-year effort to restructure middle, junior high, and high schools in four medium-sized cities. The study points to some valuable lessons about just how difficult the restructuring process is, including (a) one should not expect change to happen rapidly and promise too much too soon, (b) top-down reform without the input of principals and teachers does not work, and (c) much needs to be done to train and develop staff for new roles and responsibilities in restructured schools. The main point here is that school reformers must build a foundation of human commitment and organizational support before attempting changes in core instructional and curricular practices.

Of particular interest during the courtship phase is how teachers, principals, and district administrators, who must come together to successfully implement the Accelerated Schools Project, view the model and its potential for improving the lives of students. We began in our study with noting the commonalities and differences across these groups and then tried to draw some implications for building early shared meaning and commitment to the Accelerated Schools process.

Different Meanings
for Different Stakeholders

Interviews with teachers, principals, and central office administrators took place after the courtship was completed and all three school staffs had voted to begin the Accelerated Schools process. The courtship was designed to be a learning and information-sharing period. Through written materials, videotapes, an invited address by Henry Levin, visits to operating accelerated schools, and in-service activities, the staffs at Bridgeport, Clark, and Seaside were introduced to the model, its rationale, and its guiding principles and were able to observe the model in action. Staff members were exposed to the model, but our interviews indicated that many still felt in the dark about what the Accelerated Schools process fully meant. Yet they were beginning to construct their own meanings based on the courtship experience, and it is these initial meanings that were captured in the interviews.

Looking across the stakeholder groups (principals, teachers, and three central office administrators directly involved in the project), there were some shared meanings that related to the model's three guiding principles of unity of purpose, empowerment coupled with responsibility, and building on strengths. However, there were also some divergent points of view about what Accelerated Schools meant and what it could do for school and students. There were likewise commonalities and differences across the three school sites.

Principals

Overall, the three principals tended to agree more than they disagreed on what Accelerated Schools meant and what it could do for their schools. What principals focused on most in discussing the meaning of the model was its potential to empower both the school site and the teaching staff. "We create our own schools" was a common view of all three principals. In the words of the Bridgeport principal:

Accelerated Schools isn't a menu. It isn't a cookbook, it isn't a recipe. It is something you make yourself. No one else can tell you what the outcome is going to be like. They can give you some ideas of what the process was like for them and what the outcome was for them, but nobody else can really lay it out for you. This is a powerful strength, but it is also very difficult. Because in our profession we are used to having new programs come with a real recipe. We are not really used to being treated as thinking professionals.

All three principals likewise felt that empowering teachers with more decision making *and* responsibility was a key strength of the model, pointing out that this will lead to better problem solving and decisions and to a more professional teaching staff. A second strong theme that the three principals focused on was unity of purpose. They all saw the Accelerated Schools Project as a means of bringing focus to the school agenda and unifying the staff and parents—in the words of the Seaside principal, "a pulling together of the entire school community." Finally, a third common theme was student success. All three principals felt strongly about the principles of "Accelerate, don't remediate" and of building on student strengths in developing teaching strategies.

Although there were many commonalities among the principals, there were also some important differences. At Bridgeport, the principal, who had many years of experience, felt a greater sense of urgency about the need for change and viewed the Accelerated Schools Project as a powerful site-based management strategy, a strategy she felt comfortable with because of her experience in implementing site-based management at her previous school. She was ready to do this again at her new school and viewed the Accelerated Schools process as a "better framework" for site-based management than what she had used before. At Seaside, the Accelerated Schools Project was seen as a way to improve communication within the school and to protect the school from the onslaught of district-mandated reforms. The Seaside principal also saw the Accelerated Schools Project as a professional development opportunity for himself: "Any way that I can add another tool to my professional repertoire, you know, I felt would have been beneficial." Finally, at Clark the principal was focused on using Accelerated Schools principles to help students become more engaged in school and learning, and thereby help solve discipline problems. The Clark principal, who like the one at Seaside was new to the principalship, also saw the Accelerated Schools Project and its training as an opportunity for her own professional development as well as the development of her staff who wanted more involvement in school decisions.

Teachers

For teachers, there were a variety of views about what the Accelerated Schools Project really meant and what it could do for the school, but also some common themes across all 24 teachers who were interviewed in the three schools. Teachers focused on some of the same global concepts that principals did; particularly, empowerment, and to a lesser extent, unity of purpose. The sentiment here was that the Accelerated Schools model would allow all of the staff to be in charge *together*, as represented by the following comment from a Seaside teacher:

There was a group that always, I think, pretty much ran a lot of the educational administration choices in the building. This is why I think this would be a good model because there will not be one top person. We'll all be in charge. Hopefully, this will work. And if it doesn't, that will be because some people can't quite relinquish that kind of power. I think that's another thing. There is no key person. The principal up there, of course, has final say and is accountable to the district. But I think this program is trying to say, at least the principal was giving all his power to his professional people and then parent volunteers, and any other support people. I think that's good. I think it should be a group effort instead of one person controlling.

Referring to the responsibility that goes with empowerment, one Clark teacher commented,

There are some things that I see Accelerated Schools helping, and that is in bringing more parents in, and also in maybe taking some of the load from the principal as far as budget, and not only that, but the heat for how well children are doing seems to fall on her shoulders. I think we should all have an active responsibility in setting the climate for the school and implementing programs and working to bring these children to where they should be, to their potential. I think that not only will it make the principal's job in working with parents easier, but my job maybe a little more interesting. I don't feel now that we have a lot of say in how funds are used in the building. . . . So I see this as a way of working as a group.

These comments reflect the thoughts of many teachers in the three schools who viewed building the capacity of the staff to work more productively together as a major benefit of the Accelerated Schools model.

In general, teachers were more apt to focus on teaching, learning, and student success, in contrast to principals, who mentioned student and teaching issues, but were more focused on the operation of the school. Many teachers saw the potential of the motto "Accelerate, don't remediate" for their students and for bringing better teaching practices into the school for children in at-risk situations. The Accelerated Schools Project was seen as a way to "help students who may get lost along the way," to treat the whole child, to stop labeling and stigmatizing children, and to build on strengths. Teachers also saw the potential for improved practices that would increase student engagement, esteem, and achievement. Finally, it should be pointed out that each school had a handful of cynics, teachers who either worried that the Accelerated Schools Project was another passing fad or felt that the model was ill equipped to address *real* school problems like over-crowded classrooms and inadequate budgets.

All teachers echoed some common themes, but there were also important variations across the three schools. These variations suggested that teachers tended to view the model's potential largely in terms of their school's most pressing problems. For example, at Bridgeport (the school with the lowest achievement test scores and a very poor reputation in the district and community), teachers saw the Accelerated Schools Project as a way to lift staff morale, raise expectations for everyone, and increase student motivation and achievement. At Seaside (a school at which participants eventually formed a staff communication cadre because of communication problems identified in taking stock), a repeated theme was using the Accelerated Schools Project to "focus" the staff and improve communication and collaboration among teachers. Finally, at Clark (a school where there had been several strong teacher leaders present for many years), the Accelerated Schools Project was seen as a way to equalize decision-making power among all staff. Thus, teachers were concerned not only with global concepts like building capacity, empowerment, unity of purpose, and student success but also with how the Accelerated Schools Project would address the everyday problems in *their* school that made their jobs difficult and hindered student success.

Central Office Administrators

The central office administrators had a markedly different perspective on what the Accelerated Schools Project meant, although they certainly shared some of the same sentiments with teachers and principals about the importance of local school decision making, teacher empowerment and capacity building, and accelerating rather than remediating students who lag academically. District administrators tended to take a more systemic and visionary view of the change process—the Accelerated Schools Project was a means to ensure that the *whole* school changed rather than just "bits and pieces." The strongest theme among the two curriculum department administrators who had helped initiate the Accelerated Schools effort was that the project should be more than just a change in organizational processes and amount to something that permeates the classroom and has a strong impact on children. In the words of the curriculum director:

My caution and my major concern is that there not be too much emphasis on the structure and the organization because I think structure and organization can vary and still succeed, but the structure and organization can become the end in itself and can become meaningless activity. And I think it's really important that not happen. So if the focus stays on curriculum and instruction, the goal is to improve instruction for kids. The goal is to accelerate the learning of all kids. And if that's always kept front and center, the committees [cadres] are a tool toward that end. I think there have been lots of innovations tried and the tools become the end. That's my biggest caution and my biggest worry. You can actually end up sucking out a lot of energy into organization and it actually detracts from the focus.

Similarly, the district administrator overseeing the three schools believed that a model like Accelerated Schools must do more than change organizational decision making to ensure that decisions focus on important matters that affect students. Otherwise, shared governance becomes "like a hamster wheel" where time is spent making

decisions about relatively unimportant matters. Finally, also related to
the view of whole-school change, all three administrators believed that
the Accelerated Schools process was a means to a school becoming a
place of "continuous improvement" and "self-renewal."

The district administrators, as expected, tended to adopt a more
political view of the Accelerated Schools Project in addition to seeing
the model for its educational worth. This is not to say that they saw the
model as pure political opportunism. On the contrary, all three were
genuinely committed to the model and in fact viewed themselves as
district risk takers, who to some extent had gone out on a limb to bring
the Accelerated Schools Project into the district. However, they all saw
the political side too and felt that the time was now right for Accelerated
Schools, given a strong push from both a new superintendent and from
state legislators toward site-based management. Also, all three schools
were so-called targeted schools that had been identified by the school
board for serious improvement efforts to raise low student test scores,
and the Accelerated Schools Project was an opportunity to do something to address this problem.

In summary, there were many common views of the Accelerated
Schools Project across the three stakeholder groups: the importance of
school and teacher capacity building and empowerment, the need to
accelerate rather than remediate, and the need to create a unity of purpose within these schools in order to move forward. These views reflect
a beginning internalization of the three Accelerated Schools guiding
principles. In terms of the model's principles, at least, the three groups
generally seemed to be on the same wavelength.

Moving beyond general principles, however, there were some important differences across the three stakeholder groups. Teachers
seemed most concerned with solving the everyday problems of the
school; at the other extreme, the central office administrators involved
in the project were most concerned with achieving systemic rather than
piecemeal change. In particular, there was a concern about changes in
school decision making truly impacting teaching practices. The administrators were also more astute about the political situation, and in this
case, how the political context supported the Accelerated Schools Project. Principals fell somewhere in between, being concerned with their
local school problems, but also seeing Accelerated Schools as means to
whole-school change.

The results also indicated a different sense of urgency across the
three schools, with the Bridgeport staff feeling the greatest need for

change and the strongest push for change from its principal. Two points are noteworthy here. First, of the three schools, Bridgeport was the "lowest of the low" in student achievement. It had the worst reputation of the three schools, including some very negative press coverage for its students having the lowest achievement scores in the district. Second, the Bridgeport principal was of the three the most experienced principal and someone with strong convictions about the positive value of empowering teachers. She had previous experience in implementing site-based management. At Bridgeport more than Seaside or Clark, the principal seemed to be setting the tone for change during the early courtship period. These leadership issues are discussed more fully in Chapter 7.

The descriptive results point out that some shared meaning can be formed around a strong set of guiding principles through courtship activities, but also that different individuals and groups can hold different attitudes and views based on their own assessment of the problems, their organizational position, their experience, and the school history and context. In the next section, two larger interpretive themes are discussed, which provide deeper insight into the process of developing shared meaning and commitment.

Two Countervailing Forces: The Model's Ambiguity and Fit

During the early courtship phase, participants were beginning to form personal meanings as described above, but were also struggling with what a change project like Accelerated Schools really meant. What was surprising (and a little discouraging) was that after 3 months of learning about and discussing the model, school staff members still felt largely in the dark about the Accelerated Schools process. We represent this finding as a sense of *ambiguity* about a change model that defines the guiding principles and process for change, and then challenges school staff members to create the changes themselves.

Many of the teachers in all three schools expressed a sense of ambiguity, but the sentiment was strongest at Seaside. The two less-experienced principals also expressed some feelings of ambiguity, whereas the more experienced Bridgeport principal did not. The teachers' sense of ambiguity centered around the model being more of a set of guiding principles and a process of change than a packaged curriculum and instruction program. From two different Seaside teachers:

I think a lot of people came away [from the Henry Levin address] still saying, what is an accelerated school? I think people want someone to tell them this is what it is and they don't realize that we have to create it. [Question: That's a paradigm shift.] Yeah, it's a huge one in education given all the prepackaged things in the past.

Maybe it's inherently fuzzy because it says we're going to take and work with this particular school to decide what this school needs and how we're going to push all the kids as hard and fast as possible. So in this sense it will probably be different at every school, and there is no boilerplate model, that it must in essence change from school to school.

From one Bridgeport teacher talking about comments she heard from others:

A lot of comments about what does this mean, what do we do. It's really hard to self-start this kind of thing because we don't have a blueprint. And I guess that's the point that you don't have a blueprint. You make it yourself.

Although most teachers seemed frustrated and uncomfortable with the inherent ambiguity of the model, one Seaside teacher expressed a more positive attitude:

I just think it's kind of vague in the way it's been introduced. I'm comfortable with it, but I've heard from others that they're not. As a teacher you just hear all kinds of new things that are going to save the world and they fade away. It's easy to dismiss things when you don't really have a grasp on what it is. Maybe I don't either. But I think probably it's up to us to make it what it's going to be. I feel like if you go into it positively, you can make it more than it's even supposed to be.

This last teacher was not uncomfortable with the model's ambiguity, but her comments also reflect a theme expressed by several other teachers as well—that too much prolonged ambiguity can lead to a loss of enthusiasm for the model (i.e., "easy to dismiss things when you don't really have a grasp on what it is").

As mentioned above, Seaside teachers expressed more discomfort and ambiguity than teachers from the other two schools. There were some important differences in how the three principals presented the model that help explain this difference. At Seaside, the principal was a vocal advocate for the Accelerated Schools Project during the courtship phase. In contrast, the Bridgeport principal was a strong advocate of the principles and ideas behind Accelerated Schools (such as building on strengths and group problem solving), but did not push the model per se. For example, at an early introductory exercise during the courtship, she designed a short in-service activity that focused on building on strengths without mentioning the Accelerated Schools process. At Clark, the principal soft-pedaled the model during courtship because she did not want to push it on her staff, which she felt did not take well to being told what to do. Perhaps a more important difference was that at both Bridgeport and Clark, teachers were given the opportunity to consider the Accelerated Schools Project along with other change models whereas the Seaside teachers were not presented with alternatives. The procedures used for voting on the model also differed in an important way. Seaside teachers were asked to sign their names to a voting ballot, compared to secret ballots at the other two schools. One Seaside teacher described the courtship and voting process as "being influenced" but falling short of being "coerced." There clearly seemed to be more pressure and less free choice at Seaside during the courtship process.

This cross-school comparison points to two distinct styles of presenting the model and gaining teacher commitment and support: direct pressure versus giving teachers the opportunity to "discover" the model for themselves and then vote on it without undue pressure. The more pressured approach represented by Seaside seemed to heighten anxiety and create more ambiguity and discomfort. Teachers perhaps felt that although their principal was really behind the model, they still felt in the dark about what the model really meant and why they were pursuing it.

The discussion to this point has focused on the initial ambiguity that is a natural part of a change process that empowers staff members to create their own schools. Although ambiguity can be a negative force for change, there was a countervailing positive force, which we call *fit*. Teachers and others told us that what kept them moving forward in the early stages of high ambiguity was a sense that the Accelerated Schools Project was a good match, or fit, for themselves personally, for their students, or for the school and district. Many teachers, and especially those new to the teaching profession, felt that the Accelerated Schools Project was a good match for their training, preparation, and personal educational values. The building and central office administrators believed that the Accelerated Schools Project was a good fit for where the schools wanted to go anyway (i.e., increased teacher professionalism and site-based management). Perhaps the strongest sense of fit was that the curricular and instructional philosophy of Accelerated Schools reflected principles and practices already in place in schools and the school district (e.g., whole language, enriched curriculum, cooperative learning, and "push-in" rather than "pull-out" Chapter 1). One central office administrator told us that the curricular and instructional philosophy of Accelerated Schools "fits this district like a glove." Some teachers felt that the classroom practices advocated in the Accelerated Schools Project were "something we were already doing and therefore could do even better than other accelerated schools." This sense of fit seemed to dampen the sense of worry about the model's inherent ambiguity.

The sense of fit was most evident for the Bridgeport principal. She expressed, with conviction, a personal philosophy of teacher empowerment and enriched learning that echoed Accelerated Schools principles and values. She also had the strongest vision of what an accelerated school meant for the classroom teacher. In contrast, Clark's principal felt good about the Accelerated Schools model, but had some reservations about some of the curricular and instructional practices advocated in the model. At Seaside, there was simply a less strong vision for how the model fit where the school wanted to go, even though the principal viewed the model as the right thing to do.

Lessons Learned About Building
Shared Meaning and Commitment

This first part of our study of the courtship process led to three key conclusions:

- Courtship activities and a clear set of guiding principles can help create cohesion and shared meaning among a diverse group of stakeholders in the early stages of an Accelerated Schools change project.
- The meaning of change differs by organizational role; the different perspectives of teachers, principals, and central office admin-

istrators must be addressed throughout the Accelerated Schools implementation process.

- Teachers, more than other school stakeholders, experience a strong sense of ambiguity, but this can be counteracted by paying attention to the model's fit with the school's vision and direction.

What we hope this study reveals is that staff understanding and acceptance of Accelerated Schools change can be enhanced by a well-planned courtship experience. In the three schools under study, it appeared that courtship activities were successful in creating at least some degree of initial shared meaning as these schools embarked on the Accelerated Schools journey. What drew participants from various organizational roles and schools together was a set of clear change principles—the model's three guiding principles of unity of purpose, empowerment coupled with responsibility, and building on strengths. Perhaps most appealing to school staff members is the Accelerated Schools promise to empower teachers and communities to create their own schools. Many individuals from all three stakeholder groups (teacher, principal, central office administrator) were also excited by the idea of "Accelerate, don't remediate" and hence showed some recognition that school restructuring is really about students and student learning.

People in different organizational roles and different school settings, however, see the meaning of an accelerated school change in their own unique way. District administrators take the most systemic and visionary view, understanding the need for organizational changes supporting better teaching and learning in classrooms, and viewing the Accelerated Schools Project in a larger reform context. Teachers seem to focus more on how the change will address more local and isolated problems in their school, issues that have an immediate effect on their work lives and the success of their students. This is consistent with much that about we know about the sociology of teaching and how teachers adopt a "practicality ethic" when evaluating change projects (Fullan & Stiegelbauer, 1991; Lortie, 1975; Rosenholtz, 1989). Principals can be visionary and think systemically, but the differences across our three schools suggest that this is more difficult for inexperienced principals. Principals who have been previously involved in a school restructuring process have a clearer sense of how the Accelerated Schools model can be translated into a vision of change for *their* school. They have more in their repertoire to draw from, whereas inexperienced principals must rely on the abstract principles inherent to the model. We were unable to interview parents for this study, but we would guess that parents bring in yet another perspective that further complicates the dynamics of developing shared meaning and commitment.

These different role perspectives are important to consider as the change effort moves from courtship to implementation. The results suggest that teachers have the most potential to view the Accelerated Schools Project as a "program" to solve small problems rather than a means to systemic change and accelerated student learning. Over time, however, teachers should be able to see the larger potential of the Accelerated Schools process as they become more involved in cadres, steering committees, and whole-school decisions. Thus, involving everyone in the group work becomes an important means for achieving a deeper shared meaning and commitment over time. This means that as the implementation proceeds, cadres must include a cross-section of all important stakeholders, including students in accelerated middle schools. The steering committee and the school as a whole must meet frequently to work through the difficult change issues that the participants are likely to disagree on.

If meanings differ by organizational role and school context, then a well-planned courtship experience becomes a way to build in a vision for change via the model's formal guiding principles and deeper values (e.g., collaboration, community involvement, and equity in student achievement). Strong guiding principles and core values can provide people with an *emotional* attachment that is part of the personal commitment to change. Courtship activities can be designed as the first opportunity to air conflicts and address different subjective meanings as the change process begins.

Although courtship can be used to build some initial shared meaning, the Accelerated Schools model will still seem vague because it provides only the change principles and process while leaving the real work of change up to the school. This creates feelings of ambiguity and discomfort, especially for teachers. It is the teachers, after all, who must change first and foremost if we view the Accelerated Schools process as a means of building staff capacity. In the accelerated school, teachers will be on the front line of school decisions and will be the implementors of curricular and instructional changes. Even though many teachers are drawn to this new professionalism, they are certainly more used to operating in the world of prepackaged curricula and other mandates from above. They are more used to being told what to do than to being the creators of their school's destiny.

It is no wonder that teachers approach this new role with both excitement and anxiety. What we interpreted as ambiguity in our interviews might also be attributable to some lack of trust—that is, a sense that this is yet another reform from "on high" and a fear that "this too shall pass," as one of our teachers expressed it. On a more personal level, some teachers may also mistrust their own capabilities to become decision makers and problem solvers given their training and preparation. This is where training and development plays a role in ensuring that teachers have the skills and self-confidence to carry out what is being asked of them.

As one teacher warned, this sense of ambiguity (and perhaps mistrust) should not be taken lightly, because people eventually lose interest in something that they do not understand. As the change process unfolds, teachers' discomfort or mistrust can be dealt with by keeping them highly involved and having them experience success in early activities like taking stock, creating the school vision, and setting improvement priorities. However, staff members will not fully realize what being an accelerated school means until they become engaged in cadre work and see changes in their students. Thus, timing and a brisk pacing of activities (especially through the first year) become a means of holding teacher interest and commitment.

If ambiguity is a given, then a countervailing positive force for change is the fit of the model. Principals and outside facilitators must pay attention to where the model fits well with what teachers and schools are already doing or want to do as part of the vision for change. Pointing out how the model fits and how it can help the participants do the things they want to do even better can help alleviate the discomfort and fear that is part of the beginning change process. A second way to counteract ambiguity is through a constructivist method of presenting the model that forces teachers to come to grips more quickly with what the Accelerated Schools process means for themselves and their school. This is part of the leadership role that is discussed in Chapter 7.

APPENDIX

Research Methods

At the time of the study, both of us were facilitating and studying the implementation process at the three accelerated schools. We had worked for over 3 years with the district curriculum department, the area superintendent, the three school principals, and with many staff members and parents to stimulate and facilitate this restructuring process.

In this research, we used a qualitative case study methodology to document and understand the courtship and early implementation process in this Accelerated Schools Project. The analysis involved looking at both the Accelerated Schools Project as a whole (i.e., all three schools working together under the guidance of a district-supported leadership team) and at key differences across the three school sites to better understand the effects of contextual factors. The study was conducted in the tradition of participant observation in that both of us, acting as university facilitators, were involved in helping design and carry out the courtship and implementation activities that we were at the same time studying. This allowed something of an insider's view and an opportunity to study the change process as it was unfolding rather than after the fact. This approach helped us more fully understand the organizational and human dynamics of the change process. The approach, however, does have some limitations in that we were not totally neutral parties, but were ourselves stakeholders in the change process. On balance, however, the advantages of the approach far surpassed its limitations.

To help minimize any personal bias of the researchers, all interviews were tape-recorded and then transcribed and coded before the field notes were analyzed. Procedures described by Miles and Huberman (1984) and Yin (1984) were also used to increase the reliability and validity of qualitative data. Both researchers worked together in collecting data at all three schools, giving us a built-in perception check during the analysis phase. Finally, the key research findings were presented and discussed with each school principal in order to identify any inaccuracies or omissions. For the most part, the principals confirmed the accuracy of our findings. They shared our interpretations of events or gave us additional insights, which we then included in the results.

The following data sources were used:

- Semistructured interviews with the following key informants: 24 teachers from the three schools; each school's principal; three key central office administrators (the curriculum director, another curriculum administrator, and the area supervisor) who were directly involved in the project; and two school board members (to learn more about the district and political context)
- Meeting notes from monthly leadership team meetings and retreats held by the leadership team, all of which we ourselves participated in
- Our own observations and notes as we worked with the leadership team and the schools on courtship and early staff training and development activities
- Numerous visits to the three schools, which provided opportunities for unstructured observations of school and classroom life
- Informal conversations with some parents and staff members
- Background and demographic data on the schools and neighborhoods

It should be noted that at the time of this study, all three schools had been "launched" through the Accelerated Schools process. Participants had completed the process of taking stock and writing a school vision, had set school priority areas, and were beginning to implement the new shared governance structures. The key-person interviews, which were the main data source for this phase of the research, were conducted *after* the courtship activities and the voting were completed, but *before* the official "launch," which included 2 days of intensive training provided by the National Center for the Accelerated Schools Project at Stanford. Thus, the views expressed are the initial conceptions of the model based on courtship activities and prior knowledge.

The analysis is both descriptive and interpretive. In presenting our findings, we tried to interweave both rich description (including the words of the participants themselves) and more generalized interpretations about building shared meaning and commitment.

5

Making Change Our Friend

CHRISTINE FINNAN

School Change: Friend or Foe

In his 1993 inaugural address, Bill Clinton exhorted the citizens of the United States to "make change our friend and not our enemy." Clinton's call was for all Americans to welcome change as a part of our culture. After 2 years in office, President Clinton has found that it is hard to make change a friend, especially when there is no clear consensus on how and why we must change. Many of us trying to improve schools hope school communities will make change a friend, but are discouraged when change does not come easily. Why isn't change embraced by the nation and by schools? As Michael Fullan (Fullan & Stiegelbauer, 1991) writes, "If a healthy respect for and mastery of the change process does not become a priority, even well-intentioned change initiatives will continue to create havoc among those who are on the firing line" (p. xiii). Too often, we do not fully appreciate the complexity of change and do not provide the right kind of help to those trying to create change.

Fullan and Stiegelbauer's (1991) warning is echoed in the literature on school change. Studies often portray schools as resistant to change (Cuban, 1984, 1992; Sarason, 1990; Schlechty, 1990; Wehlage et al., 1992). This is usually true when change designed at the federal, state, school district, or university level is imposed from the outside. These school reform initiatives, no matter how well meaning, are often resisted, avoided, or altered beyond recognition when they are implemented in schools (Berman & McLaughlin, 1977; Fullan & Stiegelbauer, 1991; Sarason, 1990; Wehlage et al., 1992). Those left to implement the initiative (usually teachers) have little investment in its goals or desire to see it succeed.

The literature indicates that interventions fail because reformers ignore the implementation process (Bardach, 1980; Berman & McLaughlin, 1977). Too little attention is given to how an intervention is presented to the school community and how the school community is expected to implement it. Many reform initiatives offer in-service training with no follow-up (Joyce, Wolf, & Calhoun, 1993; Little, 1993). Teachers may be motivated to make changes, but when change does not occur easily, no one is available to provide help and guidance.

Research has also found that reformers ignore the influence of school culture on shaping the intervention (Sarason, 1990; Wehlage et al., 1992). The school culture, or the "interlocking ideas, practices, values, and expectations that are 'givens' not requiring thought or deliberation" (Sarason, 1982, p. 228) has a profound influence on how—and if—a school changes. Too often, reformers assume that all school communities will have the same response to change, and they are frustrated when change is adapted and altered to make sense within each school's unique school culture. There is little or no effort made to understand what makes each school unique or what past experiences school community members have had with reform efforts. School cultures are frequently seen as barriers to change, not as a changing, dynamic feature of the school.

Finally, for a variety of reasons, most reforms are fleeting, and as Tyack and Tobin (1994) state, fail to become ingrained in the "grammar of schooling." Too often, we are impatient for results and do not allow time for the reform to become embedded in the school.

To say that school communities resist change is accurate to a point, but it is also somewhat misleading. School communities deal constantly with change. Budgets are cut, administrators are moved, student populations change, laws and policies change. School communities accommodate all of these changes, even though they may not welcome them. So, the issue for school reform is not that change is foreign to schools; it is that change is usually not welcomed by schools.

Although the literature on school change is discouraging, school reform efforts continue. Those of us associated with the Accelerated Schools Project are still optimistic about the model's usefulness for bringing about lasting change in schools. As Henry M. Levin describes in Chapter 1, the Accelerated Schools Project was designed to avoid many of the problems associated with failed school reform initiatives:

- The project is not imposed from the top; school community members choose to implement it.
- Considerable attention is paid to the implementation process, including continuous support from a trained coach.
- The philosophy of the project encourages schools to build on strengths, including strengths in the existing school culture, and the process (especially the taking stock phase) provides school community members an opportunity to make the school culture explicit and to document the ever-changing nature of the school culture.
- The project incorporates the recognition that change takes time, especially to build trust, open communication, and accept the responsibility associated with empowerment.

In this chapter, I provide a description and analysis of how each of these features of the project design influenced the implementation process in one middle school in northern California.[1] The data collection (which took place in 1990-1991) centered on the school community's first year in the project. In the study, I followed the implementation of key stages of the Accelerated Schools process (initial buy-in, training, taking stock, developing a vision, and the inquiry process) and documented the degree to which school community members internalized the project philosophy. I also focused on how the existing school culture and other factors influenced school change. The data were generated through ethnographic interviews, observations, and document review.[2]

The following section provides a description of the school and its culture when the Accelerated Schools Project was first implemented. Data describing each of the factors listed above are then presented to provide a picture of how these design features encouraged the school community members to see change in a positive light.

Calhoun Middle School

Calhoun Middle School is a downtown school in a large school district serving over 30,000 students. The district is both geographically and demographically diverse. The immediate surroundings of the school are dominated by the city and county government buildings, including the courthouse, jail, and police station. The homes are largely older bungalows, and although many are well kept, drug activity does occur in some of the vacant homes. Most of the residents of the neighboring bungalows and apartment buildings are low income and Hispanic. The larger community served by the school district is one of the most affluent in the country. Until recently, jobs have been plentiful, but most of the jobs require specialized training and higher education. Unskilled and semiskilled manufacturing jobs have become increasingly scarce because the high cost of living in the area drives manufacturing operations to other communities. Although the school district serves a racially diverse population, many schools were segregated until the school district agreed to comply with a 1985 federal court order to desegregate. Until 1986, prior to the desegregation order, Calhoun's student population was almost completely Hispanic.

The student body represented an ethnic mix, achieved largely by the desegregation order. In the fall of 1990, Calhoun served 617 students, of whom 55% were Hispanic, 39% were other White (of which 64% were of Portuguese descent),[3] 5% were of Asian, Filipino, or Pacific Island descent, and 2% were African Americans. Calhoun was under-enrolled because it could not admit Hispanic students (even though there were many on a waiting list) unless it could attract more non-Hispanic White students.

Calhoun had difficulty attracting non-Hispanic White students because student achievement was poor and the student body was polarized both ethnically and academically. Twenty percent of the students were in gifted or accelerated classes, and 60% to 70% were eligible for compensatory programs. Few students were in the middle. Internal segregation was quite visible. The top 20% of the school was composed primarily of non-Hispanic White and Asian American students, whereas Hispanic children were disproportionately in the compensatory programs.

When the Accelerated Schools Project began in September 1990, the school resembled a traditional junior high school, despite its label of middle school.[4] The curriculum, instruction, and organization were like those found in many junior high schools. The school day was divided into six periods, 50 minutes long. Students changed classrooms at the sound of a bell.[5] Students were grouped in classes according to their ability. Language arts and social studies were labeled "accelerated," "regular," or "sheltered."[6] Math classes were tracked according to students' readiness to take algebra. Many students were also served in special classes, such as a Chapter 1 compensatory class, special education classes (self-contained and pull-out), and an "opportunity class" for children who appeared destined to drop out because of behavior problems.

The governance of the school was primarily from the top down. The principal and vice principal for curriculum made most of the decisions.[7] Teacher input into decisions was primarily through department heads. The 42 teachers were represented by 7 department heads who met monthly to discuss school issues.[8] The classified staff (teacher's aides; campus supervisors; secretarial, janitorial, and cafeteria staff; bus drivers) had little or no input into schoolwide decisions; they did not attend either faculty meetings or steering committee meetings. Parent involvement was limited. A home-school club existed, but only a few parents were active, and few of the active parents were members of minority groups.

Staff morale at Calhoun was low. Teachers were discouraged for two reasons. First, many of them had invested a great deal of time and energy in an earlier change initiative,[9] and their plans had been abandoned. Second, many of the teachers had developed strong attachments to a principal who had recently been transferred to another school without any warning. One teacher summarized the feeling of many:

> It was horrible. For those of us that had worked so hard, it was like getting slapped in the face because our new administrator came in, and I guess maybe he heard too much about, "Well, this is the way we do things." We didn't want to see our program destroyed, and he got very defensive, and it was like we learned right away we couldn't talk about that.

Factors Encouraging
Acceptance of Change

Buying Into Change

As the preceding illustrates, Calhoun was ripe for change. Relations between the staff and administration needed improvement, and teacher morale was low. The school organization was not conducive to creativity or innovation, and there were few avenues for communication across the school community. Students were unmotivated and were not achieving as well as hoped. The situation called for change because many members of the school community would not tolerate the existing situation much longer.

On first glance, it seems as if this situation would stifle any efforts at positive change and that the school community would resist any change efforts. Staff members surely would have resisted change brought in from the district or by their new principal. The negativity and antagonism that existed when the Accelerated Schools Project was introduced could have easily overwhelmed other change initiatives. However, the veteran teachers at Calhoun had already demonstrated an interest in change and a willingness to work hard to achieve it, and the administration and central office saw the wisdom in the Accelerated Schools model and were committed to making it work. In one sense, given the overriding sense of negativity, they had nothing to lose.

The Calhoun staff did not have an extended courtship (see Chapter 4) with the Accelerated Schools Project. The administrators and several staff members participated in a focus group to shape the design of the Accelerated Schools middle school component, but the majority of the staff did not hear about the project until a few days before the end of the 1989-1990 school year. After a brief presentation on the project and many hard questions, the entire faculty voted unanimously to join the Accelerated Schools Project.

Several teachers said that they voted to join the project because the philosophy fit closely with their own. They felt that the project made sense and that it would allow them to teach the children the way they had always wanted to teach. Two veteran teachers explained their reaction:

> This is the thing that attracted me to the program, was that it was so consistent with my philosophy—my own personal philosophy of the way things should be done. And I said, "Hear! Hear! Finally I have somebody who knows what's supposed to happen."

> I'm not the kind of guy that says, "Hey, this looks good! I'll jump on the bandwagon." I think the concept of the project is a valid one. It is grounded in a lot of common sense. I regard myself as a commonsense, practical kind of guy. When I read the original proposal, it just made a lot of sense to me.

Other teachers were more skeptical. They expressed reservations about the feasibility of accelerating the learning of some of the children because they felt the children were too far behind, did not value education, and created too many disruptions in class. They had also seen reform projects come and go. They voted to join the project because they felt they did not have much choice:

And those of us who have taught a while—20 years—I've gone through districts, and I've gone through different programs, and they're all new, and they're all revolutionary. And they fall by the wayside. And what I see as the nitty-gritty is what happens in my classroom on a daily basis, working with the kids, working with the discipline problems and the lack of motivation in a school like this with Hispanic kids whose culture doesn't value [education].

I'm really skeptical. It's because I've done it before. There's been so many times that we come in, and they say, "Oh, we're going to," you know. When we got the magnet program, we did the same thing that the Accelerated Schools are talking about. We wanted to raise the academic level here, we wanted to raise the idea for student achievement, and we were on our way. And then we got shoved [and a new principal was brought in].

Although some of the more skeptical teachers may have felt that they did not have a choice about joining the Accelerated Schools Project, in fact, they did. The Accelerated Schools Project is based on the recognition that change will not happen if teachers do not want to be actively involved in making the changes; at least 90% of the faculty must vote to become involved. Because the faculty voted unanimously to join the project, the skeptics could not complain that they were forced to join. Some of them may have felt more comfortable with the project if Calhoun had engaged in a longer, more thorough courtship process, but time and early signs of change helped sway most of the skeptics. One of the negative teachers quoted above was very positive about the project by the end of the year. In June, he commented, "Time heals." He went on to say,

Definitely, there have been changes. No one can deny the fact that the time has been well spent to get to a sense of common purpose. The project has pulled the school together. It has helped the attitude of students. It is a self-esteem builder for students.

The project also moved ahead because enough of the faculty embraced the philosophy and saw the utility of the process. They saw the project as theirs, rather than something imposed from the district or from the National Center for the Accelerated Schools Project, and they were able to move ahead. This group of dedicated teachers also helped win over the skeptics.

Systematic Implementation and Close Follow-Up

The Accelerated Schools Project is both a philosophy and a process. If it were limited to a philosophy, the Calhoun staff would have engaged in several days of staff development to internalize the philosophy and would have been left to implement the philosophy on their own. School communities, including Calhoun's, have considerable experience with this approach to change, and they report that it rarely works. They do not know how to apply the theories or philosophy to practice, and no one is available to help them. However, in the case of the Accelerated Schools Project, the process and close follow-up by coaches provide a vehicle for changing the school in ways consistent with the philosophy.

The Calhoun school community moved through the early stages of the process and began the inquiry process in one year. The Calhoun faculty received 2 days of training before school started and completed the taking stock and vision processes before the winter break. Following the break, they set priorities and began the inquiry process. These processes are summarized in the Resources section at the end of the book and are described in depth in *The Accelerated Schools Resource Guide* (Hopfenberg et al., 1993).

The Accelerated Schools process provides a vehicle for school communities to move toward a vision their members create and facilitates internalization of the project philosophy. It provides a structure that enables change to occur. The process provides a means to keep the vision in sight even when other influences threaten to divert participants' focus. For example, toward the end of the first year, the Calhoun school community learned that the budget would be drastically reduced the next year. This news was very upsetting, but the school community used the Accelerated Schools process to develop strategies to deal with the budget cuts and to stay focused on the vision. A teacher commented on the effects of the budget cuts on the project and mused about what usually happens when crises of this kind occur:

> Things in this district change so drastically—especially because of money. . . . You can have great intentions, but what I'm hoping as I consider the program is . . . this [the Accelerated Schools Project] may set up a system where it's not dependent on budget or personality. . . . It's more attitude than something physical.

The process at Calhoun was also very successful because it involved everyone in the school and brought disparate people together. All of the teachers, administrators, teaching assistants, and campus supervisors[10] were involved in taking stock, vision development, and inquiry. Some parents and students were also actively involved. Teachers appreciated having the chance to work with people they rarely saw before the project started. They appreciated the process in part because it gave structure to their work, but also because it brought them into productive working relationships with other people. One teacher commented,

> This is how I view Accelerated Schools. Well, first of all, the Accelerated Schools Project has done more to get all the teachers working together than anything else in the school—anything. So, if it's going to happen, something like this is going to do it.

Involving all teachers, support staff, parents, and students in a process all but ensures that the process will continue because so many people have an interest in seeing it through.

A systematic process also ensures that plans are put into action. Some teachers at Calhoun were skeptical about the project at the beginning, because in their experience, plans are often made by a committee of teachers but are never implemented in the school. This led to reluctance on the part of some teachers to invest much time and energy into the process in the beginning. However, because the process was clearly laid out and everyone in the school was involved in making plans, they realized that the chance of implementing the plans was much greater. One teacher commented,

We are starting to feel that what we decide will be put to use and practice. Before the cadres, there was a sense that input would be put to us—that decisions were made without us. We are seeing our work put in place for next year.

The existence of a planning and implementation process does not ensure that people will use it. Another feature of the Accelerated Schools Project that facilitates change is the involvement of trained coaches who work with school communities until their members have internalized the philosophy and consistently use the process. Calhoun was fortunate to have several coaches from the national center. These coaches provided staff development and attended most meetings. The coaches did not lead meetings, but they helped the committee members learn to use the process and keep the philosophy alive. An administrator praised the coaches for, "being there when we need them, but letting us do the work." The coaches and the Calhoun staff realized that the school could not rely on the national center to transform it into an accelerated school; that was the job of the Calhoun community.

Building on Existing School Culture

Each school has a distinct culture that cannot be ignored. Without an understanding of a school's existing culture, we fall prey to stereotyping and to attempting to change what does not need changing. Change in schools also comes more easily when the existing school culture is viewed as a strength rather than a barrier. To ignore the strengths of the existing culture robs people of their past and denigrates earlier efforts to better serve children. Successful change initiatives also recognize that culture is ever-changing. This aspect of culture becomes more clear when we think of the word *culture* not only as a noun, but as a verb. To culture something is to shape the growth of it, as in culturing a plant or a lab specimen (Wax, 1993). This definition of culture is useful because it assumes change. Too often when we think of culture, we think of something static and self-contained. A culture is actually dynamic and ever-changing. It absorbs influences from outside, it accommodates changes imposed upon it, and in itself it creates opportunities for change.

The Accelerated Schools Project works with, not against, school culture. Throughout the process, especially during the taking stock stage and the problem definition steps in the inquiry process, the existing school culture becomes explicit. During the taking stock stage of the process, the school community members collect data on what the school is like now. They determine the areas to investigate, and they focus on both strengths and weaknesses that currently exist (see the Resources section for a more detailed description of taking stock). This process is not always pleasant, because the investigation often uncovers discrepancies between facts and what people have wanted to believe.

At Calhoun, the school community broke up into seven taking stock groups.[11] Each committee decided how to collect data and developed questions to include on master surveys to staff, parents, and students. The surveys focused on communication between home and school; cultural issues; attitudes of students, staff, and parents; expectations for students; attitudes toward parent involvement; school climate issues; and curricular, instructional, and organizational issues. Before the surveys were distributed, the parent survey was translated into Spanish and Portuguese. Committees also examined student records and standardized test scores and obtained data on parental involvement in the home-school club. This process lasted about 4 months.

When the committees reported on their findings, it was evident that the data were not completely consistent with the perceptions nurtured by the school culture. For example, teachers believed that the school treated all students fairly. They felt that they had developed a strong program for all children. A veteran teacher's comments illustrate the level of enthusiasm for their program:

> We put together a fabulous program. I was so excited about our magnet program, and the 3 years that we had it, it was wonderful. The level of academics here—the whole atmosphere of the place changed. It was really positive. We had parents who were excited about sending their kids here, and it was really successful.

The taking stock data pointed to some disturbing holes in this belief. The program may have been successful for some children, but the majority did not benefit from it. Teachers were shocked, and many tried to deny the fact that the school was polarized—although 20% of the students were in gifted and talented classes and 60% in remedial classes. More disturbing, the student population was internally segregated— the non-Hispanic White and Asian American children were disproportionately in the "accelerated" classes, and the Hispanic children in the remedial classes.

Once this information was made public, people began to discuss the validity of commonly held beliefs. One veteran teacher finally felt free to verbalize an observation she made several years earlier:

> They [the non-Hispanic White students] got all of the attention and privileges and the benefits and so on of the desegregation program. And I know for a fact that the other kids felt left out. They said, "Why do they do everything and we don't?" Because there was a lot done for them, really. Since I've been here before to compare, I have a basis for comparison, and I can see that too. Of course, I wouldn't say that to the children. Even the children saw it.

The taking stock process encourages school communities to build on the strengths of their school culture. Taking stock is not a needs assessment. The school community members are encouraged to look for the strengths as well as the needs of the school and to determine their own areas to explore. The Calhoun staff members were pleased to report many strengths in their program and in themselves. For example, they were able to report considerable community involvement and a small number of committed parents. Attitudes for students, parents, and staff were generally positive.

Through this process, they realized that the staff members have a lot of pride in themselves as teachers. This pride made it difficult for them to accept the implied criticism of some of the taking stock findings. When some teachers became defensive about data showing that 57% to 70% of students were below grade level at every grade, a teacher encouraged them to build on their strengths to bring their newly created vision to life. By appealing to the teachers' strengths, he was able to calm their fears of criticism.

The Accelerated Schools Project provides a direction for school culture change. Although school cultures are constantly changing, the vision and the Accelerated Schools process help "culture" the change. An important way that change is cultured is by involving everyone in the process of developing and celebrating the vision. At Calhoun, everyone had an opportunity to contribute to the vision and to publicly celebrate the vision. A bold plan was developed to march over 600 students through the busiest part of town to deliver copies of the vision to key public officials. Even some of the people who were skeptical about the idea of the march and of the value of a vision were moved by the experience:

> I would suspect that a lot of people thought like I did, before —Why are we doing this? This is really stupid. A waste of time. A lot of people dragged their feet. A lot of teachers said, "Oh well, I'm not going to go on that walk." It turned out everybody in the school did it. I mean everybody. It turned out to be pretty amazing. I mean, I wish you could have seen 700 people walking. It could have been a total disaster—on public streets! Kids were absolutely amazing. It was really neat.

The vision and the vision celebration "cultured" a change in the expectations for children. Prior to the vision celebration, Calhoun never had whole-school assemblies. The administration and staff were concerned that the students would misbehave. When they allowed the entire student body to participate in the vision celebration, they realized that they underestimated the ability of the students. Throughout the school year, they reminded themselves that the students could live up to higher expectations.

Allowing Time for Change

The Accelerated Schools Project coaches repeatedly told the Calhoun school community to allow time for change to take place—significant change does not come quickly. A Mae West quote—"Anything worth doing is worth doing slowly"—was repeated throughout the year. Participants were frequently reminded that systemic change usually takes about 5 years. Time is usually required for two critical elements to take hold: trust and communication, and acceptance of responsibility for decisions.

Trust among the teachers and administration was low when the Accelerated Schools Project began at Calhoun. Many of the teachers felt deceived or cheated by their new principal, and they scrutinized the administration closely before they allowed a more trusting relationship to develop. One teacher explained why she doubted the structure of decision making at the school would change:

Well, I can see where [the Accelerated Schools Project] could [make a difference], but I'm not really sure how far the district and the administrators will let it proceed. I mean honestly, it was kind of a blow last year that some of the questions that are asked—and they wanted input—I mean, it's kind of like a farce because you'll give the input, and it will be pretty unanimous in a certain direction, and then. . . . And so it takes away the integrity and the trust.

By the end of the school year, teachers were beginning to let down their guard and trust their administrators. Because the assistant principals participated in inquiry cadres with the teachers and the administration supported the recommendations of the faculty in relation to budget cuts, a more trusting relationship was beginning to develop. The principal noticed a definite change in the attitude of teachers:

Many of those who are committed to the school in a leadership way now were the constant gripers. [They] used to come in braced for a fight. It was a real "us and them" feeling before. That is gone.

Open communication among all members of the school community is essential for trust to develop and for change to be welcomed. The Accelerated Schools Project had a profound impact on the nature and level of communication among members of the entire Calhoun school community. Teachers and support staff found that they were working with colleagues they previously would not have known. One teacher commented,

The departments now talk to each other. The departments stayed to themselves, but now there is better interdepartmental communication. There is a higher degree of unity for common goals. Before, they just worked to keep the status quo.

By the end of the year, there was considerable talk of interdisciplinary work. Teachers were actually talking to colleagues in other departments about joint work, rather than sitting in department meetings bemoaning the obstacles to interdisciplinary work. Teaching assistants and campus supervisors (people who patrol the school grounds and supervise students on detention) welcomed their new inclusion in decision making. A campus supervisor said,

> It gives us closeness, togetherness—before it was like the teachers were on one side and the other staff was on the other side, but I don't know, with these meetings, it's like—I can't say it's like they're equal to us, but we feel just the same as they do.

Avenues for increased family involvement were opened through the Accelerated Schools process. The Calhoun staff members knew that it would take time to achieve widespread parent involvement, but they were encouraged by the enthusiasm of the few who were involved. One parent described the changes he saw at Calhoun after the Accelerated Schools Project began:

> It is like night and day. Teachers talk to parents. They talk to children. There is excitement. Excitement in the kids. They are part of meetings; they make speeches; they want to be visible. If parents know what's going on at school—even if it is just one teacher, they will try to have the same relation with all teachers. We must expect teachers to care about kids.

Just as it takes time for communication to become more open and for trust to develop, it also takes time for people to realize that they can be decision makers, but that as decision makers they must assume responsibility for their decisions. A sense of powerlessness pervaded Calhoun when the Accelerated Schools Project began, but this was being replaced by a growing sense of personal and group efficacy by the end of the first year. Staff members began to realize that they could make a difference at the school. They were both excited and frightened by the thought of having influence and responsibility. One teacher said,

> I think the faculty is really happy about having the empowerment, the right to make decisions and be in on the process. They don't realize as many other people don't—fail to realize—that rights also carry their burden of responsibility.

The principal commented that he likes the idea of empowering teachers because it gives them more freedom to do what they want:

The best curriculum is what the teacher is excited about. It doesn't matter what it is. Accelerated Schools has done that. It's hard to convince teachers that they have the freedom to do it—to get over doing what the principal wants.

Related to an increase in group efficacy was increased personal efficacy, most obvious in a blossoming of creativity and initiative. As one teacher commented at the end of the year, "Accelerated Schools rejuvenated us. It made lots of us more creative." There were many examples of teachers taking small chances within their classes that they may not have taken before. Several teachers seemed to rediscover creativity that had laid dormant, or they felt more freedom to try the things that previously they may have been afraid to try. Time was needed for individual risk taking to become more universal and more frequent.

Although many changes occurred at Calhoun during the first year with the Accelerated Schools Project, they were subtle, incremental, and difficult for those at the school to see. Most staff members realized that subtle changes had occurred in the school and in many of their classrooms, but they were still impatient to see more dramatic change. One teacher summarized the feelings of many:

It seems like nothing is happening, but actually it is. Underneath, something is happening. I get frustrated too. I want to be doing something, but then I think that I don't want to be doing the wrong thing. So I think, it's important that we do take the time. Playing "Respect" once a week is the only thing I can see that we're doing, but my attitude is changing. I used to say, "Oh, families don't take time to really understand," and I never asked why they didn't. I feel that I just want to do something, but do what? We might do the wrong thing.

Conclusions

As the above description illustrates, the school community at Calhoun was beginning to embrace change as a positive force in the school culture. These data are limited to the first year of project implementation. The challenge for all schools is to maintain momentum. Many people feel that initial changes are easy; change may merely be the result of the novelty of the intervention. It is important to document these early changes, but it is also important to continue to monitor the momentum and direction of change over time. Reports from Calhoun indicate that after 4 full years in the project, positive changes are still being made. My experience implementing the Accelerated Schools Project in South Carolina reinforces my belief that change can become a positive part of a school's culture, especially when a process for guiding change exists. Why are accelerated schools able to make change their friend whereas other schools resist change? I offer five explanations:

First, in accelerated schools, the participants are *creating* change; they are not *being* changed. This is an important distinction and relates to the Accelerated Schools principle of empowerment coupled with responsibility. Often when initiatives are introduced the objective, whether implicit or explicit, is to change people. Wehlage et al. (1992) criticized the New Futures project for implicitly trying to change the students in the project schools, rather than changing the schools. Other projects have failed because they tried to change teachers, administrators, and/or parents.

The lesson to be drawn from the Accelerated Schools experience is that people do not mind being changed (that is what learning is about) if they *choose* to be changed and are able to create the change. Barth (1990) suggests that schools become "communities of learners" because it is through learning that we change and improve. One reason why Calhoun's principal had a difficult first year was because he did not support the change the teachers were creating when he took over as principal. Until the Accelerated Schools Project started, change was imposed on all but a few of the staff, and they resented it. Changes will always be imposed on schools (budget cuts, administrative changes, student population shifts), but school community members will respond better to these changes if their school culture encourages them to find the positive in change.

Second, the Accelerated Schools Project is successful in creating a climate for change because it fosters trust and communication. The process helps the school community develop a unity of purpose, which in turn leads to trust and improved communication. Change can be frightening if those planning the change are not trustworthy and if communication is limited. The administration at Calhoun realized that both trust and communication were a problem and that they could use the Accelerated Schools process to gain the confidence of the school community. By supporting the efforts of the staff and by sharing information through the cadres and steering committee, trust gradually began to develop, and staff members no longer resisted putting time into creating change. The governance structure created through the Accelerated Schools Project also fosters trust because it opens new avenues for communication. People who previously had no opportunities to interact work together on cadres, and this opens communication across grade levels and between departments. As communication flows more freely, trust develops.

Third, change comes naturally when a school community truly begins to hold high expectations for everyone. Holding high expectations implies change. When we hold high expectations for ourselves and others, we are challenged to do more. In doing more, we change. The experience of the vision celebration at Calhoun is an example of how holding high expectations of the students created change in the school. They expected the entire student body to behave well during the celebration (an expectation they had never held before), and the students lived up to this expectation. Since the vision celebration, Calhoun routinely holds assemblies for the entire student body rather than the grade level assemblies they held previously. By stating implicitly or explicitly that we expect a lot from you, students, staff, administrators, and parents grow and change.

Fourth, change occurs more easily in a school where a process for change exists. The Accelerated Schools Project is essentially a process of continual change. The inquiry process is graphed as a circle because it is a never-ending cycle of change. It is difficult for accelerated schools to return to the comfort of the status quo because the inquiry process requires constant examination, experimentation, and assessment. Although change is the primary goal of the Accelerated Schools process, it also protects the successful practices from needless change. By developing and testing hypotheses about why problems exist, cadre members develop a better understanding of problems and where their own strengths lie.

Fifth, change in schools usually involves responding to multiple and unrelated initiatives and programs. The Accelerated Schools Project provides an umbrella for comprehensive and integrated whole-school change. For example, the same year the Calhoun staff began the Accelerated Schools process, they also initiated Project Equity, a project aimed at accelerating the progress of students in mathematics. The second year they implemented an aerospace project. Neither project was brought to the school through the Accelerated Schools inquiry process, but they both fell under the umbrella of Accelerated Schools.

The goals of the projects were shaped by the vision the Calhoun school community developed for the entire school.

In this chapter, I describe how the Accelerated Schools Project works with a school community to make change a positive part of its school culture. In conclusion, I want to return to the use of the word *culture* as a verb. To culture is to grow something in a prepared medium. When scientists culture something in a lab or a test plot, they guide change toward an objective. They have a thorough understanding of the organism they want to change, and they have developed and tested hypotheses about why the organism is as it is. They prepare the medium in which the specimen will grow to enhance the chance of successfully reaching their goal. The process of culturing is nearly identical to the inquiry process. Scientists culture organisms; school community members culture their school culture. A school is not a medium that can be controlled, but through the inquiry process, members of a school community can "prepare their medium" (the school) by understanding the nature and degree of problems and by building on the strengths they have identified. Through this process, they create an environment in which everyone is free to experiment, change, and grow.

Notes

1. This study was funded by the National Center for the Accelerated Schools Project through funds from the Chevron Corporation. Special thanks are extended to Henry M. Levin, Director, and Wendy Hopfenberg, Associate Director, for their support, encouragement and openness throughout the course of the research. See Finnan (1992, 1994) for a more complete account of this study.

2. This study was conducted largely through interviews with teachers, support staff, administrators, parents, and students at Calhoun and with coaches from the national center. Interviews were taped and transcribed. I also participated in many meetings, observed in classrooms and assemblies, and reviewed documents made available by the national center, the school, and the district. Data analysis occurred throughout the data collection period as well as after. For a more complete description of the data collection see Finnan (1992).

3. Many of these students came from families that recently immigrated from rural communities in the Azores off the coast of Portugal. Their parents did not receive extensive formal education.

4. Larry Cuban (1992) recently examined the history of the junior high school and middle school movements and found that most middle schools resemble junior high schools.

5. The only deviation from a typical middle school schedule was a 2-hour language arts block designed to improve reading and language arts skills for the students. The 2-hour block had been designed by Calhoun's language arts teachers the previous year. The decision to require 2 hours of language arts forced the elimination of all but one semester of electives.

6. Sheltered classes were designed for students who were still not fully proficient in English. They were no longer in Limited English Proficient (LEP) or Non-English Proficient (NEP) classes, but their English-language comprehension and vocabulary were not strong.

7. At the beginning of the 1990-1991 school year, the administrators decided to create an administrative team, primarily to deal better with discipline and guidance issues. The vice principal for discipline and guidance (new this year) created a team with a resource teacher and a community liaison worker. They each took a grade level and worked with all of the students in that grade level.

8. Of the seven departments, the language arts department was the largest and most influential. The other departments were math, science, social studies, special education, physical education, and electives.

9. As part of the desegregation plan, the district established a number of magnet schools to attract a mix of students to each of the schools. Calhoun was designated a technology magnet school. Thousands of dollars worth of equipment was given to the school to provide state-of-the-art experiences for children. The school was closed and a new staff was hired. A group of teachers were paid to develop a new curriculum for the school during the summer before the magnet school opened.

10. Campus supervisors were responsible for patrolling the halls to ensure that no one entered the school who did not belong there and to be sure that students were in class. They also supervised students who had to do campus cleanup duties as a part of detention.

11. Calhoun had the following taking stock committees: community, attitudes, achievement, discipline, family involvement, school organization, and curriculum and instruction.

6

Building Communities of Inquiry

Linking Teacher Research and School Restructuring

EDWARD P. ST. JOHN
JAMES MEZA, JR.
LEETTA ALLEN-HAYNES
BETTY M. DAVIDSON

Teacher inquiry has been widely advocated as a means of improving schools (e.g., Gideonse, 1990; Holly, 1989; McKernan, 1989). It has been argued that collaborative teacher learning is necessary for effective teacher inquiry focused on improving student learning (Holly, 1989). However, projects that promote teacher research cannot have a direct impact on curriculum and instructional processes unless schools are structured to make use of their work (e.g., Jacullo-Noto, 1992; McKernan, 1989). Therefore, it is desirable to link teacher inquiry and school restructuring through the use of teacher research.

The Accelerated Schools Project encompasses a comprehensive school restructuring process that emphasizes teacher inquiry (Hopfenberg et al., 1993). Indeed, both classroom-level inquiry and organizational inquiry by teams of teachers are integral to the change process (see Chapter 2). In this chapter, we examine the first-year implementation

AUTHORS' NOTE: An earlier version of this chapter was presented at the Southwest Educational Research Association Annual Meeting, Austin, Texas, January 1993. The authors would like to thank Henry M. Levin, Professor of Education at Stanford University, for his advice and support. The financial support for the Louisiana Accelerated Schools Project, provided by the Louisiana Board of Elementary and Secondary Education, is gratefully acknowledged.

of the Accelerated Schools process in eight schools. The analysis focuses on the experiences of teachers in a restructuring process that emphasizes teacher inquiry. We first provide background on teacher inquiry, then present the analysis of the school restructuring and consider the implications of the study findings. The research approach used in the study is described in the chapter appendix.

Linking Teacher Research and Restructuring

The idea of collaborative teacher inquiry in U.S. education can be traced to John Dewey (McKernan, 1989), who argued, "It is impossible to see how there can be an adequate flow of subject matter to test and control the problems investigators deal with, unless there is active participation on the part of those directly engaged in teaching" (Dewey, 1929, pp. 47-48, cited in McKernan, 1989). Thus, teacher inquiry has long been considered integral to education. However, mass systems of public education have historically undervalued teachers, their participation in decisions, and their inquiry into ways of improving schools. Recently, researchers have argued that teacher inquiry can play an important role in school restructuring (Gideonse, 1990; Jacullo-Noto, 1992; Holly, 1989; McKernan, 1989). Advocates of teacher research articulate a vision of teacher professionalism that has the potential, in theory at least, to transform learning environments (Gideonse, 1990). However, research generally indicates that teacher research has been only marginally successful because administrators do not see teacher research as integral to the governance process and researching teachers are usually isolated from school decision processes (Elmore, 1990; Holly, 1989; Jacullo-Noto, 1992).

The idea that teacher inquiry should be linked to the restructuring process by making such research integral to school decisions seems to be a crucial issue facing school reformers. Most schools, especially those that serve at-risk students, are subject to district and state policies that usually limit their capacity to initiate change. In the conventional model of schooling, teachers typically feel as though they are instruments of school policy, which has a deprofessionalizing and deskilling effect on teachers (Davidson, 1992; Miron & Elliott, 1991; Miron & St. John, 1994). Making teacher inquiry an integral part of the school restructuring proess may make it possible to change this dysfunctional pattern, especially if school administrators change their leadership style from one that emphasizes providing directions and answers to one that emphasizes facilitation of teacher inquiry and empowerment (Davidson, 1992; Meza, St. John, Davidson, & Allen-Haynes, 1993/1994; Miron & St. John, 1994; St. John, Allen-Haynes, Davidson, & Meza, 1992).

Communities of Inquiry

The Accelerated Schools Project is a restructuring process that takes a step beyond most restructuring methodologies, many of which emphasize participation for its own sake (Elmore, 1990). Democratic organizations have the same potential for perpetuating dysfunctional patterns as autocratic organizations (Argyris, Putnam, & Smith, 1985). The concept of empowerment used in accelerated schools emphasizes the teachers taking personal responsibility for their work (Hopfenberg et al., 1993; Levin, 1987c), which has the potential for overcoming dysfunctional patterns.

Schools that serve at-risk students usually face at least two types of dysfunctional patterns: They are estranged from the dominant power structure in their community, and they are internally divided, which inhibits effective action (Miron & St. John, 1994). The process of taking personal responsibility involves teachers in critically examining these dysfunctions and identifying and enacting new organizational strategies aimed at overcoming them. This involves a fundamental transformation in the school from a divided community with factions blaming each other for the school's problems to a unified organization with teachers collaborating in meaningful inquiry into how to solve the problems they discover. Indeed, open inquiry in the school community may be essential to this transformation (St. John, Miron, & Davidson, 1992).

Critical questions facing the Accelerated Schools movement are: How do learning communities of teachers form? How do teachers learn to take responsibility for building communities of inquiry? These questions are the central focus of the present study. Rather than focusing on research skills per se, we are concerned with the learning process of teachers. This process of building an inquiring community of teachers is considered especially crucial to schools that serve at-risk students, because the conventional pattern of schools is less effective in these settings (Levin, 1987c). Our research approach to this study is described in the chapter appendix.

Building Communities of Inquiry

At each of the eight schools included in the Louisiana Accelerated Schools Project during the first year of the project, the major first-year milestones planned for the project were completed. School communities took stock of the school, using diverse research methodologies; developed vision statements for their school; and used the vision to set priorities. They also restructured their school governance structures to rely on teacher cadres making use of the inquiry process to identify and test new approaches to solving the problems they identified. In this chapter, we document the emergence of communities of inquiry within the schools. Four processes were evident: *universal participation* in training and taking stock; *healing internal divisions*, based on insights gained in the taking stock process; *realizing hidden strengths*, based on deep reflection on conditions in the school; and the *action inquiry process* within the school.

Universal Participation[1]

The concept of unity, one of the central concepts in the Accelerated Schools Project, was easily understood by participants in the summer training session in New Orleans, which included teams from each school. Interestingly, an inequitable situation was set up in the schools by virtue of the fact that only about one third of the teachers from each school attended the summer session. The schools contended with this disparity during the year through the design and execution of school-based training and the provision of opportunities for other teachers (those who did not attend the New Orleans session) to get involved in the Accelerated Schools network.

As long as the Accelerated Schools Project remains an activity of a few in the school, it has little chance of taking hold in a meaningful way. Most school reforms have a similar fate: A few people are trained in the principles and process; these few have responsibilities for executing the process (and possibly for training others); and the new process (or technique) usually is not widely accepted, which creates an atmosphere conducive to failure. The Accelerated Schools Project could easily fall into this type of reproducing pattern if steps are not taken in the schools to secure wider involvement.

The site visit teams were interested in how the Accelerated Schools process had been communicated to the teachers who had not attended the New Orleans training, whether these teachers felt they understood the principles of Accelerated Schools (and how the concept differed from what they had previously done in the school), whether they were involved in the taking stock process, and whether they had a personal sense of vision about the future of the school. As part of the interview process, an effort was made to talk with teachers who had not attended the New Orleans training, as well as teachers who had attended the training. Each of these factors is discussed briefly below.

School-Based Training. It was abundantly evident from the interviews that each school had organized a school-based training process and that most, if not all, teachers had attended the school training. In all eight schools, the teachers who had attended the summer training (six to eight teachers, plus the principal) were involved in planning the training. In some schools only a subgroup of the teachers who attended the New Orleans training were involved in planning and executing the training, whereas in other schools, all of the teachers who attended the summer training had been involved. In all cases, the university staff were involved in the in-school training process.

The school-based training sessions were uniformly shorter in duration than the summer session. Thus, the full range of experiences and information given by the project team in the summer session could not be repeated in the school-based training. Nevertheless, the school-based training provided an introduction to the process. The fact that not all the information provided in the summer training was covered in subsequent in-school training contributed to the inequities and established those who had attended the summer sessions as the in-school experts. The disparity in knowledge was not reduced substantially by the school-based training because the expertise of those who attended the summer training increased by virtue of the fact that they participated in the design and execution of the school-based training.

Exposure to the Philosophy and Process. It was evident that the concepts behind the Accelerated Schools Project—the three principles, and in most cases, the systematic design of the process—were communicated in the school-based training sessions. In interviews conducted in the middle of the first year, those who attended only the school-based training could generally explain what these concepts were, but they had not always internalized the concepts. Several teachers had questions about the meaning of the principles and doubts about whether they could really be implemented. Despite school-based training, the Accelerated Schools process still ran the risk of being a project that sounded good at an espoused level, but that was not acted on in any meaningful way.

On further reflection, it seemed to us the presence of these doubts was not a negative phenomenon, but showed that these were experienced teachers who had seen reform fads come and go. One of the reasons why we reached this conclusion that the presence of widespread personal doubts was not necessarily problematic was that most of those who attended summer training also harbored doubts. Many of those who attended summer training had a better understanding of the principles and process, but some had doubts about whether they could be implemented in their school and whether they could actually implement them. That personal doubts by teachers were expressed to members of the project team who made the site visit was considered a ositive sign. It communicated that many in the schools were listening to what they had been exposed to, were thinking about what it really meant for their school, and could openly express doubts with each other and with the project team.

Involvement in the Taking Stock Process. There was nearly universal involvement in the taking stock process in all of the schools. Each school formed several committees to investigate different aspects of the school and made efforts to ensure there was a mixture of people on each of these committees. Some schools assigned people to committees at random. Others allowed teachers to self-select. Still others asked teachers to indicate their priorities, then mixed people into groups—a practice that gave everyone a choice without subgroups of friends being clustered on the same committees.

The taking stock process had several advantages for the schools. One advantage was that virtually everyone got involved in the hard work of taking stock at all eight schools. Taking stock involved doing investigative research on the school: conducting surveys, interviewing, attending group discussions, and so forth. By getting actively involved in doing research on the school, most teachers began to internalize some aspects of the process and to see that this process might really be different from most other change processes. Involvement in the taking stock process helped to remove lingering doubts. In fact, it was common for teachers who expressed their doubts in midyear interviews to volunteer to attend subsequent quarterly meetings later.

The second advantage of universal involvement in the taking stock process was that it helped to build a sense of unity. By being involved in taking stock, teachers began to feel a personal investment and commitment. Most communicated a sense of having worked hard in the process. Some were bored with the process and felt they had beaten a dead horse. Others felt enthusiastic. But the fact that almost everyone was involved gave them some common experience.

Finally, the process of being involved in taking stock gave teachers an opportunity to think about their school and what it might become. Some schools had already developed preliminary vision statements when the site visits were conducted, others had not. Thus, in some cases teachers could say what the school vision was and at other schools they could say only what they thought should be in it. Most teachers had a personal sense of vision for their schools. Usually, they expressed their vision in terms of the children's academic progress and self-esteem. Thus, the purpose of the Accelerated Schools Project—to better serve students in at-risk situations (or "all students" as some teachers and principals prefer to express it)—was integral to the way most teachers thought about the future of their school. The fact that most teachers, in all of the schools visited, shared this sense about the importance of their students served as another indicator of a building sense of unity.

Healing Divisions

One of the patterns evident from the taking stock process was that all eight schools were internally divided. Our research on two schools involved as pilot sites during the prior year found that (a) there were internal divisions, or factions, in the schools; (b) there were divisions between the schools and the communities they served; and (c) the capacity to heal these divisions may be necessary for success (Miron & St. John, 1994). Both types of divisions were also evident in each of the eight schools included in the state network.

The divisions within the schools took many forms. Interestingly, these divisions were usually openly discussed in interviews, which indicates a growing awareness in the schools. In some schools, there were tensions between the races. Racial tensions ran particularly high in the schools visited before the November 1991 Louisiana gubernatorial election (Duke vs. Edwards). In some, there were divisions between grade levels, with teachers in the upper and lower grades blaming each other for academic problems in the schools. In some, there were divisions between those teachers who got along with the principal and those who did not. And in a few schools, all of these divisions were voiced in interviews. In our view, the fact that these internal divisions could be discussed was a positive development, indicating an awareness of problems facing the schools and an openness with the project team.

There was also some evidence of healing some of these internal divisions in most of the schools. For example, at one school a group of teachers who historically had not been involved in schoolwide activities had become actively involved in the Accelerated Schools process. At another school, a school leader who had not thought much about the impact of the divisive gubernatorial election commented that the school staff had recognized there was a problem and had begun to talk about it.

An even more visible sign of the desire to heal these internal divisions was evident at a principals' meeting conducted during the third quarter, where a suggestion was made to have a retreat to discuss how to deal with issues of race in the schools. A retreat was held in the summer to discuss racial tension and harmony. The fact that internal divisions have become an important issue for school leaders is an indication that the problems will be addressed and, it is to be hoped, healed with time.

These schools were all viewed with some negativity by outside communities, possibly because they served the underclass. Participants developed an awareness of this problem as part of the taking stock process. For example, in some schools there were poor response rates to community surveys. Interestingly, the healing of these divisions began with the taking stock process, which usually involved parents as well as teachers. In addition, most schools identified community relations as a topic for a cadre, focusing a work group of teachers and parents on finding ways of involving the community in the school and gaining external financial support for the school. These groups usually focused on finding business partners, as well as finding better ways of involving parents in the school.

Realizing Hidden Strengths

The deeper participants probed in the taking stock process, the more they realized hidden strengths. Very often, they discovered that the causes of school problems can be turned into opportunities for improvement. Indeed, potential strengths often seem hidden in the thorniest of school problems, like diamonds in the rough. Several examples of this discovery process were evident in interviews conducted during the evaluation site visit.

In one school, an assistant principal reflected in an interview on what she had learned from the taking stock process. In one instance, she commented on the family structures of children in the school. Most students were African American children from single-parent homes; many lived in housing projects. She observed that in many of these homes, older siblings had responsibilities for helping to raise their younger siblings. She extrapolated that peer tutoring processes could probably be developed in the school that complemented and built on this hidden strength. In another instance, she observed that because the school was extremely large (about 1,000 students), there was little opportunity for teachers or students to interact across grade levels. After discussing this situation further and making the link to the potential peer tutoring processes, she observed that they had opportunities in the school to restructure the configuration of classroom assignments, perhaps having multiple grade levels in the same classroom clusters. This might allow for increased interactions of teachers and students across grade levels, or even for thematic approaches to curricula that created "schools within the school." These observations illustrate a capacity to go beneath the surface of a problem to identify hidden strengths that can be built upon.

Another example of seeing the potential on the other side of a problem emerged from interviews and discussions with teachers in an inner-city school with a Montessori program for preschool through third grade. The teachers in the Montessori program felt isolated—they had few opportunities to interact with teachers in the regular program—and their Montessori students often transferred to other schools rather than matriculating into the regular program. This situation was symptomatic of a deep division in the school. In interviews and dialogues, teachers in both the Montessori and regular programs expressed the view that the Montessori program was an accelerated model of teaching and learning and that the whole school could benefit from the experience of this isolated group. By the third quarterly meeting, there was evidence that some teachers had begun to explore this potential.

In another school, the Accelerated Schools Project was one of several new, innovative, schoolwide projects being implemented. The teachers were enthusiastic but seemed on the verge of burnout. Based on the interviews and follow-up discussion, it appeared that they could learn a great deal about what might work in transforming the school's curriculum and instructional processes by assessing what they had learned from the new reading programs and other innovations currently being tested in the school. There was discussion that an assessment of current activities could help them to gain more focus and begin pulling together to counteract the feeling of being pulled apart and moving in too many directions at once.

The Inquiry Process

The inquiry process seems integral to the transformation of schools that serve students who are at risk of dropping out. Not only is the process the cornerstone of the Accelerated Schools methodology, but a recent study of three schools that had made major improvements in their test scores found evidence of teacher-based inquiry at both the school and classroom levels (St. John, Miron, & Davidson, 1992). Of course, it is not possible to determine a causal linkage from a few case studies, but it appears there might be such a linkage. The Accelerated Schools literature (see Chapter 2; Hopfenberg et al., 1993) refers to classroom-level teacher inquiry as "little wheels" and school-level inquiry, conducted by teams within the school, as "big wheels." Evidence of both levels of inquiry in the eight Louisiana schools is reviewed below.

From our observations of, and experiences with, the start-up of the Accelerated Schools process, we have observed two types of teacher inquiry. The first is an emerging sense of community among teachers within the school. There is substantial evidence that a sense of community is developing among teachers in several schools in the network. Indeed, a few such examples have been openly discussed. In Accelerated Schools, this sense of community seems closely linked to the process of building unity and gaining experience in the inquiry process.

Second, there were many examples of the little wheels of inquiry (see Chapter 2) in the schools. In about half of the schools, teachers immediately began the process, experimenting with new approaches to instruction soon after they returned to their school after summer training. However, in the other half of the schools, teachers expressed frustration because supervision practices inhibited classroom inquiry. Thus, the factors that inhibit or promote the little wheels of inquiry merit closer scrutiny.

In the spring of 1992, there was limited evidence of big wheels of inquiry (see Chapter 2). Of particular concern is whether there is an orientation toward designing pilot tests (school-based experiments) that have disconfirmable hypotheses. By a disconfirmable hypothesis, we mean a hypothesis that can be proven to be wrong or in need of modification.

The second aspect of creating communities of inquiry is the full implementation of the inquiry process in school-based cadres, including the steering cadre. There is growing evidence that many teachers in these schools now understand the inquiry process at an espoused level. The dialogue about the inquiry process at the last two quarterly meetings demonstrated a depth of conceptual understanding. However, none of the schools had actually pilot-tested new plans at the time of the site visit.

The Accelerated Schools inquiry process includes three ways in which teachers test their hypotheses in action: testing hypotheses about why the problem exists (assessing whether hypotheses about the causes of the challenge "hold water"); assessing alternative strategies, using the cadre's shared understanding of the challenge and of the school vision to decide which strategies to pilot-test; and evaluating the results of pilot tests to see if the strategies actually address the problem. Because cadres in most schools had not yet engaged in the formal inquiry process at the time of this study, the big wheels of inquiry were not yet in motion.

Thus, after a year of reorganizing—of creating a foundation for working together—the teachers in these schools appear ready to engage in the big wheels of inquiry about how to make their school work better. However, unless a teacher can identify experimental hypotheses that are disconfirmable—where it is possible to show hypothesized relationships that do not work in the way they are intended, possibly because of unintended outcomes—and can be publicly tested, it is difficult to transcend the self-sealing logic pervasive in schools and most other organizations (Argyris, 1993; Argyris et al., 1985). The Accelerated Schools inquiry process seems to create opportunities in schools to test disconfirmable hypotheses. The challenge for the Louisiana Accelerated Schools Project is to facilitate in schools the design of pilot tests that use disconfirmable hypotheses as means of taking responsibility in the change process.

Lessons Learned

Our principal conclusion is that school communities need to establish an organizational capacity—a shared sense of community that supports open inquiry—before they begin to restructure the organization.

We found that the little wheels of inquiry were evident in many of the schools, but that the big wheels of inquiry had not yet emerged by the second semester in the Accelerated Schools Project. This relationship caused us to speculate that the little wheels may be necessary to foster school-level inquiry. This suggests that building a transformational capacity in schools is closely linked to the process of creating teacher inquiry processes in schools.

It has been observed that "for a community of inquirers to emerge, there must first be shared understanding and a common purpose" (Rogers & Polkinghorn, 1990, p. 16). Our investigation supports this argument. Engaging teachers in research aimed at understanding the school as it is "here and now" is a first step (Stage 1). This creates a foundation for more in-depth inquiry about how to make the school work better. If a foundation of openness is created in the first stage, then it may be more likely that teachers will engage in the public testing of disconfirmable hypotheses as the restructuring process continues (Stage 2). The eight schools included in this study appear to have processed through this first stage during their first year in the project.

The first stage of the Accelerated Schools process, building capacity, followed a similar pattern at the eight schools. It started with nearly universal participation in taking stock, which resulted in a heightened awareness of internal divisions and efforts to heal them. In the process, the school communities also began to discover hidden strengths and to identify experiments that could build on these strengths.

A long-term goal of the Accelerated Schools process is to have all students performing at or above grade level by the time they leave the school. It is expected that this school transformation process will take about 5 years (Accelerated Schools Project Team, 1991; Levin, 1987c). In the initial phase, the emphasis is placed on building capacity. The capacity for school-based inquiry appears vital to this school transformation process. Further, it appears this capacity builds through the taking stock process. By being involved in taking stock, teachers gain insight into the strengths and weaknesses of their schools. In addition, as a result of their involvement, teachers get to know each other better. This knowledge of themselves and the school has two benefits: It helps heal internal divisions, and it builds teacher inquiry skills.

The historic division between groups of teachers in schools is an underlying issue that can potentially impair the restructuring process. Open inquiry by teachers can increase their understanding of these divisions and help them find ways to overcome or heal them. This not only requires a change in leadership styles (St. John, Allen-Haynes et al., 1992), but also active inquiry by teachers. Schools that begin healing these internal divisions are in a stronger position to improve.

These findings have implications for practitioners in schools and colleges of education who are engaged in restructuring processes. Restructuring is a complicated process that cannot be achieved by simply completing a set of predefined tasks, such as taking stock and developing a vision. Rather, a process of individual discovery and learning is needed to ignite the school transformation—to build the capacity for restructuring. This individual learning process by school-based reformers can be enhanced by an emphasis on open dialogue. The challenges facing these reformers are to find ways to foster the emergence of communities of inquiry within schools and to facilitate inquiry about how to solve crucial school problems.

Note

1. In this study, we included interviews with teachers but not parents. Therefore, we cannot make a claim that all parents were involved. However, a follow-up study of these schools indicated that full parent participation has not yet been achieved (St. John, 1995).

APPENDIX

Research Methods

Multiple data sources were used to develop an understanding of how teachers and principals learn to engage in a process of building an environment that supports teacher inquiry. Here, we describe the research and analysis methods used in our study.

The design for this study was based on the principles of action science (Argyris et al., 1985; Argyris, 1993). The action science process involves using interviews and observations to help build an understanding of organizational patterns, organizing findings to provide meaningful feedback, and conducting change seminars. The original design for the research for the University of New Orleans Accelerated Schools Center (St. John, Miron, & Meza, 1991) used this approach. During the first year of the project, our senior author led an interview team to each of the eight Accelerated Schools and conducted reflective discussions at state-level Accelerated Schools meetings, providing feedback on learning patterns observed in the schools. In this chapter, we use interviews, observations, and reflective dialogues at feedback sessions generated through this action-oriented research process.

First, we conducted a series of training sessions that introduced teams from the eight schools to the Accelerated Schools process, including a summer training session for teams of 8 to 12 representatives from each school; in-service training conducted at the school sites, designed and executed in collaboration with those who attended summer training; and quarterly meetings involving principals and other school leaders in supplementary training and reflective dialogue about the learning process. The evaluations, observations, and reflections resulting from these meetings were important sources of information for this study.

Second, teachers and principals were actively engaged in research at their schools. During the fall they undertook a comprehensive assessment, "taking stock." They coordinated surveys of teachers, parents, and students; reviewed school records (attendance, test scores, etc.); and developed lists of the strengths and weaknesses of these schools. After developing vision statements, these school communities then identified gaps between the vision and the status quo; they then reorganized into cadres (or teams) to address critical deficiencies. We had access to this school-based research as a supplemental data source for this study.

Third, we conducted interviews with six to eight teachers and the principal at each school as part of the first-year evaluation. In these semistructured interviews, we asked teachers how they had been involved personally in the Accelerated Schools process; what they had learned from the process; and what their personal visions were for their school. The interviews included a comprehensive set of questions to probe the interviewees' perception about most aspects of the school community.

In addition, considerable attention was given to observing teacher behavior. As aspiring action scientists, we observed behaviors during training and site visits and inquired about behavior changes during the interviews. In the formal interviews, participants were asked to give their direct observations and to reflect on the personal meaning of the experiences derived from this process. Observed behaviors and interviewers' comments were used here as evidence of change in personal "theories in use" (Argyris & Schön, 1973; Argyris et al., 1985). To develop an understanding of the patterns that emerged, we conducted frequent reflective dialogues. We shared our perceptions of what was happening in the schools, hypothesized ways of dealing with problems that arose, and assessed the results of our interventions. These sessions were intended to develop our own skills in reflection, observation, and coaching.

Reflection

Creating an Environment to Sustain School Change

CHRISTINE FINNAN

The three chapters in this part provide a rich description of the context in several different instances surrounding implementation of the Accelerated Schools Project during the capacity building phase. They also illustrate that the important changes occurring during this stage are not so much implementing the steps of the process as beginning an internal cultural transformation in the schools. This cultural transformation and beginning the Accelerated Schools process are intricately interwoven. The Accelerated Schools process allows a transformation to take place. The processes of vision development, taking stock, and inquiry provide a vehicle for making the existing school culture explicit and give school community members the tools to create a community of inquiry. At the same time, the cultural transformation allows the process to work. If a school community does not embrace change, its members will merely go through the motions of implementation and little will be accomplished.

As I read the three chapters, I reflected on the authors' guiding messages in light of my experience as an Accelerated Schools coach. Since completing the study at Calhoun Middle School, I have coached or trained coaches for 13 elementary schools in South Carolina. I asked myself if these messages about the need to create shared meaning before implementing the project, to see change as a positive force, and to create communities of inquiry fit my experience as a coach, or if they were the interesting musings of researchers. I feel strongly that these are important messages for any change agent (be it a coach, principal, teacher, school board member) because they are grounded in experience.

Although each of the chapters stresses a specific message, themes run through the entire part that are picked up in all of the chapters. These themes highlight the interweaving of the implementation of the Accelerated Schools model and the cultural transformation of the school.

The first theme is the importance of building shared meaning during the capacity building phase. This is a central message of Kushman and Chenoweth in Chapter 4, but it also underlies the point St. John et al. make in Chapter 6 that through universal participation in the early steps of the Accelerated Schools process, school community members begin to build a unity of purpose and come to better understand the perspectives and concerns of members of different role groups. In Chapter 5, I point out that during this process, a school's culture becomes more explicit and school community members develop a better understanding and appreciation of what binds them together and what makes them different.

Another theme carrying across the three chapters is that school communities begin to see change as a positive force. Rather than change being imposed upon them from beyond the school (e.g., by the district, state, university), it is something the school community chooses and, eventually, welcomes. This is the central message of my chapter, but it is also reiterated in the others. For example, Kushman and Chenoweth stress the importance of providing a thorough exploration of the Accelerated Schools model as well as other restructuring models during the courtship stage. This offers all school community members an opportunity to understand what they will be doing and to share an enthusiasm to change. When school communities are able to buy into the process with a complete understanding of the philosophy and process, they are more apt to embrace change as something positive. In describing how teachers can become frustrated researchers if their efforts are not tied to a systematic restructuring process, St. John et al. state that teachers more willingly view this change in their role as positive if they can clearly see that their efforts are rewarded.

Another theme found in the three chapters is that the capacity building stage is a time for everyone to learn to accommodate to ambiguity. The Accelerated Schools Project is not a kit that can be brought into a school and adopted step by step. Rather, it provides an opportunity to reflect and to take responsibility for change. All three chapters provide examples of people who find this opportunity uncomfortable. Although they desire to be treated as professionals, teachers are used to being told what to do. Being offered no more than some guiding principles and a process to make decisions is in no way familiar to most teachers. As school community members work through the process and begin to develop trust in themselves, in each other, and in the school administration, they begin to appreciate the opportunity to guide change in the direction they feel is best. As Kushman and Chenoweth point out, the ambiguity of the project provides a broad enough framework for diverse school community members to see the fit between the Accelerated Schools model and their vision for their school. This relates to a point that I make in my chapter: The Accelerated Schools model provides a framework for school culture change, but it does not prescribe how the school culture will change.

A final theme that emerges from the three chapters is that a rethinking of roles within the school community occurs during the capacity building phase. As St. John et al. describe, the school community members begin to embrace the notion that they are a community of inquiry —that thoughtful, systematic reflection and research should guide all of their decision making. This rethinking of their roles contributes to a growth in their sense of personal efficacy. Once school community members see the results of their decision making, once they see that they can make a difference, they become much more creative and more comfortable taking risks. I make the point in my chapter that this process fosters trust and improved communication. School community members are more likely to trust decisions when they know that the decisions are a product of a systematic inquiry process. Kushman and Chenoweth essentially call for the creation of a community of inquiry prior to implementing a restructuring initiative. Their emphasis on building shared meaning before embarking on change is the first step in creating a community of inquiry.

The characterization of capacity building within accelerating schools as interweaving learning to follow steps in a process and transforming the schools' cultures is an expansion of a more typical definition of capacity building. Often, capacity building is limited to learning new skills. This more expansive characterization is in keeping with a more expansive view of how we should educate all children. Through providing an education to children, schools are essentially in the business of building their capacity, and until recently, most schools defined building capacity as teaching skills and content knowledge to children. Children learned to follow the steps of a process that resulted in graduation from high school or college. Recently, the definition of capacity building for children has been expanded. Schools continue to teach relevant skills and content, but they also help children create a vision of themselves as capable of living up to high expectations of being lifelong learners and inquirers. The kind of transformation we want children to make—to become active agents in their own learning—is very similar to the change we want school communities to make in their culture. In both cases, capacity to grow, to learn, and to succeed is being built.

PART III

The Role of the Principal in Accelerated Schools

INTRODUCTION

Simeon P. Slovacek

The chapters in this part address the changing role of the principal in an accelerated school. This may be one of the most important parts of this book, because although principals do not have the power to transform a traditional school to an accelerated school single-handedly, they certainly have the power to block or derail this process. Much of the initial training to launch a school as an accelerated school has focused on parents, teachers, and other nonadministrative school staff. Principals have been essentially left to fend for themselves in defining their new leadership role in the restructured accelerated school. This has created some confusion and, in some cases, a power struggle, as the new role of the principal emerged. The confusion may in part be a natural outgrowth of the empowerment of teachers and staff, exacerbated by the lack of specific guidelines for principals.

In *The Accelerated Schools Resource Guide*, Hopfenberg et al. (1993) do an excellent job of explaining and illustrating the philosophy, the process, and changes that occur in many areas of an accelerated school. However, even this seminal work spends less than 2 pages out of 387 on the role of the principal. Since the publication of this work, the National Center for the Accelerated Schools Project at Stanford has undertaken and published more definitive works on Accelerated Schools principals (Christensen, 1994). It has also conducted several workshops specifically for principals of new and existing accelerated schools. The four chapters in this part also help to fill this need by presenting both the perspective of researchers who have examined the changing role of the principal in accelerated schools and the perspective of principals themselves.

Chapter 7 by Chenoweth and Kushman begins at the beginning: The earliest phase of restructuring for an accelerated school is labeled the "courtship" phase. It is where the school staff, including the principal, engage in discussion of the need for change and attempt to garner support and commitment to begin comprehensive restructuring using the Accelerated Schools model. Much learning takes place during this process as the staff members familiarize themselves with the model and its implications for their school. The chapter is quite telling in that it shows the thinking of both principals and staff engaged in the courtship process. Clearly, there is a lot of uncertainty about the process and everyone's role at the beginning of becoming an accelerated school. The approach that principals choose to take, be it hands off or that of a change agent, has implications for how swiftly the school becomes accelerated.

Chapter 8 by Davidson and St. John uses a case study approach to document changes in the leadership style of accelerated school principals after the first or second year into the process. In the four cases studied, the role as facilitator and transformational leader was a new one for all the principals involved. The study looks first for evidence of change in the leadership style of the principals during the first year(s) of becoming an accelerated school. Also, the factors facilitating or inhibiting this changing role are identified. The authors found substantial variation in the extent to which the role of the principal changed in the four case study schools.

Chapter 9 by Christensen uses the critical incident technique to identify, classify, and rank key behaviors of accelerated school principals. The resulting taxonomy of behaviors represents a considerable addition to the body of research about accelerated school principals. The taxonomy is also contrasted with the behaviors of principals in other school restructuring and reform movements.

The final chapter in this part, Chapter 10 by Mims, builds on the work of Christensen. Mims focuses on the reflections and words of the principals of seven accelerated schools who have worked with implementing the Accelerated Schools model from time periods ranging from 1 to 4 years. The principals responded to six interview questions discussing their roles before and after their school became accelerated, aspects of the accelerated school that made their role easier, aspects that made it more difficult, and suggestions for help in assisting themselves and other principals of accelerated schools with the process.

✍ 7

Building Initial Commitment to Accelerate

THOMAS G. CHENOWETH
JAMES W. KUSHMAN

In this chapter, we examine the role of the principal in building staff commitment during the earliest phase of an Accelerated Schools change project. This earliest phase, or "courtship," is where initiators of school change engage the school staff in a discussion of the need for change and a model for change, and attempt to garner the initial commitment and support needed to embark upon a comprehensive school restructuring. The goal of the courtship phase is to begin building a shared meaning and commitment around the Accelerated Schools model and to achieve a critical mass of staff support so that efforts to restructure the school can begin.

Compelled by powerful ideas and pressed to make school change happen quickly, school leaders frequently ignore or underestimate the importance of building commitment and creating shared meaning during the early stages of the change project. This chapter is intended to guide school principals who initiate and implement whole-school restructuring projects. It provides a framework and a means for understanding the preimplementation and early implementation activities that are necessary for sustained commitment and success of long-term change projects such as the Accelerated Schools model. In our study, principals emerged as central to building commitment to school change. This does not preclude the possibility that in other schools or different situations, teacher leaders or program coaches might emerge as the primary initiators of school change.

This study is significant because the role of the principal has been largely ignored in the current reform literature (Bradley, 1989, 1990; Chenoweth, 1992; Griffiths, 1989; Sagor, 1991). Only two papers—by Letendre (1991) and Christensen (1992)—on principal leadership in accelerated schools were discovered. The comprehensive volume *The Accelerated Schools Resource Guide* (Hopfenberg et al., 1993) devotes only two pages to the principal. This sparsity is difficult to comprehend, especially given the effective schools research literature stressing the importance of the principal's strong instructional leadership. For example, Smey-Richman (1991) reports, "There is nearly universal consensus in the effective schools literature that in order to improve the achievement of low-performing students, the principal needs to play a major role in providing instructional leadership" (p. 69).

Leithwood (1993) posits that the effective schools research literature is a management literature that demands "control" strategies by the principal. The restructuring movement of the 1990s, however, emphasizes teacher leadership and professionalism and calls for "commitment" strategies by the principal.

In this chapter, along with Chapter 4, we present a qualitative study of the courtship process in three accelerated schools located in an urban district in the northwestern United States. It is somewhat unusual to study the preimplementation activities of a change effort, but our hope is that this research will provide insights into two important areas. The first area (covered in Chapter 4) is how different stakeholder groups (teachers, principals, and central office administrators) view the Accelerated Schools Project at the end of a courtship process and what these different viewpoints imply for building shared meaning and commitment as the implementation unfolds. Of concern here are the dynamics of building shared meaning out of the many personal and role-bound meanings that individuals bring to a change project. The second area of interest, covered in this chapter, is the role of leadership in building commitment and understanding during courtship and early implementation. In our study, principals emerged as being central to building staff commitment to school change.

In essence, these two companion chapters address the larger question: What does it take to build the kind of early commitment to a school change project that will keep staff energized and involved through a long-term restructuring? This study will be of most interest to Accelerated Schools change initiators and leaders, but we also believe that the results apply to similar whole-school change models that require the long-term commitment of different stakeholder groups.

The Setting and Courtship

We use the implementation of Henry M. Levin's (1987b) Accelerated Schools model as a vehicle for studying the courtship phase of a systematic school restructuring process. The three schools involved in this study—which were given the pseudonyms of Bridgeport, Clark, and Seaside—are among the lowest-achieving elementary schools in their region. Despite a number of effective teachers and numerous classroom curricular/instructional improvement projects, these schools have remained "stuck" with the lowest 5% of district students in third-grade student achievement in both mathematics and reading. A socioeconomic ranking of area elementary schools, based on attendance, student mobility, and parent education and income levels, reveals that the schools are located in the one of the city's most disadvantaged areas. Further, within this school attendance area lies the largest concentration of public housing in the region. These housing projects have traditionally been racially segregated and pose numerous sociological problems to the schools and the community.

The three schools are "sister schools" located within several miles of each other and are together embarking on the implementation of the Accelerated Schools model under the guidance of a leadership team comprising the three school principals; a teacher representative from each school; the district administrator with direct line authority over the three schools and his instructional specialist; a curriculum department administrator; and ourselves, who serve as university coaches. This leadership team led the three schools through a 3-month planned courtship before the final decision was made to implement the Accelerated Schools Project.

The purpose of this courtship was to give the three school staffs enough information and time to learn about the model, an opportunity to discuss the model among themselves, and a chance to observe the model in action through school visits so that they could make an informed choice about whether or not to embark on the Accelerated Schools path. The actual courtship activities included (a) attendance by the leadership team at a 1-week Accelerated Schools summer academy conducted by the National Center for the Accelerated Schools Project at Stanford University, (b) dissemination of written materials and video-tapes about accelerated schools to the staff at each school, (c) short presentations and interactive exercises meant to introduce Accelerated Schools concepts, (d) a visit by Henry Levin to observe the three schools and make a presentation to their staff, and (e) visits and one long-distance conference call by teachers to operating accelerated schools in the region. At the end of these activities, the three school staffs were asked to vote on the model and all three voted affirmatively (with vir-tually 100% agreeing within each school) to begin the process of becoming an accelerated school.

Finally, we recognize that this study is in a sense a study of exter-nally imposed change in that the Accelerated Schools project was initi-ated by central office administrators working with university facilitators and offered to the schools to adopt on a voluntary basis. Thus, the task of convincing school staff to adopt the model became paramount. What we describe as courtship in this chapter may be de-scribed by others as wooing or selling. Accordingly, the importance of courtship activities, especially in external change projects, must be rec-ognized and underlined.

Overview of the Chapter

Following this introductory section are sections on the conceptual framework we employed and our results pertaining to the role of the principal. Key patterns of leadership focusing on principal under-standing and vision are discussed. We conclude with a section on les-sons learned. The research methodology employed is that of a qualitative case study. We conducted our study in the tradition of par-ticipant observation in that both of us, acting as university facilitators, were involved in helping design and carry out the courtship and imple-mentation activities that we were at the same time studying. For fur-ther discussion of methodology, see the appendix to Chapter 4 of this volume.

Framework for School Change

The Accelerated Schools Project is one of several prominent na-tional restructuring models for schools serving at-risk students. It is a model for transforming a school through an interweaving of school process and school content changes to create a school where local problem solving and continuous improvement become the means to accelerated student learning. Like all models of restructuring, however, it is based on a particular point of view about what needs to be changed most and what the focal point of the restructuring should be. Using Elmore's (1990) typology of school restructuring models, Levin's Accelerated Schools Project is perhaps best described as *reforming the occupational conditions of teaching*, by creating a school organization in which teachers assume greater responsibility for identifying and solving the school's problems and for cultivating their own teaching practice as well as the practice of their peers. In accelerated schools, building teacher capacity is the key to accelerating the learning of all students. The model also includes elements of what Elmore (1990) calls *reforming relationships between schools and their clients* in that it stresses building an inclusive school community that engages parents and other community members as partners in education.

This discussion may help place the Accelerated Schools Project within the context of the school restructuring movement, but it tells little about the model's successful implementation, which of course is the major focus of our study. In conceptualizing this research, we have developed a four-phase change model to describe the successful implementation of an accelerated school. The hypothesized four phases of successful implementation are the following:

- Courtship
- Training and development
- Changing school structure and culture
- Changing classroom practices

In the courtship phase, initiators of the reforms (in this case, school principals, district administrators, and university facilitators) engage the school staff in a discussion of the need for change and a model for change, and in the end garner the initial commitment and support needed to embark upon a major school transformation such as the Accelerated Schools Project. The goal of the courtship phase is to begin building a shared meaning and commitment around a particular reform model and to achieve a critical mass of staff support so that efforts to restructure the school can begin. In our study sites, an extended process of courtship (approximately 3 months) was deliberately built into the project.

In the training and development phase, school staff members receive training in the skills, knowledge, and attitudes that are required for the model to succeed. In accelerated schools, the requisite skills and knowledge include working in teacher teams, developing group process and meeting skills, using an inquiry process to identify and solve school problems, and having knowledge of instructional and curricular practices that create powerful learning experiences for all children. Part of the training and development is to instill in teachers the work norms of collegiality and continuous improvement.

In the third, or structural and cultural, phase, real changes in school structure and culture are introduced, experimented with, and refined for the particular school site. Changing school structure and culture are placed together because they must be integrated and must support each other. In the Accelerated Schools model, changes in school structure and culture include implementation of a new governance structure and decision-making/leadership roles for teachers and principal, creation of a collaborative and team-oriented work culture, increased parent and community involvement, and a continual focus on a school vision and goals that are developed by the entire school community.

Finally, the last and most critical phase for student learning is the classroom practices phase, in which structural and cultural changes pass into the classroom and lead to real changes in the curriculum and teachers' instruction and practice. It is only when this last phase is in place that widespread improvements in student learning can be expected to occur.

This four-step process corresponds roughly to what Rosenblum and Louis (1981) have called the rational model of school change, whereby change is viewed as a logical, sequential process of readiness, initiation, implementation, and continuation (a framework originally developed by Berman & McLaughlin, 1976). We propose our four-phase model only as a heuristic device for understanding some essential steps in successfully implementing the Accelerated Schools Project. The actual change process is hardly as linear and sequential as this framework suggests. For example, training and development is really an ongoing activity, and cultural change, we would argue, can begin as early as the courtship, when new ideas are introduced, discussed, and assimilated among staff members. We also believe that change is best viewed within a systems framework, recognizing that planned change is embedded within an existing school structure, culture, and environment that can either support or impede the school's transformation (see Rosenblum

& Louis, 1981). Nonrational processes as well as rational planning are part of the change process, most notably the political forces and personalities within and outside of the school that define the context for change.

The central premise of our research is that in the press to make school reform happen quickly, schools tend to pay insufficient attention to the early foundational phases (i.e., courtship, training and development, and laying the groundwork for changing the school's culture) and move quickly into changing organizational structures and classroom practices. This is a tempting approach because it is these latter changes (particularly those in the classroom) that are most directly tied to student improvement. Yet the research on school change has pointed to the folly of proceeding without sufficient foundation. School change efforts tend to fail when they are purely top down or centrally designed with little consideration given to building teacher commitment, ownership, and personal meaning; when they fail to provide needed training and professional development; and when they ignore school culture and history (Berman & McLaughlin, 1976; Fullan, 1982; Hall & Hord, 1987; Rosenblum & Louis, 1981; Sarason, 1971).

A recent example is provided in a study by Wehlage et al. (1992) of the educational component of the Casey Foundation's New Futures program. The study involved a Year 3 midcourse assessment of a 5-year effort to restructure middle, junior high, and high schools in four medium-sized cities. The study points to some valuable lessons about just how difficult the restructuring process is, including (a) one should not expect change to happen rapidly and promise too much too soon, (b) top-down reform without the input of principals and teachers does not work, and (c) much needs to be done to train and develop staff for new roles and responsibilities in restructured schools (Wehlage et al., 1992). The main point here is that school reform efforts must build a foundation of human commitment and organizational support before changes in core instructional and curricular practices are attempted.

The Role of the Principal

In this section, we offer examples of what school principals can do to promote commitment and build staff capacity during the earliest, or courtship, phase of the change process. These examples emerged as patterns of leadership pertaining to *understanding* and *vision*. Several key findings emerged from our research and are presented below.

Understanding

Understanding the Model. Principals need to understand the model fully before introducing and trying to clarify it for teachers and staff. We met two types of teachers in our experience working with Bridgeport, Clark, and Seaside schools. The first type, clearly in the minority, felt very comfortable with the model and wanted to use it to build on their previous training and methods they were currently using as individual classroom teachers. They had no problem understanding and accepting that the Accelerated Schools model is a process, not a package or cookie-cutter approach for school restructuring. They felt excited about the prospect of empowerment and having the opportunity to shape their school into what they wanted it to become. They looked forward to improving school communication and working more collaboratively with their colleagues.

The second type of teacher we encountered felt they didn't fully understand the Accelerated Schools model. They responded,

Where do we go? What does this mean? What do we do?

It's really hard to self-start this kind of thing because we don't have a blueprint.

You keep hearing that each school will evolve differently. Well, what's the same?

How principals responded to these types of questions and concerns was critical to building early staff commitment and capacity for moving the process along. At Bridgeport —the school moving fastest and farthest along in implementing the Accelerated Schools model—the principal was an experienced veteran. She had moved to site-based management at her previous school. She felt that the Accelerated Schools model and being part of a national network offered a "better framework" for school change than the one she had previously developed on her own. She felt confident about the first steps she had taken with her staff and basically would not do things differently if she were going to start the process over. This principal also demonstrated an astute and critical understanding of the model and its dynamics.

I was thinking about "Accelerate, don't remediate"—academic outcome benefits for students rather than remediate and trying to dummy down the curriculum, pulling kids out, fixing them and then sticking them back in, not really having a classroom teacher be central to what happens to these kids.

There is going to be lots of ambiguity even way into the process and we have to be willing to have that. Because Accelerated Schools isn't a recipe. It is something you make yourself, no one else can tell you what the outcome is going to be like. They can give you some ideas of what the outcome was for them, but nobody else can really lay it out for you. . . . In our profession, we are used to having new programs come with a real recipe.

Teachers at Bridgeport School referred to their principal's leadership style as the following:

She does what she says she will. I really feel she's going to follow through.

She comes to staff meetings with lots of wonderful ideas and asks for input, which is wonderful.

Very dynamic. Willing to embrace new ideas. Energetic. She's always got something going on.

She's modeled a lot of things already for us.

It was really interesting to watch a cooperative lesson being done on us. You know, it was really good modeling.

Clearly, the Bridgeport principal demonstrated a conceptual understanding of the Accelerated Schools process. But she also demonstrated to her staff that she possessed the requisite leadership skills to operationalize what she understands, that is, follow-through, participatory management skills, a certain charisma, and the ability to model what she believes in.

The principals of Seaside and Clark schools were novices with only 1 and 2 years of experience, respectively. Both, however, had spent a week at a Stanford University summer academy learning about the Accelerated Schools model. The principal of Seaside school, when asked what he would do differently during the early phase of introducing and clarifying the model for staff responded,

> I wish I would have had a better handle on the whole Accelerated Schools Project, so that I could have answered some of the questions as to what exactly is the accelerated school. I really didn't know, I still don't know 100% because we haven't created it yet.

Teachers at Seaside school referred to their principal's leadership style as

> He is very easy and goes along with what we want.

> He really tends to let people take over.

> He kind of sits back and observes.

> He's easy to get along with. Sometimes, I think that the follow-through doesn't come for what we talk about that we want to do.

> He doesn't tend to bring things up. Sometimes, he's not aware of what's going on or problems unless it's brought up to him.

> I think he is very caring, always willing to listen, not aggressive, kind of a passive leader.

The principal at Seaside demonstrated some self-doubt and a limited conceptual understanding of the Accelerated Schools model. Further, his leadership style appeared to be administrative or maintenance oriented rather than proactive. He does not become actively involved and defers to staff requests.

The principal of Clark school echoed similar concerns to the same question—"What would you have done differently during the early phase of introducing and clarifying the Accelerated Schools model for staff?"

> Maybe, I should have given them more information. . . .
> Maybe, what you need to do at the very beginning is share the
> ambiguity of the concept. . . . Do they need lots of stuff in their
> boxes? Do they need lots of verbal things? Do they need video
> presentations or whatever? Do they need support people to
> come in? You have to be prepared with answers . . . because
> people are going to ask questions and they want answers.

Clark teachers characterized their principal's leadership style as

> I have sat down and talked to people one on one in small
> groups. The principal has not. She has been saying that she
> doesn't want to persuade people one way or another, but I
> think that she really hasn't said enough. She could have shared
> more information than she has. Because she doesn't want peo-
> ple to say, "Well, you talked me into it or whatever."

> I think she is really concerned and wants to do things. But I
> don't think that she is quite sure how to do it effectively.

> I think that she probably has a lot to learn as far as leadership
> and directing.

> She doesn't become involved.

> Sometimes, I am not sure that she is working from a basis of
> understanding of what's going on in the elementary class-
> room.

The principal at Clark school also demonstrated self-doubt and a
great deal of second-guessing about presenting and clarifying the Accelerated Schools model. In addition, she did not become actively involved during the courtship phase. She wanted staff members to feel
it was their decision to become an accelerated school. A number of
staff members felt that she did not understand or know what to do.

Certainly, it is important for principals to allow room for different
points of view, for underlying disagreements, and for various staff concerns during the earliest phase of introducing and clarifying the model.
But for staff, it appears to be most critical for the principal to be actively
involved, modeling the process, and sending strong signals of being

knowledgeable, confident, and possessing a "can do" attitude. Clearly the principal of Bridgeport school fulfilled these demands and the principals of Seaside and Clark schools did not.

Understanding the Change Process. Principals need to understand the change process and develop a game plan. Careful management of the restructuring process is critical, with a realization that change takes time, that it has predictable stages, and that there are no simple solutions. Bridgeport's principal clearly articulated the steps she took. At the opening faculty meeting in September, she held a 3-hour workshop with a catered dinner in a local church.

> I just used Accelerated Schools stuff because I thought it sounded neat to me, neater than the stuff I had used before. I didn't really do that with the thought that I am trying to pave the way to move to Accelerated Schools, I just thought it looked good. As it turned out, that was a really great move.

> I never mentioned Accelerated Schools at that workshop, I didn't say boo about it. We did an Identifying Strengths activity, a Building on Strengths activity, we did that little grid about where decisions are made, because that was an issue that had come up.

> When people went to hear Levin, and also to some degree when they saw the videotapes, there was a reaction of, "Oh, you know, we are already doing that," or "I knew about it already." It wasn't so much we don't need this, but they felt some sense of pride or accomplishment in having done it.

The principal of Bridgeport school subsequently held a staff meeting focused on the key elements of the Accelerated Schools model, the three guiding principles, curriculum, instruction, and school organization. She began the meeting by saying,

> Change is in the air. We do not have a choice about whether or not to change. We can't remain the same. But we do have a choice about how we will change.

Rather than directly explaining the key elements of the Accelerated Schools model, the principal designed a cooperative learning "jigsaw" activity so that staff members ended up explaining the model to each other in small groups. Chart paper was used and advantages and barriers were listed. "Burning" questions that remained were also listed. A conference call with teachers at the first accelerated school, Daniel Webster in San Francisco, was conducted. The staff of Bridgeport also visited Daniel Webster, which had been an accelerated pilot school beginning in 1986. The entire process was carefully orchestrated by the Bridgeport principal and no stone was left unturned, so to speak.

> I gave people a chance to explore, look at, talk about, think about, play with, read about, dialogue with so that they really had to digest new ideas and bring them back to the whole staff.

> More than pumping a lot of paper at staff, I made an effort not to give tacit messages that this is what we ought to be doing and you better like it.

> I wanted to have it genuinely be open and above board. Let's take a look at this. Let's explore it. So that there isn't the sense that, yeah, she really wants to do this so we better do it better.

This is a powerful example of principal leadership and an intuitive understanding of the change process in the earliest phase of a school restructuring process. Leadership was indirect or constructivist in nature. Staff members were led to feel they were ultimately making the decision to become an accelerated school. It became a relatively easy decision for them to make because they felt the model actually validated and reflected what they were already doing. A central office curriculum specialist succinctly captured the Bridgeport principal's constructivist approach:

> She sets up learning situations so that people will experience them and get excited about them and therefore want to do it. It's just like a teacher in a classroom. If you want to get your kids excited about something, you set up the right experiences and they are going to jump right in.

She's one of these natural leaders. She's just able to get that excitement about whatever it is that's going on. She just presents herself in such a way that I'm here working with you. The people know that she's in control, but yet she's not taking control.

The principals of Clark and Seaside schools presented the model in a much more traditional, direct, but fragmented fashion, although their staff members also visited an accelerated school in the region as part of the courtship. Along the way, both principals expressed doubts about sustaining the change process:

I am really kind of in a quandary right now not knowing what the next step is. The people are asking what is next? A couple of them have maybe even forgotten about it because they are involved in so many things.

There are a lot of things that I wonder about. Am I up to this? And there is so much to sort through.

Information was presented. The principals tried to answer a barrage of questions. Henry Levin made a presentation. Videotapes were made available, information was placed in teachers' mailboxes, and visits to another accelerated school in the region were arranged. When voting, the Seaside principal even asked staff to sign their ballots, and the Clark principal deliberately distanced herself from the voting process. Yet although the staff in these two schools eventually voted to become accelerated schools, individuals never really seemed to own the process as the staff at Bridgeport did.

Although at Clark the principal used a more traditional and direct approach in presenting the model, she did use the inductive approach in one instance to surface and resolve some initial differences of opinion about the Accelerated Schools Project. After the Henry Levin address, there was a polarization at Clark between some teachers who felt very positively about the model and an almost equal number who were less positive or very negative. Chapter 1 teachers were particularly concerned about how the model would affect their pull-out program. Some teachers also wanted consideration given to another school improvement model. The principal set up an activity where two committees were assigned to do further research on each model being considered.

The whole staff then met to hear the reports and discuss each model. This activity provided for an open discussion and airing of concerns. At the end of this activity, everyone at the school felt, "We've had enough talk," and they were ready to vote on which of the two models they would like the school to pursue. (They chose Accelerated Schools.) This is an illustration of how building shared meaning and commitment must be more than just providing videotapes and canned presentations of the model. Courtships must also use a constructivist learning approach to surface underlying disagreements and work them through before the decision to adopt or not to adopt the model is made.

Understanding the Experiences of Other Teachers. Teachers need to visit and observe other school sites and have conversations with teachers involved in the restructuring process. No one has more credibility or is better at selling the model than another teacher. Visits to two other accelerated schools (including Daniel Webster) were arranged for interested staff at all three schools. Armed with camcorders, staff members formed "action research" teams and boarded minivans and even a Greyhound bus to visit these schools. Upon returning, they shared their experiences with colleagues. Next, the schools held an "Accelerated Schools Reach Out" in which the three staffs came together and shared videotapes and stories. Finally, the Bridgeport school staff made a conference telephone call to the Daniel Webster accelerated school in San Francisco. Twelve Bridgeport staff members crammed into the principal's office and talked for an hour to nine Daniel Webster staff members over a speakerphone.

Teachers at Clark school had this to say about their visit to one of the accelerated schools in the region:

> I think that our trip to _____ made a big difference. We voted for Accelerated Schools, but it was real shaky and people were kind of like, "Well, let's give it a try." But we still had some underlying tones from some people who were trying to sabotage. . . . There were three of us that went from this school and we are all very strong personalities. I took a third-grade teacher aside and said, "So, tell me the truth. You have been here all this time." I had met her before and she was out on yard duty. "Is this accelerated stuff really worth it?" She said, "Well yes,

because I am teaching novels," I am doing this and I am doing that.

The visit to _____ really clinched it for me. I mean, we talked and discussed all the way up and all the way back.

About understanding Accelerated Schools. . . . I think there needs to be more hands-on, personal interchanging between other schools.

Speaking to the principal in _____ and listening to the staff and parents. . . . Everybody feels as though they are part of a team. And they are an equal part of the team. This isn't our boss and we are little guys that make the machine work and do the work. We all decide, we all make decisions, good or bad, we have to live with them.

Staff at Bridgeport school reported on the conference call and their visit to Daniel Webster:

The conference call was really good because it made us know that, yes, there really was a school. . . . It was important because that was another step in connecting up with the reality of it. I think it's really hard to see theoretically. Then the people went down and that was really important because they came back with some really important impressions. . . . They were real enthused. They gave us more information and raised a lot more questions. . . . It just gives you the feeling that they've done it, it's there, it's concrete.

Daniel Webster staff is very good at responding to your concerns and really understand what teachers fear because they are not afraid to talk about what the problems were and how they solved them. They're not afraid of being really honest.

When asked to evaluate the various courtship activities, teachers clearly felt that hearing it from their peers was much more credible than hearing it from the promoters or "experts." Significantly, teachers who made the visits and conference calls now became responsible for explaining the Accelerated Schools Project to their colleagues. Staff members became actively involved in sharing their impressions and experiences. Principals were able to step back and let staff begin to own the eventual decision to become an accelerated school.

Vision

Vision is clearly related to understanding. A critical understanding of the model can lead to the development of a compelling vision. By the nature of the roles they play, central office administrators are more likely than teachers and principals to develop a systemic or visionary perspective of school change, as brought out in Chapter 4. In describing district support for the Accelerated Schools Project, a teacher from one of the schools made this observation:

> It's easier for people who are outside of the school to be more committed. They are really dealing more with the theory of it than the reality of it.

Four years ago, for example, two central office curriculum administrators and a local university professor (one of us) began exploring ways to restructure some of the district's lowest-achieving schools. All three had led significant school restructuring projects in the past and felt that the Accelerated Schools model resonated well with their past experience and hopes for the future of public schooling. One of the administrators explained,

> Our vision was one of "school improvement through staff development." We began looking for a model or process that had been replicated in a number of settings, had a track record, and could possibly be transferred to a number of other schools fairly easily. None of it's easy, of course.

> We were willing to take risks . . . and are firm believers that kids who are not succeeding in our schools are not at-risk. It's their situation that's creating their lack of achievement.

After visiting several accelerated schools in California and Missouri, a critical but visionary concern was raised by one of the central office administrators:

Based on what we saw, we were very concerned that there not
be too much emphasis placed on the structure and organization
(of the restructuring process), because if our goal is to improve
instruction for kids, the focus must stay on curriculum and instruction. . . . Otherwise the means becomes the end.

With this cautionary note, the initial central office group presented
the Accelerated Schools model to other central office administrators and
then to district principals, with the hope that some of them would become interested enough to pursue and initiate the process at their school
sites. Eventually, with the active support and encouragement of their
immediate supervisor, the principals of Bridgeport, Clark, and Seaside
schools decided to become involved.

As previously mentioned, the Accelerated Schools model was a
good fit with the principals' own personal beliefs and values (see Chapter 4). To varying degrees, it reflected and validated their personal visions. Conveniently, it came with a built-in vision and a set of guiding
principles of what their school could become. Rather than having to
develop an entirely new vision for their school from the ground up, their
job became that of clarifying and elaborating this built-in vision so that
it was understood, shared, and developed in a way responsive to their
own staff members' particular context and needs.

The principals became keepers and promoters of their school's
built-in vision rather than its primary creators or initiators. Vision was
kept by introducing it and clarifying it, which provided direction and
order in what was for many staff members an ambiguous and uncertain
school restructuring environment. The Bridgeport principal promoted
the vision by creating a sense of urgency or a press for school change
through active involvement, or pitching in, at every possible opportunity and by the continuous modeling of appropriate behaviors.

The principals of Bridgeport, Clark, and Seaside schools shared
similar values and beliefs, as brought out in Chapter 4 discussing our
courtship study. This is reflected in the fact that they decided to get
involved in the first place. According to their supervisor, they all have
the "right instincts," but as described earlier, their levels of understanding and experience differ. Consequently, their visions of how their
role might change and how classrooms will eventually look are, as expected, different. For example, the principal of Bridgeport school (the
school farthest along in the process of becoming an accelerated school)

had a great deal to say about her changing role and how she would like to see classrooms:

I won't have to be responsible for Monday faculty meetings. Teachers will take much more of a role in planning and carrying out the goals that we have set. There will be so much going on . . . there will be trouble figuring out what is happening. That is the way it was in my last school and I am sure that is the way it will be here. I won't have to initiate everything. We will be working in cadres and a steering committee. We will need to get training, group process training.

I like to see an atmosphere in a classroom of community where there is careful attention paid to that responsibility . . . a community with a problem-solving component, rather than just booting the kids out for misbehavior. And an attitude that kids who are misbehaving are misbehaving for a reason, that is usually a skill deficit and that it is primarily the classroom teacher's job to teach to that with the support we provide.

I want good concept-level math instruction . . . lots of manipulatives, lots of real-life math experiences, very little textbook. That would be the same in social studies and science. I want to see little pull-out. I want to see some really different looks at Chapter 1.

I want a curriculum that integrates around themes. You know when you are in a classroom following an integrated curriculum because it kind of looks like whatever they are doing at that point. You can tell what they are doing because they transform the hall outside. Now they are a rain forest or a coral reef. It would be kind of messy and interesting looking and not all neat and tidy and done by teachers. The trick is to stay within that integrated curriculum and yet still have some specific skill teaching when needed.

In contrast, the principal of Seaside school had very little to say about his emerging role and the type of classrooms he would like to see:

My role will change probably a little bit, but I don't see it changing significantly. I think that I will be doing basically an orches-
tration, like a conductor. . . . Just kind of making sure that every
thing is running smoothly.

I would look for student achievement to be up. I would look
for the reputation of Seaside school as a great place to be, to
have kind of circulated. I think that there is going to be more
and better communication.

I think that building on the strengths that the students come to
school with will be very important. We had a couple of kids here
last year who were attendance problems . . . they were at the
low end of the academic scale, but what they had done—I was
talking to a police officer—they had stolen a car from the wreck-
ing yard, somehow pushed it home, and made it run. If we
could build on those types of strengths that these kids have,
you know, just working and tinkering with something.

The principal of Clark school also had little to say about future
changes in her role. She had more to say about the classroom, but it was
couched in terms of addressing current school problems rather than a
vision of what might be:

I am not sure how my role will change. It just depends on how
this whole process goes. I may decide that it doesn't work, and
I may find that it works better than I ever imagined. So I want
to be open. I am going to need to be more responsible for making sure that people are doing the tasks they need to do, to
coordinate that effort.

Obviously, our kids need to be accelerated because they are
below. Maybe, it is not a good match. We have big turnover. I
hope to see some different instructional models . . . more cooperative learning activities, more cross-age, cross-grades kinds
of things, better use of personnel resources . . . Chapter 1, Music, and the [school] secretary. There is not a lot of dialogue
between classroom teachers and our specialists. What we don't
have is articulation between the grades, which I hope will impact our test scores. I think that staff are asking to make deci-

sions, but they are going to have to be responsible for the decisions they are making.

Thus, school principals were central in building staff commitment and capacity for school restructuring during the courtship phase. Patterns of leadership pertaining to principal understanding and vision emerged as central in building staff commitment to the Accelerated Schools model and moving the process along.

Lessons Learned About the Role of the Principal

The second part of our study of the courtship process led to five key conclusions:

- Principals need to be actively involved, model the process, and send strong signals of being knowledgeable, confident, and possessing a "can do" attitude.
- Principals need to understand the change process and have a game plan.
- Principals need to create experiences for staff to learn from practitioners already involved in the process.
- Principals must clarify and elaborate the vision built into the Accelerated Schools model so that it is understood, shared, and developed in a way responsive to their own school's particular context and needs.
- Principals need clear pictures of their changing roles and how classrooms might look in the future.

In a complex and ambiguous school restructuring environment, the principal needs to be actively involved, model the process, and send strong signals of being knowledgeable, confident, and possessing a "can do" attitude. Joyce, Hersh, and McKibbin (1983), in reviewing research on implementation of innovations, state, "The less explicit the characteristics and rational of the innovation, the more likely there will be user confusion and frustration and a low degree of implementation" (p. 71). Levin (1989c), in describing the principal of an all-minority Chicago Heights school, further points out, "This woman hit the ground running. She just understood the ideas right away. She really communicated the ideas with her staff. . . . They picked up on it and that school is just unbelievable."

These statements confirm that initiators of school change need to understand their particular school innovation well. This observation seems rather obvious and simplistic, yet Joyce et al. (1983) make a similar conclusion: "Results seem to boil down to the common sense proposition that the more thoroughly one understands something the more likely one is to master it and be committed to using it" (p. 71).

Ensuring principal understanding can be difficult. Some principals are experienced and able to make expert moves or decisions whereas others are novices and possess very limited repertoires. In many districts, principals are regularly reassigned. Often, there is a poor match or principals are assigned to schools in the middle of a restructuring effort not knowing what it is all about. Fully understanding the restructuring model and what it entails is critical. Information, discussions, and research need to precede the decision to implement the model and should be geared toward the school's particular context and level of development. Any ambiguity or fuzziness needs to be clarified with concrete examples.

Fullan (1982) describes two types of school principals, those who are primarily administrators and ad hoc crisis managers and those who are change agents. Change agents may become either directive or facilitative leaders. However, directive principals need to understand the purpose of the change and have a critical mass of teachers who agree with them. Facilitative leaders, on the other hand, need both understanding and the skills to turn the change process over to their staff.

Clearly, the principal of Bridgeport school is a facilitative leader. She is committed to changing her school and possesses the skills to do so. Although the other two principals had the "right instincts" to become change agents, they had less understanding, skills, or experience to initiate a whole-school restructuring process by themselves. Working with the guidance, assistance, and coaching of the project steering committee, however, they have been able to move their schools along, albeit at a slower and more laborious pace than that of Bridgeport school.

Beyond understanding the Accelerated Schools model, principals need to understand the change process and develop a game plan. It appears that an indirect or constructivist approach of presenting and clarifying the model, in which teachers are obliged to make sense of the model by actually practicing and engaging in important components of it, is far more successful than a direct approach where information is simply presented. This reflects what we know about learning, in that learners learn more and are better able to transfer what they have learned when they must make sense of it themselves in an inductive way. What we conclude is that an inductive approach to learning about the Accelerated Schools model is far more powerful than a direct or deductive approach, especially in the earliest introductory stage. Further, it makes much better sense to take this type of constructivist approach with the Accelerated Schools model because of the inherent value the model places on problem solving, critical thinking, and hands-on learning. The model reflects the aphorism, "How you teach is what you teach."

Understanding the experiences of staff already involved in the process is also very important. What these experiences indicate is that teachers felt a great deal more confident about committing themselves to the Accelerated Schools model after visiting and talking with other teachers, principals, and parents. Interestingly, they were given no recipes or assurances about what to do or how to do it. But they came away feeling that it was "concrete" rather than abstract and that in spite of continuously having to wrestle with implementation problems, the schools they visited were much better off because of their involvement in the Accelerated Schools process. Teachers in our study generally felt that learning about accelerated schools from their peers was much more credible than hearing it from promoters or experts. Perhaps the clearest lesson learned is that teachers want courtship to be an opportunity for informed choice rather than a hard sell.

Finally, understanding is more than just receiving training and reading the literature. It's related to one's worldview, or vision of what schooling is all about. Some individuals will never, as Levin (1989c) says, "have a clue" because they either have no vision or their own personal vision is out of alignment with the model of schooling they find themselves responsible for implementing. Sometimes, they get involved in school change for the wrong reasons. They use the model or program as a symbolic means of signifying that they are doing something significant about their at-risk students. A commitment is made at a symbolic or ritualistic level rather than at a substantive and transforming level, and the model is used for recognition or as a means of gaining needed resources.

The Accelerated Schools model comes with a built-in vision and a set of guiding principles of what schools may become. Rather than having to develop an entirely new vision from the ground up, the principal's job becomes that of clarifying and elaborating this built-in vision so that it is understood, shared, and developed in a way responsive to their own school staff's particular context and needs.

To be effective and inspiring, principals need clear pictures of their changing roles and how classrooms might look in the future. We conclude that ultimately vision must be directed at teaching and learning. Clearly, the vision of the Bridgeport principal is the most developed and focused. She can see her role changing dramatically and can vividly envision classrooms in the future. The Seaside and Clark principals are less certain about the roles they will play. Their descriptions of classrooms are at more at a buzzword level, that is, "cooperative learning," "higher achievement," "building on strengths," and so forth. They talk more about addressing current school problems than of the future and what their schools might become.

Murphy (1990, 1991) aptly points out that changing the core technology of schooling, teaching, and learning as a strategy for school restructuring has received little attention compared to strategies such as teacher empowerment, school-based management, and choice. He and others suggest that we should actually begin with teaching and learning and that it is entirely possible to restructure a school and have no real impact on the classroom and students (Epstein, 1988; Fullan, Bennett, & Rolheiser-Bennett, 1989). Thus, when principals' vision is not clearly focused on teaching, learning, and classrooms, the means of school restructuring may actually become the ends.

In closing, we note that our findings demonstrate how inextricably principals' understanding and vision are linked. One is impossible without the other. Our study was based on the premise that comprehensive school change efforts frequently underestimate the importance of first steps in building commitment and shared meaning for participants. The literature is replete with examples of what Sarason (1990) calls the predictable failures of school reform. We addressed the need to establish early commitment and shared meaning to a change process like the Accelerated Schools model that requires great personal energy and long-term commitment among all participants. Our findings point to the importance of intentionally building a foundation of commitment and understanding as a first step to building teacher capacity. Building capacity becomes more than imparting a new repertoire of teacher skills and should also include helping teachers build their own understanding and vision of an accelerated school early on, which becomes a shared understanding and vision as the school moves forward.

ϑ 8

Principals' Changing Roles

Analysis of Selected Case Studies

BETTY M. DAVIDSON
EDWARD P. ST. JOHN

C hanges in the role of the principal from a manager or instructional leader to a facilitator—a transformational, empowering leader—is integral to most recent school restructuring approaches, such as the Accelerated Schools Project (Levin, 1987b, 1988a, 1988c). Yet the Accelerated Schools training material gives very little attention to the role of principals (Hopfenberg et al., 1993), and research on how the role of principals changes as part of the restructuring process in accelerated schools has been quite limited.

In this chapter, we examine changes in the roles of principals in four accelerated schools. One began the Accelerated Schools restructuring process in the fall of 1989, the other three the following year. We consider both how the principal's role changed in these schools and what factors facilitated these transitions. The chapter contains four parts: background on the role of principals, a description of the research approach used in this study, an analysis of the changes in the role of principals and the factors that influenced these changes in the four schools, and conclusions and implications.

Background

Public interest in school improvement intensified in the 1980s. As a result, teaching and schooling underwent a spate of examinations

169

resulting in school reform movements that prioritized top-down decision making (Boyd, 1989; Dunlap & Goldman, 1991) and emphasized "instructional" leadership (Leithwood, 1992) on the part of the principal. The more recent literature on school restructuring, however, suggests a substantially different role for principals, which we examined briefly.

The Principalship

The literature provides a panoply of definitions describing the traditional role of the principal. Several authors argue that the principal determines the organizational relationships within and about the school. Keedy (1990), Lipham and Daresh (1970), Lipham and Rankin (1981), and Austin (1979) state that this traditional image depicts the principal as both maker of initial decisions and determiner of which decisions are to be shared with others in the school.

This traditional view of leadership appears inadequate for the challenge of school restructuring now facing schools. Leithwood (1992) defines *instructional leadership* as a focus of the "administrators' attention on 'first-order' changes—improving the technical, instructional activities of the school through the close monitoring of teachers' and students' classroom work" (p. 9). This definition of instructional leadership makes it similar to transactional leadership, which is generally defined as an exchange of services for various kinds of rewards that the leader controls, at least in part (Burns, 1978; Leithwood, 1992). Mitchell and Tucker (1992) note, "Transactional leadership only works, unfortunately, when both leader and followers understand and agree about the important tasks to be performed" (p. 31). According to Bass (1987) and Sergiovanni (1990), transactional practices appear to be central in maintaining an organization—getting the day-to-day routines carried out. Yet as Leithwood (1992) emphasizes, "Such practices do not stimulate improvement" (p. 9).

Sarason (1990) maintains that the blame for the "predictable failure of education reform" rests, in large measure, on existing power relationships in schools. Leithwood (1992) notes that instructional leadership is "an idea that has served many schools well throughout the 1980s and the early 1990s. But . . . no longer appears to capture the heart of what school administration will have to become" (p. 8).

In the light of current restructuring initiatives designed to take schools into the 21st century, the traditional role of the principal needs to change to that of facilitator, keeper of the dream, or transformational leader (Bolman, Johnson, Murphy, & Weiss, 1991; Fullan, 1992; Leithwood, 1992; Levin, 1988a; Sergiovanni, 1992). Leithwood (1992) states, " 'transformational leadership' evokes a more appropriate range of practice; it ought to subsume instructional leadership as the dominant image of school administration" (p. 8). Roberts (1985) describes transformational leadership as "leadership that facilitates the redefinition of a people's mission and vision, a renewal of their commitment, and the restructuring of their systems of goal accomplishment" (p. 1024).

Sashkin (1988) describes the new role of the principal as a visionary. However, Fullan (1992) argues that good principals do not create a vision independently and impose it on others; rather, that effective principals develop a collaborative culture in which participants build vision together. In a conversation with Brandt (1992a), Thomas Sergiovanni states that he has abandoned his earlier views about leadership and now believes that professionalism and leadership are contradictory (Brandt, 1992a). Sergiovanni (1992) further notes, "The more professionalism is emphasized, the less leadership is needed. The more leadership is emphasized, the less likely it is that professionalism will develop" (p. 42).

Research Approach

The Accelerated Schools process provides a methodology for fundamental school restructuring. The new images of the role of principals as facilitators and transformational leaders is highly compatible with the Accelerated Schools process. In this study, we focus on the change in the role of principals in schools engaged in the Accelerated Schools process. It examines the change process in four Accelerated Schools. All four are elementary schools that were in the midst of the restructuring process at the time of our site visits in the spring of 1991. Three of the schools neared completion of their first year of the process and were about to enter the inquiry (or implementation) stage. The fourth school was ending its second year and had one year of experience with the new environment. The analysis of the four cases focuses on (a) whether there was evidence of change in the role of the principals in these four schools, and (b) what factors facilitated or inhibited change in the role of principals.

We used the case study research method, which involves an assortment of research methodologies, including interviews, direct observations, document review, archival records, participant observation, and surveys (Yin, 1984). The names of the schools were changed to protect the confidentiality of the interviewees. The specific approaches used to collect and analyze information on the four schools is included in the chapter appendix.

Analysis

We examine changes in the role of principals in four accelerated schools. Our analysis is presented in four parts: overview of the schools; the initial role of principal; the role of the principal at the time of the site visit; and factors influencing change.

Overview

Each of the schools is located in an urban public school system in the southern or southwestern sections of the United States. Two were located in the same large urban district in a southern state (Griswald Elementary School and McBride Elementary School); one in a medium-sized urban district in the same state (Forest Elementary School). Griswald, McBride, and Forest were in the initial phase of implementing the Accelerated Schools concept. They were selected because we had the opportunity to study them as part of the University of New Orleans Accelerated Schools Project.

The fourth school was located in a suburban district adjacent to a large urban center in a southwestern state (Cedarcrest Elementary School). The motivation of the principal and the teaching staff to execute the project based on their beliefs in the concepts of the project and the successful implementation of the first year of the project led to the selection of Cedarcrest as a model for the present study.

At Griswald Elementary School, dedication ceremonies for the building that currently houses the school were held on February 15, 1939. The school is located in the inner city of a large southern city. The community consists of low-income families living in single-family residences. The student population of Griswald, for the 1990-1991 school year, was 320, with a faculty of 24 teachers and a principal. The ethnic background of the student population was 100% African American. Grades prekindergarten through 6 are taught in the school. Griswald has a history of longevity in the number of years individuals serve as principal: The previous principal served for 15 years, and his two predecessors had held the position for a total of 35 years. In the fall of 1989, a new principal was appointed and made the application for the school to be included in the Louisiana Accelerated Schools project.

McBride Elementary School is situated on a 7.15 acre site in a large metropolitan area in the South. It opened its doors in 1959. Homes in the area are primarily privately owned, single-family dwellings. For the 1990-1991 school year, the enrollment of McBride was 406 in Grades prekindergarten through 6. Sixty percent of students qualified for free lunches, 12% received reduced-price lunches, and 28% paid the full price for lunch. The ethnic composition of the student body was 99% African American and 1% White. The faculty consisted of a principal and 26 teachers. The administrative history of McBride is brief in that until 1980, only two persons served as principal. In the fall of that year, the current principal, the third in the history of the school, was appointed.

Forest Elementary School was built in 1955. It is located in a large metropolitan city in the South, in a neighborhood of single-family residences. The majority of families have incomes below the poverty level. Ninety-eight percent of the student body participated in the free or reduced-price lunch program for the 1990-1991 school year. During the same school year, Forest had a population of 401 students in Grades prekindergarten through 5 with a faculty of 22 teachers and a principal. With the exception of 10 White children, the school population consisted of African American students.

Cedarcrest Elementary School is part of a suburban school district near a large city in the Southwest. The majority of the district is made up of middle- to upper-class families and has the reputation of being a private school district for upper-class, Anglo children. However, Cedarcrest was separated from the other schools in this affluent district by railroad tracks and a freeway, in the words of the current principal, "a double barrier." At the time Cedarcrest was constructed, the neighborhood consisted of middle-class homes, and the school enrollment was 99% Anglo and 1% Hispanic students. However, the demographics of the neighborhood rapidly changed. The student population for the 1990-1991 school year was 989, 78% Hispanics, 11% other Whites, 5% African Americans, 5% Asian Americans, and 0.1% other. The faculty consisted of 70 teachers, 2 assistant principals, and a principal.

The Initial State of the Schools

Three of the schools exhibited characteristics that justified placement in the extreme quatrain on the left side of the continuum (see

TABLE 8.1

Traditional Scale				Accelerated Scale
Extreme	Moderate	Neutral	Moderate	Extreme

Table 8.1)—Griswald, Forest, and Cedarcrest. Prior to becoming accelerated schools, all three were dominated by a principal with an authoritarian and autocratic leadership style. The teachers at Griswald were satisfied with the operation of the school under this leadership. Three of the teachers interviewed were members of the Griswald faculty before the change process, and all three agreed, "There were no major problems." One remembered that, "We had good leadership." The school ran smoothly, the teachers recalled, because the former principal handled the discipline problems and made the decisions. The teachers expressed comfort with the authoritarian style and the fact that the principal maintained responsibility, especially for discipline.

Forest also exhibited characteristics of the extreme traditional mode. The leadership style of the principal was domineering and controlling. One teacher remembered, "And it was pretty much what she said was the way it was going to be." Of the seven teachers interviewed at Forest, five had been members of the faculty for a number of years. The consensus of these five interviewees was that control of the school emanated from the principal but was influenced by a small group of the teachers with longevity on the Forest faculty. The teachers that were not members of the in-group felt—and were— isolated. As a result, there was very little interaction among the faculty; creativity and self-esteem were at a low point.

Cedarcrest was assigned a new principal the year before it started as an accelerated school. All six of the teachers and the assistant principal who had been at Cedarcrest during some or all of the years during which the previous principal served indicated that management was authoritarian. One teacher explained, "It [the school] was run primarily in a very traditional approach and basically all the decisions were made from the top down and passed on." Others indicated that the prior principal "went strictly by the book," "made all the decisions," and "played favorites." As one teacher recalled, "It made the climate full of a lot of tension." The environment at Cedarcrest was intimidating and demoralizing for all segments of the school community due to the top-down approach utilized by the former principal.

The leadership style in one of the schools, McBride, could be classified as moderately traditional. The principal inherited a school community accustomed to and conditioned by the authoritarian, top-down leadership style of her predecessor. All but one of the teachers interviewed at McBride had been on the faculty for 10 or more years and agreed that both teachers and parents had little opportunity for decision making or input into school decisions. One teacher stated, "We [the teachers] were told what to do and we did it." However, most of the teachers enjoyed a good rapport with the principal. And the principal had been making efforts to change her traditional approach even before the Accelerated Schools Project. She felt that her endeavors fell short until some of the members of the faculty retired and were replaced by, in her words, "younger and/or fresher people." Because of the principal's predisposition toward a more facilitating role and the fact that many of the teachers indicted they had a good rapport with her, we classify her leadership style as moderately traditional.

The principals of Griswald and Cedarcrest had served at their respective schools for 1 year before the implementation of the Accelerated Schools process. In contrast, the principal of Forest had been there for 7 years and the principal of McBride for 9 years prior to the adoption of the Accelerated Schools Project.

Status During the Site Visit

We found more variation in the extent to which the role of the principals had changed in the schools at the time of the site visit. The role of the principal had changed to an Accelerated Schools mode in two of the schools—Cedarcrest and McBride. The most extensive change was evident in Cedarcrest, the school that had been in the Accelerated Schools Project for the longest period. The new principal arrived at Cedarcrest with a vision and the knowledge that empowerment and professionalization on the part of the school community would bring that vision to life. All of the teachers interviewed acknowledged that she was the catalyst for the change that occurred at Cedarcrest. One teacher expressed the attitude of the entire school community when she stated, "She was the one that brought it [the Accelerated Schools Project] to us and showed us what to do and how to get there." The leadership style used by the new principal at Cedarcrest correlates with the attributes of the extreme quatrain on the right side of the continuum. In this case, a new principal came with a new image of leadership and was able to act on it.

There was also evidence that the role of the principal at McBride had changed to an Accelerated Schools mode from a moderately traditional mode. Four of the five teachers interviewed at McBride related that a modification had occurred in the leadership style of the principal. One stated that the staff was encouraged "to speak out. Come up with ideas. Really discuss whatever our problems are and try to come up with a solution." This shift on the part of the principal from decision maker to facilitator produced leadership qualities that correspond with the attributes in the moderate quatrain on the righthand side of the continuum under the accelerated scale.

At the time of our site visit, the leadership style of principals in two of the school remained in a traditional mode. In one of the schools, there had been modest change, but in the other the principal's role remained in an extreme traditional mode.

At Forest, one of the schools that retained its long-term principal, the principal was not the catalyst for the change that occurred at Forest, but at the time of our site visit she had begun to question some of her authoritarian traits. One teacher observed:

And I see her [the principal] as more comfortable with her role. I've seen her more willing to take chances and to give faculty members the leeway to experiment. I think she's become much more open and available, and trusting of us.

Even though a softening had occurred in the autocratic leadership style of the principal, two problematic areas remained. First, the division in the faculty that existed before the adoption of the Accelerated Schools process still existed. During the interviews, several teachers stated that a group of four or five teachers still have the ear of the principal. Second, the teachers felt the principal's lack of organizational skills resulted in confusion and dissatisfaction on the part of the staff. They noted that she changed meeting times at the last minute, or even canceled meetings altogether. The school calendar was not accurate. The time frame for faculty meetings was never followed.

No change in the principal's role was evident at Griswald, in spite of the fact that there had been a change in principals. Each of the teachers interviewed at Griswald saw little headway being made in implementing the Accelerated Schools process. All of the teachers indicated that the reason for the slow progress was the leadership style of the principal. The ranking teacher related the feelings of the others:

> They [the teachers] feel that [the principal] isn't supportive of anything that's done. They feel that he is very critical of things that are done.

The principal espoused the principles of Accelerated Schools model, including empowerment, but he was critical of the teachers because he did not think they were knowledgeable about the curriculum aspects of the Accelerated Schools Project. The principal's attitude, coupled with resentment on the part of the staff, led to a stand off. Thus, the top-down environment changed very little in the school, in spite of the Accelerated Schools Project training.

We saw substantial variation in the extent to which the role of the principal changed in the four case study schools. The implementation of the Accelerated Schools process created a change in the leadership style of the principal in three of the schools—Forest, McBride, and Cedarcrest. In the case of Cedarcrest, the change was dramatic—from an extremely traditional principal's role to an extremely accelerated role. At McBride, there was a transition from a moderately traditional mode to a moderately accelerated mode. In Griswald, in contrast, there was no change, and the teachers in the school were extremely dissatisfied with the principal.

Factors That Influenced Change

We found evidence in the case studies that six factors combined to facilitate—or inhibit—change in the role of the principals in schools. Our summary analysis of these factors, presented below, is based on an in-depth analysis of each of these factors (Davidson, 1992).

First, district offices had a minor influence on the restructuring. Two of the schools—Griswald and McBride—were in a large urban district in which no commitment had been made to move toward site-based management in 1990-1991. The principal at McBride, who had been in her role for 11 years at the time of our site visit, used the Accelerated Schools process to distance her school from district policies and go her own way. In contrast, the principal at Griswald, who was new to the school, had previously been curriculum specialist with the district office. He used the Accelerated Schools process as an opportunity to promote many of his curricular ideas, which were consistent with district policies.

The other two schools—Forest and Cedarcrest—were in districts that had moved toward site-based management. At Forest, the decision to initiate the Accelerated Schools model was made as part of a site-based management process. Cedarcrest experienced little district resistance to the process, but received no district support either.

District movement to site-based management policies can help to foster the Accelerated Schools process, but the absence of site-based management policy does not necessarily inhibit the process if the principal ignores (or reinterprets) district mandates.

Second, there is an apparent relationship between the role of the principal and the role of teachers, at least in the Accelerated Schools studies. Teacher empowerment appeared to be a crucial aspect of the Accelerated Schools Project. The role of teachers changed, in varying degrees, in three of the four schools due to the implementation of the Accelerated Schools Project (Davidson, 1992). At McBride, Forest, and Cedarcrest, the change process had a positive effect. The role of the principal did not change at Griswald. In the schools that experienced change in leadership, the teachers indicated they felt more empowered. Movement toward a facilitating style enabled teachers to begin experimenting with curricular change (the "little wheels" of inquiry). These findings support the arguments by Levin (1987b) and Brunner and Hopfenberg (Chapter 2) that success in empowering teachers appears to have great potential for curricular improvements.

Third, a relationship between change in pedagogy and change in the role of the principal was also evident, although it was not a simple, one-directional relationship. At the time of our site visit, Griswald exhibited curricular changes. Teachers were using math manipulative and whole-language approaches. However, it also appeared that these ideas had been promoted by the principal rather than chosen by the teachers. In this case, the curricular changes resulted from top-down leadership.

Both Forest and McBride exhibited slight changes in curriculum during the 1990-1991 school year. At McBride, teachers were actively involved in planning for curricular changes—a writers' workshop and an Afro-centric curriculum—that were implemented in the 1991-1992 school year. At Forest, team teaching was being utilized by several of the first- and second-grade teachers. A number of the teachers interviewed mentioned "going beyond the textbooks" and "looking for real motivational activities."

At Cedarcrest, there was substantial curricular change, with the introduction of team teaching, thematic education, and a variety of other innovations that had already resulted in large gains in students' test scores. Thus, the three schools that showed the most change in the leadership style of the principal—Forest, McBride, and Cedarcrest— were best able to make meaningful changes in pedagogical processes.

We draw four tentative conclusions about the relationship between curricular changes and the role of the principal:

- It is possible to implement curricular changes even when the principal utilizes the top-down, authoritarian style of leadership.
- When the principal assumes the role of facilitator, the teachers have more opportunity to become empowered.
- An emphasis on empowerment changes the role of the teachers and enables implementation of meaningful curricular innovations (little wheels of inquiry; see Chapter 2).
- Curricular innovations implemented by teachers, as a result of their own inquiry processes (little wheels), have great potential for improving student learning.

Fourth, a relationship between the leadership style of the principal and parental involvement was also evident. The three schools that evidenced change in the role of the principal also exhibited major changes in parental involvement. Parents at McBride, Forest, and Cedarcrest were involved in cadres and were actually part of the change process, as well as participating in more typical ways, such as attending PTA/ PTO meetings, donating time to assist with field trips, and so forth. These changes were not evident at Griswald, where there was also little change in the role of the principal. Thus, change in the role of parents seems closely related to change in the role of the principal in the Accelerated Schools process. Indeed, changes in attitudes the principal holds about parents may influence the ability of the school community to embrace the Accelerated Schools methodology (St. John, 1995).

Fifth, technical assistance from university faculty played a minor role in the change process in three of the schools. Cedarcrest initiated its Accelerated Schools process without assistance from university consultants. After the school's success with test score improvements, Accelerated Schools specialists at a local university learned about and visited the school. Thus, Cedarcrest illustrates how schools can restructure without outside help. Staff at the other three schools were trained in a university-based program and were given technical assistance with the implementation of the process. In interviews, principals and teachers indicated this university support was helpful. However, the success of the schools was variable. And the university consultants had little influence on the predispositions of the principals. If the principals believed in empowerment, then they were open to coaching. The principal with a less-open attitude toward teachers was also reluctant to use coaching from the university. We conclude that technical assistance from university specialists can help with the transition to the Accelerated Schools model, but it does not guarantee success.

Finally, it is possible that the length of time a school is involved in the Accelerated Schools process influences the extent of change in the principal's role. The school that had been in the Accelerated Schools Project for 2 years prior to our site visit showed the most extensive change in the principal's role. That the principal's role had not changed as extensively in the other three schools may be attributable to the fact that these schools remained at the initial capacity building stage discussed in previous chapters.

Lessons Learned

This initial study of the implementation of the Accelerated Schools process in a select group of schools illustrates that (a) the Accelerated Schools Project can foster a change in leadership to a more facilitating (or empowering) approach, and (b) change in leadership appears to facilitate change in curriculum, instruction, and parent and community involvement. However, changing the leadership style of principals is a complex process that cannot be easily transferred from one school to another or from university trainers to schools. Instead, it takes a great deal of dedicated effort.

The principals, and their capacity to change their leadership styles, were probably the most important single factor in the success of the Accelerated Schools Project in four schools. Two of the schools had new principals who initiated the process. In the school that changed the least, the new principal had an authoritarian approach and seemed unable to change his style even with coaching from university faculty who provided technical assistance. Teachers consistently indicated that his controlling approach and his temper prevented them from taking risks. In contrast, the other new principal brought in a new style that engaged teachers. She seemed to have a deep personal commitment to the philosophy of the Accelerated Schools Project. Her leadership style allowed all members of the school community to become agents for change.

Two of the schools had long-term principals who had previously functioned with authoritarian styles. Thus, both needed to change their styles. One of these principals found this a difficult transition and some of the teachers harbored doubts about whether she would be able to make the transition. However, she did make some changes during the year. The other principal had long been looking for an opportunity to change the school and readily embraced Accelerated Schools concepts.

Thus, the predisposition of the principal seems critical. Indeed, the assignment of a new principal to a school does not ensure change unless the new principal has an authentic orientation toward empowerment. However, it is difficult to judge whether a principal is truly willing to empower others or merely espouses the rhetoric. Griswald was selected for the Accelerated Schools Project because the principal appeared to be very supportive of such principles, yet parents and teachers indicated he did not have an empowering approach to the project.

Teachers' experiences help them judge whether principals really believe in empowerment. If teachers think their principal does not believe in empowerment, they do not take risks (Meza et al., 1993/1994). However, if the principal's approach to empowerment seems genuine, then teachers can begin to take the risks necessary to change their role in school.

District restructuring, especially the movement toward site-based management, also appears to be an important aspect of the change process. Districts with site-based management have fewer obstacles to implementing the Accelerated Schools process. However, a district orientation toward site-based management in itself does not explain why one school changes and another does not.

Universities can provide training and technical assistance that help facilitate the empowerment process, but other forces in schools can inhibit change even if university assistance is provided. And there is no guarantee that university facilitators have the personal skills and knowledge to actually help schools with this difficult change process. The craft of facilitating school restructuring needs to be refined both by school leaders and outside facilitators, including university faculty. There is a clear need for continued inquiry into how change in leadership can best be fostered.

Appendix

Research Methods

Data Sources

Institutional documents were collected and analyzed. Test scores, attendance records, parental involvement and attendance at meetings, memoranda, administrative documents, grant applications, vision statements, surveys, and brainstorming papers were used in the change process and were also examined in the case study.

Interviews were conducted at each school site with teachers, administrators (principals and assistant principals), and others (e.g., social workers and parents). The principal at each of the schools was consulted to identify the parents and teachers to be interviewed. An attempt was made to talk both to those who supported and to those who resisted the change process. An interview guide used for the study asked questions about (a) the status of each school before the implementation of the Accelerated Schools concept or change process, (b) the status of the school at the time of the interviews, and (c) the factors that facilitated or inhibited change in the schools. A total of 35 people were interviewed for the study.

Each interviewee was questioned about the status of the school before the restructuring process and at the time of the site visit, as well as about factors that influenced the change process. Questions about histories and current status of the school related to five dimensions: (a) relations with the central office, (b) the role of the principal, (c) the role of teachers, (d) the role of parents and the community, and (e) pedagogical processes in the school. In this chapter, we focus on the role of the principals. However, changes in all of the factors have been analyzed (Davidson, 1992) and will be discussed as they pertain to the topics of the chapter.

Field notes were taken during the site visits. Most of the interviews were taped, and after each interview a written record was made of each session, using a method recommended by Lofland and Lofland (1984). These records contained (a) summaries and notes of what was said, (b) recorded transcription of important responses, (c) notes on methodology, and (d) personal emotional experiences. Each taped interview was typed verbatim and the transcript was sent to the interviewee for review and verification of facts. In the case of the few interviews that were not taped, due to technical difficulties, the transcript was typed from the field notes and sent to the interviewee for review and verification of facts.

Case studies were developed and analyzed for each of the schools (Davidson, 1992). The names of the schools and interviewees were changed in order to disguise the real identities and foster respondents' openness. Disguising was also important because the analyses critically examine the extent of change in each school and the reasons why change occurred.

Analysis Methods

Two analysis methods were used. First, a continuum was developed to assess the extent of change in the role of principals. One side of the continuum (the left) represented the characteristics of the traditional mode of school organization: top-down decisions with the principal as the authority figure. The other side of the continuum (the right) represented the extreme characteristics of the Accelerated Schools model: bottom-up decisions with the principal as the facilitator. Each side of the continuum was further divided into "extreme" and "moderate," indicating degree of the characteristics on either end of the continuum. The middle quatrain of each continuum was considered neutral, or as exhibiting the qualities of both types of leadership. For example, the extreme quatrain would assume virtually *all* the characteristics of the top-down mode, in the case of the left dimension, or of the participatory mode, in the case of the right dimension. The neutral category assumes a combination of relations. The distinction among the five quatrains assumes predominance of one form of relations or the other. The continuum is shown in Table 8.2.

The assessment of the initial status of the schools, before the Accelerated Schools process, focuses on the role of the principal. Judgments were made about quatrain on the continuum based on the following criteria:

1. Did the principal pay more attention to rules and regulations than relationships?
2. Did the principal maintain a sense of control through the enforcement of rules and regulations, along with taking total responsibility for pertinent information and decision making?
3. Was the principal an active listener and team participant?

TABLE 8.2 Assessing the Extent of Change in the Role of Principals

Traditional Scale				Accelerated Scale
Top-down within school				Bottom-up decisions
Principal as authority				Principal as facilitator

Extreme	Moderate	Neutral	Moderate	Extreme

Griswald (1) and (2)

Forest (1)   Forest (2)
————————————>

Cedarcrest (1)   Cedarcrest (2)
——>

                              McBride (1) McBride (2)
                              ————————————>

---

4. Was the principal able to identify and cultivate talents among faculty and staff, work productively with parents and the community, and keep the school focused on goals they all agreed upon and understood?
5. Did the principal have the training and specific techniques to encourage cooperative group processes such as problem solving or goal setting?
6. Did the principal assume the role of facilitator?

The responses obtained in the interviews and the direct and participant observations were used to make judgments about placement. To assess the organizational structure of each school before the implementation of the Accelerated Schools process, judgments were made based on the responses of teachers who had been members of the faculty prior to the adoption of the process. The continuum was used to assess the extent of change in the role of principals. Interview results are presented to illustrate the judgments used to place schools on this continuum.

Second, analyses of other factors included in the full study (Davidson, 1992) are reexamined in these schools. The other four factors were analyzed using a similar methodology to the one developed for principals. The results of these other analyses are only discussed as they pertain to changes in the role of principals.

℘ 9

Toward a New Leadership Paradigm

Behaviors of Accelerated School Principals

GEORGIA CHRISTENSEN

The technologically complex, ethnically diverse, and increasingly global scope of postindustrial U.S. society has placed extreme stress on a school system designed for life in the 1920s. Although diverse constituencies recognize the necessity of transforming schools, still under debate is how to achieve this and with whose participation (Sergiovanni, 1992). My research focuses on the work of the Accelerated Schools Project, one of the nationally recognized models of school transformation, and highlights the role of principals as change agents in this model. This chapter begins with some general background on different prominent responses to calls for school reform and then moves to a more specific analysis of the accelerated school and the role the principal plays in this transformation process. The analysis hinges on a detailed and comparative taxonomy of the behaviors of principals in accelerated schools, relating accelerated school stakeholders' opinions about important principal behaviors with those identified in the literature on principals and school change. This taxonomy allows for the development of a general portrait of effective principals' behaviors and enriches existing profiles of school leadership with extensive empirical data. The final section provides conclusions and implications derived from the study for the design of training and development programs for principals as well as contributions to research on administrators in restructuring schools.

Responding to the Call
for School Change: Restructuring

One of the national responses to the call for change is school restructuring (Ascher, 1993; Ascher & Burnett, 1993; Brandt, 1992b; English & Hill, 1990; Lieberman et al., 1991; Sailor, 1991; Wilkes, 1992). *Restructuring* "is an effort that is trying to change the basic beliefs about the nature of schooling and its practices as well" (G. R. Smith, Tourgee, Turner, Lashley, & Lashley, 1992, p. 1). Current school organization comes from a turn-of-the-century design with some modifications along the way. The postindustrial age, the information age, and the global village concepts of today demand very different student skills and outcomes, which must be supported by new school structures.

In the 1980s, states and districts across the United States sponsored groundbreaking restructuring initiatives (e.g., California, Chicago, Dade County [Florida]). At the heart of the restructuring movement is the assumption that better decisions about students, policies, and programs happen when those most directly affected by and responsible for implementation participate in the process. Building on this assumption, restructuring efforts focus on changes in the nature of teaching and learning; the decision-making processes in schools; teachers' working conditions; and the relationship between schools, their clients, and the members of their community (Hallinger, Murphy, & Hausman, 1991, pp. 1-3; Sailor, Kelly, & Karasoff, 1992).

In a restructured school, change is a prominent theme. Restructured schools transform the way teaching and learning take place; teachers' working conditions; the manner and level at which decisions are made; and the relationships among the school staff, students, and members of the school community. In the restructured school, one finds more shared decision making and overall involvement among the various stakeholders than in a traditional school (Fullan, 1993; Fullan & Stiegelbauer, 1991). There is a sense of collaboration among staff and integration in the areas of the curriculum, instruction, and organization of the school. Flexibility, risk taking, sharing of information, and problem solving are integral to the life of a restructured school. The culture of the school is student based and student centered.

A major restructuring model in the United States today is the Accelerated Schools model inspired by Professor Henry M. Levin and developed by his colleagues at the National Center for the Accelerated Schools Project at Stanford University as a response to the growing urgency to address the needs of students caught in at-risk situations

(Chenoweth, 1992; Guthrie & van Heusden Hale, 1990; House Subcommittee, 1992; Levin, 1989a; Stefkovich, 1993). The Accelerated Schools Project contains in one model all the characteristics of a restructured school, but adds to it an underlying philosophy about education and a process to enable the systematic transformation of the school that honors the unique characteristics of the particular site (Hopfenberg et al., 1993). The Accelerated Schools model is focused on the premise that *all* children have the right to receive a high-quality, enriched educational program that enables them to enter the mainstream of education, by building on rather than disregarding their background and experiences. To do this, all members of an accelerated school work together to systematically address selected prioritized challenges, the resolution of which provides more enriched learning environments and moves students in the school to higher levels of achievement and learning.

Transforming a traditional school, in which hierarchy is firmly rooted and decision making is often the prerogative of one individual seeking to meet externally imposed demands, into an accelerated school, in which high levels of participation and a clear focus on selected objectives are the norm, is a daunting task. Such a transformation requires considerable changes from all members of the school community, particularly the principal.

The role of the principal in a traditional school and a restructured school is quite different (Brandt, 1992a; Murphy & Hallinger, 1992; Nadler & Tushman, 1989). The overall behavior of the principal in a traditional school is that of a policy compliance officer who enforces mandates from outside the school. The role is a reactive one, with little flexibility relative to the outside forces of the traditional structure. The principal of a traditional school is part of the hierarchical structure and thus operates in an autocratic manner as a middle manager at the local school site. In the traditional school we see the principal as a static compliance manager who reacts to directives from outside the school and operates out of a top-down model of leadership and decision making, generally in isolation from the other members of the school community.

In an accelerated school, the principal's primary role is expected to be that of a transformational leader, one who contributes to and enables change in the school (Hallinger, 1992; Leithwood, 1992; Seeley, 1991). There is a high degree of collaboration on the part of the principal in a restructured school with all the stakeholders in the local school community in addressing decisions affecting all aspects of the school that influence student learning (Sagor, 1991). The principal serves in a proactive manner as a facilitator of change and a risk taker. Table 9.1 provides a comparison of the principal's role in these two distinct settings.

Although the literature is replete with analyses of and frameworks for change, it offers very little theoretical or empirical discussion of how principals actually operate in, facilitate, and adapt to this context. Granted, the principal's role changes as the school changes, but who contributes to the changes in schools and how? What part does the principal play in school change? What are the new "best practices" for principals in this restructured school model? To date, there are relatively few rigorous studies of the principal's role in change either in a traditional school or a restructured school.

The literature provides somewhat of a divided analysis of the role of the principal. A few of the studies suggest that the principal contributes no more to change than do other constituents. The majority of the studies identify the principal as the key player or most influential member of the school and thus most responsible for change. The somewhat ambiguous nature of the literature leaves many unanswered questions about the principal's role. It is difficult to obtain a holistic view of the principal's role in bringing about change or specific details about what is new and different in the principal's role. My review of current research highlighted the need for a detailed study on the actual behaviors of principals. The purpose of my exploratory study was to look at the role of the principal in the Accelerated Schools transformation process. More specifically, the question under investigation was: What are the behaviors of a principal that contribute to the implementation of the Accelerated Schools philosophy and process?

The Methodology

To address my research question, I consulted with the National Center for the Accelerated Schools Project at Stanford University. Together, we developed criteria for selecting the accelerated schools and principals for the study, which included at least 3 years' experience with the Accelerated Schools philosophy and process, stability in the principalship, and similarity in size and student population characteristics. In addition, we determined that varying degrees of progress in transformation would provide a richer portrait of schools' change processes and

TABLE 9.1 Major Characteristics of a Traditional School and an Accelerated School

The Traditional School	The Accelerated School
Organization	**Organization**
Hierarchical, top-down structure	Empowerment coupled with responsibility
Bureaucratic, remote-control changes	Formal Accelerated Schools process
Teacher isolation/autonomy	Total staff involved in each level of gover-
Subject area departments	nance: cadres, steering committee, SAW
Isolated classes/departments	Cross-department cadres
Fixed scheduling	Flexible scheduling
Separation of all staff	Building on strengths of all school members
Principal as manager	Principal as one of the facilitators
Limited parent/community involvement	Active involvement of parent/community
Maintenance oriented	The inquiry process
Central office monitoring compliance	District is part of school groups
Age-graded institution	Student-centered vision
Little/negative attention to schoolwide goals	Schoolwide vision, unity of purpose
Cosmetic, piecemeal changes	"Big wheel" and "little wheel" activities
Staff development from outside	Open to new ideas and adventures
Curriculum	Total staff decides on programs
Standardized curriculum	**Curriculum**
Basic core classes for all	Equal access to all courses by all
Standardized testing	Integrated curriculum
Stress on facts, abstract concepts	Assessment integral to inquiry process
Remediation for lower-level students	Real-world curriculum
Acceleration for upper-level students	Inquiry process part of curriculum
Tracking	Student participation on cadres and
Textbook serves as primary source	committees
Electives and extra activities for gifted	No tracking
Isolated subject areas	Multiple primary sources
"Traditional" content	Cocurricular and extracurricular activities for
Controlled/mandated by outside	all
Instruction	Equity in course content
Homogeneous grouping	Cadres and SAW determine curriculum
Conventional techniques (lecture, rote	**Instruction**
learning, drill, worksheets, etc.)	Heterogeneous grouping
Teacher's guide serves as primary source for	Active, powerful learning techniques and
lesson development and presentation	strategies
Teacher-centered classrooms	Real-world experiences as primary sources
Students work independently of each other	Student-centered vision of school
Reliance on standardized tests and external	School is seen as center of expertise
assessment for evaluating progress	Group activities and cooperative learning
	Open-ended activities
	Multiple ability learning opportunities
	Alternative assessment and self-assessment

a wider range of behaviors of the principals. On the basis of these criteria, I selected five elementary schools located in four school districts.

To accurately capture the behaviors of accelerated school principals, I used the Critical Incident Technique, which is a research method for identifying and categorizing actual behaviors through the collection of critical incidents related to the role being studied (see chapter appendix). I used interviews with various constituents from each of the five accelerated schools to collect data on the behaviors of accelerated school principals and I conducted on-site observations at each school. I interviewed 60 individuals who spend time at the five accelerated schools on a regular basis, either as employees or regular voiunteers. In selecting interviewees, I attempted to maintain broad representation from the school community (e.g., positions, ages, ethnic backgrounds, genders, and experiences) to ensure characterizations of the principal from a variety of perspectives.

I developed a specific interview protocol in accordance with the directives of the Critical Incident Technique and the major constructs of the Accelerated Schools philosophy and process. During the interview, I asked each respondent to relate specific incidents illustrating what the principal did that contributed to or hindered the implementation of the Accelerated Schools process, each of the three principles of the Accelerated Schools model, and powerful learning experiences for the students. Along with these interviews, I spent 2 days at each school, during which time I visited classrooms, talked with numerous individuals at the school, participated in some of the school activities, and reviewed documentation.

Each of these activities yielded information that I categorized using the following questions: (a) What led up to the situation? (b) What happened? What did the principal do? and (c) What was the outcome? How did it lead to the implementation or internalization of the Accelerated Schools philosophy and process? Over 1,055 separate critical incidents were identified. Both positive and negative incidents were included.

With the assistance of two outside researchers—an expert in the Critical Incident Technique and an Accelerated Schools Project trainer[1]—I used these incidents to develop a taxonomy of principals' behaviors. After six revisions, the taxonomy was shared with the 2 outside sorters and 60 accelerated school principals to review for clarity and comprehensiveness. Their contributions assisted in further refining some of the descriptors and redistributing two of the discrete behaviors to a different major category.

Results and Interpretation

The Taxonomy

The final taxonomy of the behaviors of principals that contribute to the implementation of the Accelerated Schools philosophy and process contained 13 major categories and 152 discrete behaviors.[2] The 13 major categories appear in Table 9.2 along with the number of incidents that reflected behaviors in each category and the number of discrete behaviors per category (Christensen, 1994).

Although Table 9.2 was constructed using information provided by persons in accelerated schools, it does reveal some behaviors that one would likely expect in any study of effective principal leadership, including such behaviors as supporting the staff, promoting communication, exhibiting positive human relation skills, facilitating meetings, and using administrative skills. In addition, behaviors such as interacting with the state/district, promoting learning, and even promoting parental involvement are essential for any principal who is trying to facilitate change in a school. Table 9.3 lists principals' behaviors identified through a review of the existing literature on effective school leadership. A comparison of Tables 9.2 and 9.3 shows that in many instances what is required of accelerated school principals is quite similar to expectations for effective leaders in most restructured schools. This study also identified many behaviors that are unique to the implementation and internalization of the Accelerated Schools philosophy and process, for example, promoting the Accelerated Schools model, promoting the vision of the school, and fostering the process. In the following sections, I discuss those behaviors common among all effective principals and distinguish those behaviors unique to accelerated school principals.

Similarities Between Accelerated School Principals and Other Effective Principals

As mentioned above, accelerated school principals exhibited behaviors considered universal for effective school leadership. Of these generally identified principal behaviors, supporting staff was the most frequently cited. Principals demonstrated support for staff by promoting staff expertise, supporting staff initiative, and providing written and verbal praise. Other supportive behaviors included meeting with the staff members individually, in small groups, or collectively; spending

TABLE 9.2 Major Behavior Categories Identified With the Critical Incident Technique

A.	Promote Accelerated Schools Model—57* (11 discrete behaviors)**
B.	Promote the Vision of School—42 (9 discrete behaviors)**
C.	Support the Staff—148 (19 discrete behaviors)**
D.	Foster the Process—284 (24 discrete behaviors)**
E.	Promote Communication—24 (3 discrete behaviors)**
F.	Exhibit Positive Human Relations Skills—70 (10 discrete behaviors)**
G.	Facilitate Meetings—25 (8 discrete behaviors)**
H.	Interact with Students—49 (7 discrete behaviors)**
I.	Interact with the District/State—40 (5 discrete behaviors)**
J.	Promote Parent Involvement—90 (15 discrete behaviors)**
K.	Provide Resources—74 (8 discrete behaviors)**
L.	Promote Learning—102 (23 discrete behaviors)**
M.	Demonstrate Administrative Skills—48 (10 discrete behaviors)**

* Number of incidents that reflected behaviors within the major category.
** Number of discrete behaviors within the major category.

time solving problems with students, parents, or other staff members; and assisting with professional development. In total, there were 19 different ways reported in which the principals supported their staff members, including promoting staff expertise (32 incidents), supporting staff initiative (22 incidents), and providing written (19 incidents) and verbal (17 incidents) praise. These behaviors reflect how important it is for the principal to recognize and build up the staff in order for the staff to deliver its best to the students.

TABLE 9.3 Principals' Behaviors: Evidence From the Literature

Communicates goals—11
Shares decision making—10
Creates/articulates school vision—10
Develops goals—9
Exhibits human relations skills—9
Supports staff—9
Secures resources—9
Provides instructional leadership—9
Exhibits public relations skills—8
Emphasizes high expectations—7
Motivates staff—6
Manages change—6
Communicates effectively—6
Buffers staff—6
Promotes staff development—6
Evaluates/monitors teachers—6
Monitors student progress—6

NOTE: Numbers represent the number of studies that reflected the behavior.

Following supporting staff were principals' behaviors that promote learning. Over 100 of the incidents represented examples of principal behaviors that promoted learning. Accelerated school principals promoted learning by participating in school/classroom activities (16 incidents), planning powerful learning activities (11 incidents), and taking photos or videos of powerful learning (8 incidents). Their efforts were seen by staff as motivating, encouraging, and enabling learning in the school directly with the students and indirectly through the staff members.

A third frequently reported category was promoting parental involvement (in the term *parent* I include family and extended family). The basic premise for parental involvement in an accelerated school is that the parents play a key role in the education of their children. The school cannot take the sole responsibility for educating the child. Parents must be involved, and principals must encourage that involvement. As the African proverb states, "It takes a whole village to raise a child." In my research, I found that accelerated school principals promoted parental involvement through formal participation in organizations such as PTA and through informal activities with parents who volunteered at the school and were members of cadres and committees. Specifically, accelerated school principals directly solicited parental involvement (22 incidents) through telephone calls, letters, and even home visits, and communicated with parents in their own language.

Demands on educators to provide more services and opportunities for an increasingly diverse group of students seem to be ever pressing on site staff. Many of these demands require special resources in the form of materials and supplies, personnel, or special training for those currently working with the children. All of these resources—not all by any means extra—are critical. It is incumbent upon the principal to ensure the adequacy of resources, if only by providing opportunities for other members of the school community to find the specific resources and bring them to the school. I identified specific behaviors related to providing resources such as successfully writing grants (17 incidents), providing materials and supplies (17 incidents), and providing opportunities for professional development (15 incidents) as critical behaviors on the part of the principal in providing resources.

Children are the most important members of the accelerated school community. In the taxonomy, I identified 49 incidents related to ways principals interact with students. Looking at the discrete behaviors in this category and the descriptors, we can see that most of the behaviors represent informal interactions. A principal need not spend inordinate amounts of time with students or preparing to be with the students. The visibility of the principal to the students is important.

Another major category of behaviors of an accelerated school principal is interacting with the district/state. With the structure of decision making moving toward a more comprehensive and inclusive process, the school's traditional compliance relationship with the district changes. In accelerated schools, attention is often focused on the three or four challenge areas given top priority by the school community. To address these challenges, cadres proceed through a systematic process of inquiry to develop comprehensive solutions that get at the root of the challenge. Because of this situation, principals must often step up communication with district or state staff on a variety of fronts. Maintaining regular communication with district and state representatives keeps these policymakers informed of the progress being made at the school and helps them to understand the Accelerated Schools transformation process. Increasing awareness at the district and state levels is also useful in those situations in which the principals must intervene in the school's interest (e.g., to decline a program that doesn't meet the school vision, to request a waiver or variance to substitute taking stock for a needs assessment, etc.). Even though only 40 incidents reflected the need for the principal to work with the district or state, most of those (62.5 %) described a situation in which the principal either took advantage of an opportunity to, or failed to, intervene with the district/state on behalf of the school (25 incidents). Sixteen of the 40 incidents in this category were negative incidents in which the principal missed a chance to lobby for the school, to ask for a waiver, to say no to a district demand, or to request more time for the process.

Very few of the behaviors of an accelerated school principal can be performed without good skills in human relations. Not surprisingly, then, exhibiting positive human relations skills occurred in 70 different incidents. The primary behaviors present in this section of the taxonomy are being sensitive to people's concerns/feelings (15 incidents) and dealing with criticism in a nonconfrontational manner (15 incidents). Considering the strong focus on interaction among all the school community members in the organizational, curricular, and instructional components of an accelerated school, one can see the reason for the frequent occurrence of these behaviors.

Three other categories closely related to exhibiting positive human relations skills are demonstrating administrative skills, facilitating meetings, and promoting communication. These are behaviors that an effective traditional or restructured school principal should possess— and an accelerated school principal is no exception. Open and clear communication (14 incidents) and good meeting management and organizational skills (12 incidents) often go hand in hand with the smooth running of any organization. They are essential for the Accelerated Schools process to move within the school and must be operationalized through the philosophy.

Based on these categories, it appears that many of the behaviors that make for an effective accelerated school principal correspond with those required for successful leadership and partnership in any school. As I demonstrate in the next section, however, effective accelerated school principals must add additional behaviors to their repertoire to truly foster and facilitate the transformation process at the school.

Differences Between Accelerated School Principals
and Other Effective Principals

As discussed above, many of the behaviors listed in the taxonomy are applicable to principals in any leadership position. However, the most frequently cited behavior (fostering the process) determined through the Critical Incident Technique protocol related directly to the Accelerated Schools model. In addition, during interviews, respondents identified behaviors particular to the Accelerated Schools model as the "most important things" a principal must do to be a good accelerated school principal. Table 9.4 provides the most frequently reported "important things" and offers an interesting cross-check for the behaviors listed in Table 9.2. (For the complete listing of "The Most Important Things a Principal Must Do," see Christensen, 1994.)

The dual approach provided by a comparison of Tables 9.2 and 9.4 reveal those unique behaviors required for effective principalship in an accelerated school: fostering the process, promoting the Accelerated Schools model, and promoting the school vision. Each of these categories stresses the underlying philosophy of the accelerated school and highlights ways in which principals have put the three principles of the Accelerated Schools model into practice from the very beginning of the transformation process. In doing this, accelerated school principals have advanced the model; they continued to reinforce the three principles by keeping the school vision alive.

Over one fourth (27.1%) of the incidents identified behaviors relating to the characteristic of fostering the Accelerated Schools process. All of these incidents manifest a behavior that is quite particular to an accelerated school, as following the process is the major way of implementing the Accelerated Schools philosophy.

In this category are behaviors that indicate that the principal knows the process, promotes it, and follows it. These behaviors manifest the overall steps in the process of becoming an accelerated school—buying into the model, taking stock, forging a vision, setting priorities, and establishing the governance structure. They also reflect specific behaviors of following the governance process itself by using the trilevel governance structure of cadres, steering committee, and school as a whole (SAW) meetings to address the major concerns of the school, make decisions, and implement those decisions. Underlying this category is the basic use of the inquiry process as a method of solving problems and addressing challenges that occur in the school.

The participants related 24 different behaviors illustrating this category. The most commonly reported of these behaviors were using the governance process correctly (38 separate incidents out of the total represented this behavior), soliciting staff input (33 incidents), and participating in cadres/steering/SAW as a co-member (30 incidents).

TABLE 9.4 Accelerated Schools Community Members Speak: Most
Frequently Cited Things a Principal Must Do
to Be an Effective Accelerated School Principal

Be willing to let go of control—21
Be supportive of staff—18
Be present—16
Stand up to the district—15
Be a real expert on the Accelerated Schools process—14
Be positive—13
Believe that every child is a success and is smart, and build on that—12
Be open-minded; listen to everybody's opinions—12
Be sensitive to staff morale—12
Make sure all communication channels are open and remain open—11
Show appreciation to everyone—10
Use the process—10
Follow up on disciplinary consequences—10
Have a global vision or view of the whole picture—9
Build on the strengths of all—9

NOTE: The numbers at the end of each phrase refer to the number of individuals out of the 60 interviewed who stated that particular type of behavior.

Considering that the Accelerated Schools process is the primary mechanism for the internalization of the philosophy and the transformation of the school, the frequent occurrence of these behaviors is not surprising.

Promoting the Accelerated Schools model was another category of behavior that facilitated the transformation process. Principals often exhibited this type of behavior in the early stages of a school's exploration and launching, when the principal's understanding of and support for the model acted as a catalyst for staff decisions regarding it. Staff members viewed promoting the school's vision, also a process-related behavior, as being instrumental in the school's transformation process in several ways. It helped to anchor their use of the inquiry process by consistently moving decisions toward a set of objectives collectively identified by the school community. In addition, the principal's promotion of the school vision provided visible support for these collectively held goals and made it easier to use the vision as a benchmark for making difficult decisions about program development, staffing issues, and resource distribution.

Interviewees most frequently reported that an accelerated school principal must be willing to let go of control. Over one third of the respondents identified some form of letting go of control as most important. Data collected through the interviews also corresponded with data in the Critical Incident Technique taxonomy, particularly in the areas of being supportive to staff, being present, standing up to the district, and being a real expert on the accelerated school process.

The focus on process, along with the philosophical underpinnings as evidenced in the three principles—building on strengths, empowerment coupled with responsibility, and unity of purpose—are basic in an accelerated school. The principal's role in implementing the Accelerated Schools philosophy evidenced itself in numerous behaviors from the list of important things, such as being supportive of the staff; being positive; believing that every child is a success, is smart; being open-minded; listening to everybody's opinion; being sensitive to staff morale, as well as in the taxonomy developed from the critical incidents: soliciting staff input, promoting staff expertise, supporting staff initiative, providing praise, interacting with students, and promoting the Accelerated Schools model. Various dimensions of supporting the staff surfaced frequently in each taxonomy. This appears to indicate that the principal's role in instructional leadership occurs most directly through the support he or she provides to the staff. Intervening with the district/state and standing up to the district occurred very frequently in both taxonomies. The respondents not only felt these were important behaviors in an accelerated school, but they related many specific incidents in which the principals exhibited the behaviors in an effective or ineffective manner.

A Few Surprises

Selections from the current literature on principals' behaviors highlights studies on the role of the principal in whole-school change efforts (e.g., restructuring) and normatively highlights several key behaviors. Some behaviors are relatively similar to those identified in my empirical research. But the differences are provocative. Table 9.5 lists the principals' behaviors necessary for whole-school change efforts as identified in the literature.

There is a similarity between the majority of the behaviors identified in Table 9.5 and those from the taxonomies in my study (Tables 9.2 and 9.4). However, their order of frequency in reporting is quite differ-

TABLE 9.5 Principals and Whole-School Change: Behaviors Cited in the Literature

Exhibits human relations skills—7
Exhibits public relations skills—5
Communicates goals—4
Shares decision making—4
Emphasizes high expectations—4
Communicates effectively—4
Exhibits conflict resolution skills—4
Supports staff—4
Trusts others—4

NOTE: Numbers represent the number of studies that reflected the behavior.

ent in an accelerated school, with the exception of supporting the staff. I think this reflects the current realization that behaviors that support school staff are crucial behaviors in any setting, especially where reform is taking place. Because I was looking specifically at a reform strategy that related to the principal's role in whole-school change, I felt it important to compare the behaviors identified from that specific literature review with the behaviors in my taxonomies.

In Table 9.5, we see that the behaviors represented are those of an effective school administrator in any restructuring setting. The top two behaviors here, exhibiting human relations skills and exhibiting public relations skills, were present in the taxonomy of accelerated school principals but not at the top of the list in frequency of occurrence. Supporting the staff appeared to contribute to whole-school change both in the literature studies reviewed and in the critical incidents from the accelerated schools.

As we look further at Table 9.5, we find the behavior of communicating goals; we do not find that behavior in the accelerated school taxonomy. In an accelerated school, the principal is not solely responsible for communicating goals. Moreover, in an accelerated school, all members of the school community participate in the formulation of school goals as expressed in the vision, and actively work, in their cadres and with the inquiry process, to keep this vision alive in the school. Through this process, in which everyone shares in defining and working toward school goals, there is greater potential for an increased sense of commitment to implementing these goals. Rather than struggling to get buy-in from community members on his or her goals for the school, the principal participates in a united movement toward goals shared by all. Because of this, the center of expertise in an accelerated school resides in *all* the members of the school community.

In an accelerated school a large number of reported behaviors had to do with fostering the process, with specific behaviors relating to the workings of the governance structure at its various levels. This doesn't appear in general school-change literature other than through a broad interpretation of sharing decision making. In an accelerated school, the issue of fostering the process is crucial because it is through the governance process and the inquiry process that the real work of systemic reform occurs. Careful adherence to the governance process can make positive changes in communication and collaboration norms at a school. Following the individual steps of the inquiry process allows the school to make changes in a systematic manner and address root causes of often-recurrent problems and challenges. Through both of these processes, the school community's understanding of the philosophy of the Accelerated Schools model grows and is increasingly solidified in all school practices and norms.

It is noteworthy that promoting learning or even providing instructional leadership was not a significant category in the literature on whole-school change and school reform. Perhaps the focus in whole-school change literature was so broad that learning failed to surface. Nevertheless, behaviors relating to promoting learning and instructional leadership appeared third most frequently from the accelerated school incidents. Although the Accelerated Schools model does provide one strategy for developing site-based management, its central focus is on students and creating an educational environment for them in which all students excel and achieve academic success. It is because of the importance of powerful learning in the Accelerated Schools model that promoting learning surfaced as a frequently identified behavior for principals, thereby distinguishing the Accelerated Schools model as one that successfully combines restructuring with improvements in student performance and achievement.

Finally, both interacting with the state/district and promoting parental involvement were behaviors cited as important for accelerated school principals, though not for others. As accelerated school communities increasingly try to make decisions that further progress toward their vision and improve the chances for all children in the school to experience academic success, the principal has a more crucial role to play in interacting with district and state policymakers to ensure that the hard work of the school community is supported at these levels. Similarly, as the school community works in a more focused way to provide powerful learning experiences for all children, the support and involvement of families and parents becomes increasingly important. Principals can play a central role in securing this involvement and maintaining productive relationships with these community members.

Even though an accelerated school is a restructuring school, we see many differences, primarily from the fact that the Accelerated Schools model presents a specific set of practices for implementing that philosophy and thus sustaining the transformation. In this study, I have shown that some of those differences resonate with the specific behaviors of the principals. Above all, my research indicates that it is imperative for accelerated school principals to understand, foster, and follow the process with all its ramifications to bring about the transformation of their school into an accelerated school.

Conclusions and Implications for Future Work

In this study, I have compared traditional schools and principals with restructured schools and principals. I looked at the role of the principal in school change and presented the question: What are the behaviors of a principal that contribute to the implementation of the Accelerated Schools philosophy and process? I then described a method I used for identifying the behaviors of the principals in accelerated schools. Results were presented that show the behaviors of a principal that contribute to the Accelerated Schools philosophy and process. Finally, these behaviors were compared with principal behaviors identified in the literature.

The taxonomy of behaviors of an accelerated school principal developed through the use of the Critical Incident Technique suggests the need for an accelerated school principal to exhibit the characteristics of an effective traditional and restructured principal: administrative skills, human relations skills, and public relations skills. However, to contribute to the transformation of the school to an accelerated school, it is essential for the principal to understand, promote, and follow the Accelerated Schools process as comprehensively and consistently as possible in all its dimensions. In addition, accelerated school principals must develop a different relationship with district and state staff by proactively sharing information about the school's transformation process and helping to ensure that district requirements and mandates can be used to support rather than hinder the school change effort.

With the information provided by this study—the development of the taxonomy of behaviors of accelerated school principals—and the use of the Critical Incident Technique as a research method, it is evident that this research has many applications, the two most important being the design of principal development programs and the furtherance of research on principals in restructuring schools.

Principal Development Programs

A taxonomy of behaviors of an effective accelerated school principal identified in this study can contribute to the design and implementation of training and development programs for principals of accelerated schools. Because an accelerated school is a restructured school, the identified behaviors can also assist the development of principals for any restructuring school. The major behavior categories would make it easy for someone to consider specific types of behaviors around which to design a program for ongoing training for principals or even programs for those aspiring to become principals of accelerated or other schools.

Assisting Current Accelerated School Principals

The first set of implications relates to current accelerated schools and principals. The reader may recall that I shared my taxonomy with 60 accelerated school principals. They found it informative and asked many questions relating to the actual execution of the behaviors. Because the behaviors collected with the Critical Incident Technique identify those that contribute to the implementation of the Accelerated Schools philosophy and process, but do not necessarily tell us which ones are most important, it could be beneficial to use the behaviors found in the taxonomy to develop an instrument that would identify the most important behaviors. A survey could be developed that would ask the participants in accelerated schools to rank the behaviors according to their importance.

The taxonomy itself could be used by the National Center for the Accelerated School Project and its affiliated regional centers in assisting with the design of the training and support programs for coaches and principals currently involved in accelerated schools. The behavioral information that surfaced could assist in producing changes that would transform schools by apprising administrators, trainers of administrators, and others involved in restructuring of necessary behaviors and skills needed by principals in schools making the transition to the Accelerated Schools model.

If we look at any 1 of the 13 major categories, we can see the value in designing a program to assist principals in developing behaviors that would help them in their role as accelerated school principals. Fostering the process, for example, was a very frequently reported category in the taxonomy and in the open-ended question as well. The taxonomy provides numerous examples of ways a principal can promote the correct use of the Accelerated Schools process. The taxonomy lends itself to specific training sessions on various behaviors or groups of behaviors. It could be used as a basis for "problem-based learning" (Bridges, 1992). One might construct case studies that demonstrate effective or ineffective behaviors for discussion or construct problem situations in which effective and ineffective strategies have different consequences. Role-playing activities could provide opportunities for principals to demonstrate various behaviors identified in the taxonomy. They would benefit the principals by exposing them to these experiences early in the transformation process of their schools.

Preparing Future Accelerated School Principals

The findings from this study can assist in preparing future accelerated school principals. This has a two-pronged focus: (a) the findings can be built into an initial training program for schools beginning the Accelerated Schools journey of implementing the philosophy and process, and (b) the findings can be used to aid school districts and universities in their recruitment and selection of principals for accelerated schools.

As the Accelerated Schools model moves across the country and takes root in the schools, new individuals will need to be brought into the philosophy and process. The tenure of principals is quite short in many districts. The Accelerated Schools model is still too young for us to see the long-term effects on staff stability, but already there have been changes in administrators of several of the early accelerated schools. Both district and national center staff have been involved in screening and hiring new accelerated school principals. The information gleaned from the taxonomy developed in this study can serve as a component of the recruitment or interview processes.

Evaluating Accelerated School Principals

Flanagan (1954) discusses the use of the taxonomy as a basis for performance evaluation. The taxonomy of behaviors of accelerated school principals could be transformed into an evaluative instrument and used for assessment. I could imagine how the behaviors identified in this taxonomy could be arranged in a manner that would provide either a self-evaluation instrument for the individual principal or an evaluation instrument that could be used in conjunction with other forms of assessment of performance by other members of the local school community and the district.

Leadership Training for Other
Restructured School Principals

Because the Accelerated Schools model is a prominent restructuring model, the findings of this study can be made available to principals and trainers in any schools in the process of restructuring. The reader may recall that the actual number of empirical studies on the behaviors of principals in restructuring schools was quite sparse. Most of the principal development programs today grew out of descriptive rather than empirical information about the role of the principal. This study can be of great assistance to anyone planning leadership training programs for principals. Trainers and staff developers can use the taxonomy selectively to focus on those behaviors that are relevant for all principals rather than those particular to the accelerated school principal, for example, supporting the staff, promoting learning, providing resources, and demonstrating administrative skills.

Notes

1. Dr. Roger Levine, American Institutes for Research, was my Critical Incident expert; Dr. Pia Wong, National Center for the Accelerated Schools Project, was the Accelerated Schools trainer.
2. It should be noted that the purpose of this exploratory study was to highlight the behaviors of the principals that school community

members identified as contributing to or hindering the transformation of the school to an accelerated school. The respondents may have viewed their stories and the resulting behaviors as being connected in a causal way to success or failure in principal leadership in their school. Researchers using the Critical Incident Technique warn against equating frequency of occurrence of behaviors in the incidents with importance of the behaviors (Flanagan, 1954; Wilson-Pessano, 1988). However, the frequency of occurrence does indicate the prominence of the behavior in the stories related by the respondents. In this study, I do not link the behaviors in a causal sense to transformation, except in a speculative manner.

Appendix

Research Methods

The Critical Incident Technique has three essential components:

1. It is a procedure for gathering important facts concerning behavior in defined situations or critical incidents.
2. The incidents are classified in a taxonomy of behaviors.
3. The behaviors are studied and inferences drawn for the purpose of improving performance. (Flanagan, 1954, p. 335)

The Critical Incident Technique consists of five operational steps: (a) the general aim, (b) the plans for observation, (c) the collection of data, (d) the analysis of data, and (e) the interpretation of data. My general aim was to identify the behaviors of a principal that contribute to the implementation of the Accelerated Schools philosophy and process in a school.

This study provides a model for the application of the Critical Incident Technique in identifying behaviors of school personnel. Very little empirical research is available on the behaviors of school personnel, especially principals. The Critical Incident Technique is one of the most credible methods available to researchers for identifying and studying behaviors of individuals. The technique has been used in many fields throughout its 40 years of existence.

Because the Critical Incident Technique identifies behaviors that contribute to the successful implementation of a task, the taxonomy of behaviors could serve as a basis for identifying which behaviors might be most important for the principal's role. Or the taxonomy could be used as a basis to identify which behaviors might be lacking in an individual performing the task. The taxonomy I developed in this study could be arranged in the form of a survey and given to accelerated school personnel to rank for importance of performance in an accelerated school.

Considering the comprehensiveness of the Critical Incident Technique, my study could be modified to determine the behaviors necessary for a trainer or coach of an accelerated school. With the frame of reference being the implementation and internalization of the Accelerated Schools philosophy and process, this method could be used to identify the critical behaviors of teachers, paraprofessionals, or other school personnel.

10

Principals Speak Out on Their Evolving Leadership Roles

JOAN SABRINA MIMS

The act of leadership is to apply a touch of optimism, to hold high expectations of performance. Such an act may indeed make us vulnerable to betrayal and to failure.
But it also opens us to the possibility of greater human achievement, to the satisfaction that comes in helping human potential unfold, and to the pleasures that come when we call into action the noblest parts of the human spirit.

Bogue (1985, p. 29)

As the quotation from Bogue (1985) exemplifies, our conception of leadership is changing in the climate of school restructuring. Leadership is still viewed as a key component in shaping the context of student learning (Smylie, 1994), but in ways quite different from the situation for traditional schools. The purpose of this chapter is to examine the role principals play in accelerated schools and the socialization process the principals go through in adapting to the project's democratic governance structure. This chapter builds on early research by Christensen (1992) on the changing role of the principal in accelerated schools. Christensen (1992) asked five principals and two assistant principals working in five San Francisco Bay Area elementary and middle schools to describe their role as an administrator before and after their schools adopted the Accelerated Schools model and to provide examples of aspects of their role that are easier and harder under the Accelerated Schools Project. Because this research was limited to schools in only one geographic area, it seemed that we would benefit from replicating it with a different set of principals. The following discussion gives a voice to a set of seven elementary school principals working in accelerated schools in Southern California. Their responses are analyzed in light of the literature on leadership in restructured schools and in comparison to Christensen's (1992) findings.

The Interviews

In this study, seven principals from seven different accelerated schools in Southern California were interviewed in order to determine the changes they perceived in their individual leadership style as their school became accelerated. The seven principals have varying lengths of involvement with the Accelerated Schools Project. One has been involved for 4 years, four principals have been involved for 2 years, and the remaining principals have 1½ and 1 year of experience with the project. Three of the principals are male; four are female. The principals have 3 to 17 years of experience as school administrators.

Adopting Christensen's (1992) research questions, I asked each administrator to respond to a series of open-ended questions. They were asked to describe their roles as school administrators before and after their school adopted the Accelerated Schools model. They were also asked to reflect on the aspects of their administrative role that were enhanced, or made better, as a result of involvement in the Accelerated Schools Project, and what aspects of their administrative role were made more difficult. Each principal was asked to offer suggestions on what could have helped him or her as an administrator during the school's transition to an accelerated school. One interview was conducted with each of the principals.

When completed, the interview data were combined by question and analyzed collectively. In addition, the responses of the Southern California principals were compared with the responses of the Northern California principals. The responses of both groups, in turn, were compared with the literature on school restructuring and its implications for administrators.

Principals' Role Prior to
Involvement in Accelerated Schools

Organizations worldwide, including schools, have been built on the traditional concept of hierarchical leadership with the leader or manager at the apex of the pyramid (Beck & Murphy, 1993; Giroux, 1992; Halcomb, 1993; Patterson, 1993). Leadership has been characterized by the central values of power and control. Understandably, most of today's leaders obtained their present status by conforming to the unwritten but powerful rules for successful leadership.

According to Gorton and Schneider (1991), traditional leaders fall into six major categories: (a) manager, (b) instructional leader, (c) disciplinarian, (d) human relations facilitator, (e) evaluator, and (f) conflict mediator. Most of the principals interviewed indicated that their roles were more traditional prior to involvement with the Accelerated Schools Project, and their responses exemplify the categories described by Gorton and Schneider (1991). For example, in the interviews principals described themselves as managers and instructional leaders:

> In my first years as principal, I was more traditional. . . . I was viewed as the conduit for the main office, the staff instructional leader, the chief disciplinarian, the cheerleader, and the person who could fix everything.

> I am seen as the idea person. My role is trying to get people to share ideas and information, and I try to facilitate this process. I usually do a lot of research on my own and share what I find out with my staff on an informal basis or at meetings. I strive to plant seeds and piggyback on my informal observations of my staff, as well as formal evaluations of them. I try to find ideas and information that will help them. I am seen as the one with all the answers. All problems come to me.

Another principal's comments illustrate how many of the principals were placed in the role of disciplinarian and conflict mediator:

> Their expectancy of me and my role as administrator was that I was a disciplinarian, or one who would maintain order in the school. I was to discipline the students, mediate or intervene if there were interpersonal conflicts among the staff.

The interviews also provided evidence that principals functioned in other categories identified by Gorton and Schneider (1991), such as human relations facilitator and evaluator:

> My role hasn't changed much. I've always believed in collaboration. I just wasn't always sure how to do it. Still, I was viewed as the problem solver and mediator. If staff had problems with other staff members, they would come to me for intervention and mediation.

> I did all the teacher evaluations, parent meetings, and directed the curriculum. My goal was to promote high quality in the classroom. We used the clinical instruction model where I did a lot of observation and evaluation in classrooms. The staff saw me as helping things to run smoothly and as the intermediator.

These comments are consistent, not only with Gorton and Schneider's (1991) categories of traditional leaders, but also with those of the accelerated school principals interviewed by Christensen (1992). In response to the same set of questions, principals in Christensen's study made comments about their previous role, such as, "It was lonely at the top, but it was easier to make decisions," and "There was a wider range of responsibility. Politics in schools became out of hand." In all cases, principals expressed little nostalgia for their previous role.

Principals' Role After Implementing the Accelerated Schools Project

The principals in this study, as in Christensen's (1992) study, verified what research on leadership for the 21st century concludes—that the rules for success have been redefined (Crow, 1994; Smylie, 1994; Strike, 1993; Thurston, Clift, & Schacht, 1993). This is as true for leadership in U.S. business and industry as it is in education (Patterson, 1993; Vroom & Jago, 1988). Patterson (1993) rejects the great person theory of leadership in which leaders are viewed as people possessing admirable characteristics or traits, and defines *leading* as the process of influencing others to achieve mutually agreed upon purposes for the organization. Leading, unlike coercion or bossing, involves persuasion and implies a relationship among people. Current conceptions of leadership maintain that a leader is not in a static role, but rather, the role is fluid and changing and is influenced by many variables (Beck & Murphy, 1993; Christensen, 1992; Strike, 1993).

Current literature stresses the changing role of the educational leader to one of transformational leadership where there is decentralization of decision making and a more participatory and democratic climate (Lugg & Boyd, 1993; Smylie, 1994; Strike, 1993). Sergiovanni (1990) contrasts transactional leadership, in which the focus is largely on extrinsic motives and needs in order to accomplish independent objectives, with transformational leadership in which leaders and followers are united in pursuit of higher-order, more intrinsic, and shared motives and needs. The primary goal of transformational leadership is to arouse human potential, satisfy higher needs, and raise expectations of both leaders and followers to motivate them to higher levels of commitment and performance.

Reitzug (1994) describes leaders as possessing empowering behavior—behavior that encourages staff to choose appropriate practices. This contrasts with traditional principal leadership, which consisted of telling subordinates how to practice. He presents an empowerment taxonomy with three levels of behaviors used by principals to foster shared decision making and democratic governance (support, facilitation, and possibility). He also suggests a need for school leadership that focuses on how leadership supports and facilitates an ethical school environment in which principals fulfill their responsibility for moving schools forward without imposing their will on the staff. In an ethical school environment, principals remain true to their personal beliefs while honoring those of teachers and other staff.

The interviews point to a shift toward a more transformational leadership style and toward more empowering behavior among the accelerated school principals. The principals commented on a greater degree of shared responsibility in their schools, which has changed not only their role but the role of teachers and other staff members. For example, several principals commented on how they have begun to step back and let others make decisions:

The staff participates in decision making more. Rather than taking charge, I am now stepping back and giving them a chance to voice their opinions. I'm becoming more of an observer. It's very interesting to watch the cadres investigate their issues on their own.

There is a lot less of me as the center of things or as the source of ideas. I stimulate ideas, but I'm no longer the only one. I am learning to become more of a facilitator and to offer facilitation based on what I perceive the needs to be. Now, I'm trying not to have all the answers. The staff is also asking more difficult questions.

Principals noted that they see a change in staff behavior since they have begun to step back and allow more shared decision making:

Through ASP [Accelerated Schools Project] two things happen: As I become more secure as a principal, I release more. As I get more comfortable with the process, I look forward to more people taking greater responsibility. ASP helps teachers become more secure in taking leadership roles. It's wonderful to see teachers taking leadership with new decisions and knowing that I had nothing to do with it.

The trust level has also increased. A year ago, there would have been panic if I left campus for any reason. This year, I knew the school was fine. I trusted that the school would still run smoothly if I was called away from campus for some emergency.

The literature (see especially Reitzug, 1994; Sergiovanni, 1990) emphasizes the importance of a unity between leaders and followers and of creating an environment in which all remain true to their personal beliefs. According to the principals interviewed, the Accelerated Schools philosophy and governance structure are helping the schools achieve these goals:

All of the principles have been extremely helpful. . . . Unity of purpose and the vision really helped us in setting priorities, planning the budget, and becoming focused. . . . Although the vision was broad, my job was to keep it in the front, as a constant starting point. Building on strengths really helped us to change our attitudes about each other and the school. . . . The program has helped us all to develop a greater sense of professionalism.

The process has given me permission not to know all the answers, and that's been a relief for me. One thing with the process

is that as we develop focus, I'm not spread so thin. It helps me
to focus.

One principal's comments echo Sergiovanni's (1990) description of
transformational leaders joining in unity to pursue higher-order, more
intrinsic motives:

> One of the best things about Accelerated Schools is the changed
> mind-set it promotes throughout the school. When you have
> hearts and minds working together you really can do well. The
> program has gotten teachers to really believe that children can
> learn, achieve, and be challenged at high levels. It's not just lip
> service. Through this process, more teachers have moved from
> a remediation mind-set into an acceleration mind-set. People
> are more willing to invest time to enhance their professional
> skills. They want to do stimulating teaching, and they desire
> more staff development to help them in this regard. The re-
> newed energy and excitement of the staff toward the academic
> program makes me more motivated. It's great to see that people
> really do care about how children learn and are willing to do
> all they can to improve that learning process.

Difficulties Implementing
Accelerated Schools

The literature on school restructuring supports efforts to transform
schools, but it is clear that such a transformation is not easy, especially
for principals (Christensen, 1992). Although the principals in my study
and in Christensen's (1992) study were positive about the changes in
their roles, they did express discomfort, primarily the result of a lack of
clarity in roles, time, and trust. For example, a principal expressed concern that staff viewed empowerment as no longer needing an administrator—a few members of her school thought that she "should just
disappear and let them take leadership." Another principal explained
that it is not clear what decisions should be the responsibility of cadres
and what decisions should remain administrative:

> There is no manual to tell you what issues are for cadres. Not
> all issues are appropriate for the process. . . . A principal has to

know when to hold and when to fold when it comes to decisions, and what should be taken over by cadres. Sometimes the
principal needs to decide.

Principals expressed concern that involvement with the project brought
additional demands on their time:

> Visitors to the school, the additional phone calls, new schedul-
> ing concerns. . . . All these things take time. The visibility is a
> plus in terms of being positive advertisement for things that are
> good in education; still, managing the increased visibility can
> be a burden at times.

Changing roles for both the principal and the staff places strain on all
relationships and often leave people wondering who they can trust:

> The lack of clarity with what my role as administrator was to
> be made things difficult for me. I wasn't sure, and neither was
> anyone else. . . . Empowerment means we have to learn how to
> take on different responsibilities. When cadres form, changes
> in power involve making changes over a period of time as the
> cadre gains expertise in making decisions. It just doesn't hap-
> pen over night. Who's going to follow though with conse-
> quences? Who will enforce new changes and ideas? There is a
> serious limitation when it comes to who will do the enforcing.
> Some people use ASP goals as self-serving goals and not for
> children or the school as a whole.

It is not surprising that principals expressed frustration with the
transformation process. As principals commented in Christensen's
(1992) study, "It's more difficult in a democracy than a dictatorship,"
and "Cooperation is an unnatural act." The principals interviewed in
both studies were in the early stages of the Accelerated Schools transformation process. They were still negotiating changes in roles and in
expectations for themselves, the staff, and the children. This kind of
change creates discomfort and uncertainty. In response to these concerns, principals offered suggestions that are summarized below:

- Provide more staff development, more direction on curricular
  issues, and more emphasis on student achievement

- Provide pretraining for principals and improve the buy-in process
- Provide training in facilitation strategies and empowering behaviors for administrators
- Allow time to interact, reflect, share concerns, and build commitment
- Provide specific guidance with the inquiry process
- Provide a clearer definition of the principal's role in an accelerated school

Summary and Conclusion

All of the administrators who were interviewed shared the view that the principal in an accelerated school becomes one who facilitates and collaborates with the entire school community about change rather than one who initiates change, implements programs, solves problems, and so forth, as in traditional schools (Christensen, 1992). In the traditional model, administrators viewed themselves as "top down"—they were the source of all decisions and activities. In accelerated schools, where shared leadership is actualized through the governance structure (cadres, a steering committee, and the school as a whole), principals frequently saw themselves as the "keepers of the vision" with the students at the center of all decisions and actions. As one principal said,

> The principal must share the school's vision and be a part of forging that vision. Manifesting that vision takes a lot of time and a deep commitment to the process. The principal has to be the keeper of the vision, but the principal must share the same vision as the staff, or the process won't work. The principal cannot do the work alone, but the principal must be of the same mind-set as the entire school community in order for the process to move forward. If the principal does not have the vision, it's not going to happen.

Although the principal still remains the final authority in the school and the one commissioned by the district and school board as the site administrator responsible for the proper running of the school, the principal in an accelerated school becomes an integral team player through the cadre structure along with teachers, support staff, students, and parents. Everyone shares in the responsibility for the successful running of the school. The decisions are shared and so is the responsibility to implement the decisions.

When asked what were the most difficult aspects of implementing an accelerated school, the principals in the study viewed trust, empowerment, and time as major factors, along with lack of clarity about the principal's role and the need for more direction in terms of curricular enrichment. They felt that trust and shared decision making can only be developed over time, and that there is a need for consistency and commitment to successfully implement the model. Change takes time and a principal must remain energized and committed over time to remain the keeper of the vision.

The principal is critical to the success of an accelerated school. For a school to move forward with the model, the principal's beliefs must be consistent with the model. According to the mutual learning theory that provided the basis for the earlier research on administrators of accelerated schools, the organization's learning is enhanced and quickened by the fact that the beliefs and ideals of the organization (the school) are similar to those of the individual (the principal) (Christensen, 1992).

Strategies that would enhance the transition of principals to becoming effective leaders in an accelerated school include the following:

- A clearer definition of the principal's role in an accelerated school
- Pretraining for principals with an overview of the model and what to expect
- Staff development and more direction on curricular enrichment and more emphasis on student achievement
- Facilitation strategies and empowering behaviors for administrators
- Time to interact, reflect, share concerns, and build commitment
- Specific guidance with the inquiry process and assisting cadres

In conclusion, principals of accelerated schools are still defining their roles as they move more in harmony with transformational leadership strategies. Principals of accelerated schools demonstrate an openness to participation, diversity, conflict, reflection, mistakes, and risk taking. The principals in this study also demonstrate a strong desire to strengthen the model through their own adaptation to empowering behaviors. The primary goal of the administrators was to keep the focus of the model and all of the efforts of the entire school community on educational enrichment for all students. Only in this way can leadership truly shape the context of student learning.

Reflection

The Changing Role of Principals in Accelerated Schools

SIMEON P. SLOVACEK

My interest in the role of principals grew out of an observation that much of our satellite center's coaches' time and energy, particularly in some of our accelerated schools, focused on the principal and providing guidance to the principal. In 1994, the National Center for the Accelerated Schools Project sponsored a satellite center meeting in Portland, Oregon, and a second meeting at Stanford. The role of the principal was explored extensively at both. There was surprising agreement among coaches and other participants as to the challenges and opportunities principals present to the Accelerated Schools process.

Before we turn to the lessons learned from the works in this part, it is important to reflect on the strengths and the potential of principals in accelerated schools. For many reasons, principals can be important and powerful proponents and allies in school restructuring. They have the "voice and ear" of the school and the community and generally have good interpersonal skills. They are in a position to recognize the strengths of all members of the school community, and can delegate as well as provide resources to the process. Often, though not always, they are visionaries and have a systemic view of the school community and district. Traditionally, they are viewed as the instructional leaders of the school. In short, principals can play a central role in the transformation of traditional schools into accelerated schools. Indeed, lack of a principal's commitment to restructuring will thwart or even stop the process.

In what follows, we summarize the lessons learned through research, case studies, and voices from the field presented in this volume. We have also drawn on the shared experiences of numerous accelerated schools coaches and many conversations with principals of accelerated schools. Common challenges and clear opportunities emerged from these sources. In reviewing the notes taken to prepare this summary, it was surprising to see how often the same ideas were suggested by different individuals.

Thoughts about principals' roles seem to fall within two main categories. The first is *challenges* (for Accelerated Schools trainers, coaches, and practitioners), and the second is *opportunities* (for improving the process). The challenges are behaviors, perceptions, situations, events, personalities, and realities that tend to slow down the process of accelerating a school. The opportunities are ways of improving the role of the principal in accelerating a school and facilitating the process. These varied opportunities include such items as principal-specific training, ongoing support, role clarification, and networking for principals. Let us turn first to the challenges.

Challenges

- *Veto power.* Although principals cannot single-handedly transform a traditional school into an accelerated school, they certainly have the veto power to stop or slow the process. When veto power is used by a principal, it often negates the incipient yet fragile empowerment of teachers, other staff, students, and parents that normally grows out of the Accelerated Schools process.
- *No separate accelerated schools training or peer support for principals.* During the initial years of Accelerated Schools Project launchings and training, more emphasis was placed on teachers, staff, and parents. This "one size fits all" training may not meet the needs of principals. It was *assumed* that the principal would change automatically. Further, principals are often isolated from other accelerated school principals in training and at their school sites. Support networks for accelerated school principals were often an afterthought and not well formed.

- *Principal's role is unclear.* Until the past year or two, the principal's role has largely been ignored in the Accelerated Schools literature, training, launching, and coaching. The parameters of shared decision making are unclear *during* the transition from a traditional to accelerated school. In its early years, the Accelerated Schools model did not fully provide for the dramatic changes in the leadership required of the principal. Often, the principal and coaches have limited understanding of the change process with respect to the principal's role. To its credit, the Accelerated Schools model is constantly evolving with respect to the principal's role, but this makes it hard for principals to keep up with the most recent developments.
- *Rigid leadership patterns.* Some principals are not willing to change. Manager-type principals are compliance oriented and are more comfortable complying with school district mandates than with forging a new vision for the school and a new style of facilitative leadership for themselves. Sharing power is not easy, particularly in times when site-based management reforms usually hold the principal fully accountable for the school.
- *Lack of commitment.* Sometimes, principals' lack of commitment springs from a lack of understanding of the principal's role, or perhaps, the inability to give up tried and tested patterns of leadership. Some principals "talk the talk"—that is to say, they are quite knowledgeable about the Accelerated Schools model—but they don't "walk the talk." Some principals lack the passion for change. They just don't want to rock the boat and they prefer to avoid confrontation —something change and transformation typically engender.
- *Mismatch of district expectations with Accelerated Schools model.* Many accelerated schools lie in districts that have not made a commitment to support the Accelerated Schools process. Principals in such cases are caught between a rock and a hard place. The "rock" is the district staff and the principal's boss, the superintendent, who have their own agendas and expectations for job performance. The "hard place" is an eager faculty and school community who want to break the mold and push ahead on reforms that may not sit easily with school district policies and procedures and the ideas of career administrators. Superintendents still review, hire, and fire principals in many districts—a fact that does not escape the attention of principals.
- *Cultural mismatch.* There is often a cultural mismatch between the principal and the majority of parents and students (and sometimes

teachers) in the school community. This can inhibit the essential process of building mutual trust and fostering open communication.

- *Pessimistic expectations.* Among coaches and trainers, there seems to be a mismatch between the philosophy for children and the philosophy for principals at selected schools. Proponents of the Accelerated Schools Project believe that all children can learn but do not uniformly believe that all principals can learn and change.

- *Principal turnover.* Staff turnover always poses a challenge for accelerated schools, but it can be particularly problematic to have a committed accelerated school principal leave the school after a few years, to be replaced by a new principal who is unfamiliar with the process. The new person has his or her own agenda, leadership style, and expectations for the job and for the school. Sadly, in some cases, changing leadership at an accelerated school has stopped or even reversed the process.

Opportunities

- *Address principals' training needs.* We may need to refine the role of principal in the training and the follow-up. In Chapter 9, Christensen strongly entreats us to consider preservice and in-service training for principals. Principals need to participate fully in the school training, but they may need their own training as well. Many accelerated school principals need multicultural training. It may be necessary to modify the launch training to help teachers and principals clarify their changing roles. Principals should be involved in planning the school launch in order to secure their buy-in and to build on their unique strength and position within the school.

- *Address principals' support needs.* Christensen (Chapter 9) also urges supports organizing peer support groups or principal networks with frequent meetings among accelerated school principals. Sharing the taxonomy of principal behaviors could help many principals to understand their changed role. Coaching strategies could be developed that focus support for principals. Such coaching strategies must address helping principals during the transition, especially before cadres are in place. Principals themselves should secure time and resources to make multiple site visits to model accelerated schools so they can construct their own understanding of their new roles.

- *Improve the school buy-in process.* School buy-in needs to be revisited. The buy-in process needs to focus more on the principal's "fit" and the school district's support for the model. Chenoweth and Kushman in Chapter 7 illustrate that the schools with strongly supportive principals were on a faster track toward becoming accelerated. The principal's motivation should be a key factor in the selection of schools. The crucial role of the principal in school transformation must be made clearer during the courtship process. Principals need substantial district and community support. What if they don't have it? Where possible, the job description for the selection of a new principal should be tailored to reflect desirable traits. For example, seek a facilitative instead of an authoritative leadership style, as suggested in Chapter 8 by Davidson and St. John.

- *Clarify the principal's role.* All of the chapters in this part illustrate varying degrees of principals' understanding of their roles in accelerated schools. Chapter 10 by Mims, in particular, demonstrates in the principals' own words the muddling through many principals experience. Better understanding of roles could result in schools moving more swiftly through the process. Clearer parameters for shared decision making, particularly during the process, need to be developed and shared. The principals' behaviors taxonomy is an excellent starting point. Principals need to understand that they cannot run cadre meetings. If they do not trust themselves to be a rank-and-file member of the cadre they should not participate. Building on principals' strengths, coaches could perhaps develop an action plan for the first-year transformation (away from business as usual toward shared decision making) together with the principal. In Chapter 9, Christensen also suggests building the accelerated school role into the district's job description and evaluation of its principals.

- *Develop the external coaching role to better address principals' needs.* Although none of the chapters explicitly addressed this opportunity, it stands to reason that the coaching role should be expanded to develop new coaching strategies in working with principals and to clarify the coach/principal relationship. Coaches should help raise the principal's level of understanding of the model. First, coaches need to establish a trust relationship with principals in order to be effective. They should frequently revisit the principles and process of the Accelerated Schools model with the principals and prepare them to be in-house experts on the process. Coaches need to confront the principals with the problems they perceive; unaddressed problems do not go away. Coaches should be heavily involved in principals' training as it emerges.

- *Research the principal's role further.* Although these studies represent the first major breakthrough in understanding the role of the principal in an accelerated school, more study is needed on the effect of principal turnover on school transformation. Principals' input on their roles could be solicited through focus groups and workshops for principals. Research on the new role(s) of principals during the transition process and on principals' motivation, exemplary characteristics, and change processes would be welcome. More case studies of effective accelerated school principals are needed.

PART IV
Powerful Learning Through Curriculum and Instruction

INTRODUCTION
Jane McCarthy

The chapters in this part illustrate the effects of the Accelerated Schools process on the lifeblood of the school—its curriculum and instruction. Often, restructuring projects become mired down in the logistics of governance and site-based management and sight is lost of the original purpose of the restructuring effort—to enable children to succeed academically. As the following chapters attest, the Accelerated Schools model includes a clear vision of what the products of restructuring should be and focuses all efforts on the journey toward the attainment of that vision: the creation of an environment that builds on the strengths of all members of the school community so that powerful learning occurs.

The curriculum of an accelerated school provides a rich framework within which teaching and learning take place. The accelerated school curriculum embodies what we know about the ways in which all children learn and provides opportunities for maximized intellectual and personal growth. The curriculum is a carefully integrated whole that flows from a unified vision of what children in at-risk situations should know and be able to do by the time they leave the school. The curriculum is designed to enable students to think and act at high levels of complexity by providing them with relevant, motivating, and challenging experiences and materials. The curriculum builds on children's strengths and is predicated on the belief that all children are capable of complex learning when provided with appropriate curriculum and instruction.

Curriculum is equitable to all groups—racial, ethnic, sex, and socioeconomic class. It is broad in scope and interdisciplinary in nature. The curriculum includes more than textbooks and worksheets—it makes use of the child's environment as well. The community and the home are integral elements of the curriculum in an accelerated school. Language is taught throughout the curriculum. Basic skills are not taught in isolation, but woven into the very fabric of all concepts and skills. The curriculum is not remedial, but enriched and challenging. The strengths of all children are built on and all children are viewed as potentially gifted and talented.

The curriculum of an accelerated school is not a piecemeal list of facts and concepts. It is a carefully planned, holistic entity that integrates Accelerated Schools principles throughout. The following chapters provide us with rich descriptions of the impact of the Accelerated Schools process on the lives of children, teachers, and families in school communities and the resulting changes that occur in classrooms. Radical restructuring of the teaching and learning process occurs as school communities identify areas of challenge and strength and utilize the inquiry process to develop effective curriculum and instruction and to infuse every classroom with powerful learning experiences as schools change the "what," the "how," and the "context" for what is taught. Some of the changes you are going to read about started out as one teacher's pilot program; others came about as the result of the inquiry process being used by schoolwide cadres on teaching, learning, and assessment. In all instances, you will see that the enthusiasm of success was contagious, and careful attention was paid to evaluation of the effectiveness of all innovations.

The goals of all powerful learning experiences are to create students who love to learn, who are stimulated to search for answers, and who acquire the skills and motivation to become lifelong learners in all situations in which they find themselves. The schools described in the following chapters have all restructured curriculum, teaching, and learning to provide equity of access to powerful learning in order to enable all children to meet these goals.

Chapter 11 presents a teacher's description of the changes in thinking about teaching and learning that occurred in her school during the first year of participation in the Accelerated Schools Project. Olivier relates the feeling of empowerment that grew for children and teachers as they explored the philosophy and principles of the Accelerated Schools model. Her story is a moving one of challenge, frustration, and commitment.

Chapter 12 is focused on inclusion in accelerated schools. Levin and I delineate the principles, practices, and values of the Accelerated Schools model and the relationship of these to the ideal of full inclusion. Five case studies of diverse school communities illustrate how belief in the principles and practices of the Accelerated Schools model play out and lead naturally to the ideal of full inclusion and equity of access to powerful learning for all students.

Chapter 13 gives us a picture of the development of one the first accelerated schools, Hoover Elementary School, as the school community put the principles and practices into action to facilitate the success of every child in learning to read. Gonzalez and Tucher show how Hoover's early pioneering efforts informed much of the later structure of training and of the project.

Finally, Chapter 14 describes the spin-off efforts of schoolwide change as teachers create individual classrooms where powerful learning exists and the inquiry process is used by students and teachers on a daily basis. Keller and Soler provide us with the voices of teachers, students, and administrators as they explore the effects of change brought about in classrooms as a result of participation in the Accelerated Schools Project.

Taken together, these chapters provide us with glimpses of the reality of life in school communities as they embrace change and the impact on the lives of children in classrooms as they are exposed to a rich and powerful learning environment. They provide an important and personalized addition to the literature on school change by keeping us focused on what the products of that change are meant to be.

🔗11

A Teacher's Voice

The First Year of the Accelerated Schools Project

CYNTHIA J. OLIVIER

Background

Eight years as a teacher in the Louisiana public schools convinced me that nothing could alter the failing educational machine that drove children on an assembly line from kindergarten through eighth grade. This was an opinion shared by many of my colleagues in the inner-city at-risk educational community as we watched the inequalities that existed between White and Black schools in our district, and indeed, nationally.

My own university studies in educational social foundations convinced me that the gap between mostly Black students from a lower socioeconomic class and mostly White students from the middle class was not only intentional from an economic standpoint, but ever widening with the push toward neighborhood schools. My studies caused me to view the educational hierarchy with contempt. I saw my third-grade students as perpetual victims of poverty and despair. The feelings of helplessness and hopelessness that I experienced made it impossible for me to view my profession as a rewarding or fulfilling one.

The involvement of my school in the national Accelerated Schools Project caused a dramatic change in the way I viewed teaching and learning. I began to see the possibilities for creating a positive environment in which all children could learn and thrive. Our school community, J. W. Faulk Elementary School in Lafayette, Louisiana, under the leadership of our principal, John Lee, applied for funding to become an accelerated school at the end of the 1990-1991 school year. We really didn't know a lot about the project except that it had been implemented successfully in a number of at-risk schools across the nation. We received the grant and initiated the project in the fall of 1991.

The Theoretical Framework

The Accelerated Schools model was developed by Professor Henry M. Levin at Stanford. Levin's work in the area of critical theory lead him to look at education for at-risk students in a new way. If all students were to function in the mainstream of education and society, then education must become meaningful and relevant for them and build on their strengths rather than perpetuate their deficiencies.

Many educators believe that the current system of schooling is so unreflective of students' home life that failure is inevitable. In an at-risk school, traditional instruction has failed to meet the needs of its diverse population, and so the student continually falls behind (McLaren, 1989, p. 153). Levin's accelerated schools are based on making the classroom a direct reflection of the child's experience, where concepts and ideas that a child can relate to are used to "speed up" the learning process for the at-risk child. Great emphasis is placed on writing and language skills. Like John Dewey, Levin (1985) believes that the process of education is more important than its immediate product. Student writing, for example, that reflects children's interests is meaningful and educative. It has also been demonstrated that standardized test scores in accelerated schools move up to and, in some instances, beyond grade level as a result of meaningful learning experiences that build on student strengths.

The Change Process Begins

Although armed with the theoretical background of the Accelerated Schools Project, I had no idea of the dramatic change and conflict that would be necessary to transform Faulk from a school cut from the traditional mold to an accelerated school. Working with the Accelerated Schools Satellite Center at the University of New Orleans, we began our journey as a school community. It was a journey that would end with a cease-fire at the end of the first year of the change process.

First Steps—Research

To get a clear picture of the strengths and challenges of the school, we started with the Accelerated Schools process of taking stock. Various committees dealing with student achievement, community, family, district policies, and history were established, and teachers, in their "spare time," researched all aspects of Faulk. We found that academically Faulk students performed well below the norm, that the more than 1,000 students enrolled in Grades K-5 were overcrowded in classrooms, that discipline was a major concern, and that an overwhelming majority of our children qualified for the free or reduced-price lunch program, indicating that most were from families living below the poverty line. The majority of the school population had failed at least one grade level, with most falling at least two grade levels behind. It was discovered that there were several 14- and 15-year-old students in the fifth grade.

Although many of these data were routinely collected by the school and district, it was the first time that we, as a school community, had systematically looked at and analyzed the realities of our school. For the first time, we disaggregated test scores to see what they really meant. We surveyed teachers, parents, and students to understand their concerns and dreams for our school. This process of taking stock helped the school community to realize what we were up against and just how difficult our task would be to change the situation. It also helped us to begin to work together with a common goal—to find out as much as we could about the here and now before we began to make any changes.

It was an agonizing exercise, because not only were teachers asked to do research, which they were unaccustomed to doing, but they were asked to do it on their own time. In addition, requests for information made to various departments in our school district's main office were met with resistance, delays, and in some instances, no information at all. Scheduling problems made meeting times difficult, and the fact that teachers were already working a full day made it hard to ask them to come early and stay late. The value of collecting all of this information was not yet clear to all the participants. Identifying the challenges was discouraging and daunting. Then the faculty engaged in an activity that formed the turning point in the project for us.

A Visit to Hollibrook Elementary School

The entire faculty and staff of Faulk Elementary School visited an existing accelerated school in Houston, Texas. We had read about Hollibrook in the Accelerated Schools literature and we had attended a presentation given by Suzanne Still, then the principal of the school. Her inspiring story of how the Hollibrook school community had gone through the process of acceleration and made enormous changes in the school and the teaching and learning process made us eager to see for ourselves what the change process had produced. So we got on a bus and went to Texas!

At Hollibrook, located in the Spring Branch School District, in an area that had undergone dramatic demographic changes over the past 10 years, we saw the Accelerated Schools process in action and realized why we needed to gather data before we took action. In a school where 85% of the students enter speaking limited or no En-glish, where the poverty of the surrounding neighborhood is overwhelming, we were amazed to see that an at-risk school could be a vehicle for meaningful educational experiences for all students.

The interactions between child and environment at Hollibrook were truly amazing. We saw children working together on art, writing, and mathematics projects, with teachers serving as facilitators. Because of the teachers' abilities to use manipulatives and a more hands-on approach in general, classrooms suddenly came alive with sound and movement and energy. There were no desks in rows, no rules posted on walls, no cubbyholes stacked with texts, no problem children filling up the front office, and to our astonishment, even when children were on the playground the rocks stayed on the ground! Our conversations with the faculty and staff at Hollibrook gave us inspiration for what the possibilities were of becoming an accelerated school with clearly defined goals and mission.

We went back to our own school excited about our future. The hard work and sacrifice now seemed to have a meaning and purpose. We wanted our students to be excited about school and learning. We wanted them to be successful academically and socially. Our visit to Hollibrook convinced us that it could happen for our school community, too.

Second Steps—The Inquiry Process

One of the cornerstones of the Accelerated Schools process is teacher empowerment. This is embodied in the process called inquiry. The inquiry process provides a systematic way of looking at the challenges identified in taking stock, defining them clearly, hypothesizing about why they exist, testing these hypotheses, then brainstorming potential solutions, testing the solutions, and evaluating the effectiveness of the solutions.

The school community spent a day reflecting on the information gathered in the taking stock process, clustering the findings into major groupings, and then comparing the findings to the school vision we had collaboratively created. The challenges were then prioritized and teachers, parents, and administrators self-selected themselves into one of the identified "cadres," or committees, such as that for curriculum and instruction, and that for family involvement. Each cadre then used the inquiry process to deal with the identified challenges. Cadres met weekly to analyze data and then submitted plans for action to the steering committee. If the steering committee believed the inquiry process had been followed, the action plan was then presented to the school as a whole for consensus.

This process was very different from our traditional way of throwing solutions at problems and hoping some would work. It was a difficult process to implement because of the tendency to slip back into the old way of doing things (which hadn't worked very well). It was also a very time-consuming process and we spent much of our first year on the initial steps of defining the challenge areas and why they existed. However, we knew from our conversations with the teachers at Hollibrook that this was a process we could not shortcut if we wanted to see meaningful results. So we hung in there.

Because teachers are the people most directly involved with student learning, and the ones who know what needs to be done to enhance student learning, teachers should be the decision makers in the school. The old top-down model of governance that characterizes traditional schooling was no longer effective. This notion of empowerment meant that (through exemptions from the district and state boards) teachers could make changes regarding curriculum, instruction, scheduling, and policies such as those affecting discipline.

Because teachers have always been subjected to policies from above, and teacher decisions have always been measured with a sidelong glance at contractual clauses about insubordination, empowerment was the most difficult concept for our faculty of 40 classroom teachers and over 20 support and special education personnel. Before the Accelerated Schools Project, veto power was exercised benevolently by the administration. After we engaged in the Accelerated Schools Project, decisions became subject to the variety of viewpoints, opinions, philosophies, and beliefs held by the entire faculty. Although individual teachers began to be more expressive in individual classroom situations, majority rule was an old habit hard to break. The notion of consensus has been difficult to achieve and the lack of it has stymied real change schoolwide. It is an issue we are still struggling with.

Change Begins in Classrooms

As we learned to use the inquiry process, which enables us to critically view our challenges and brainstorm potentially effective solutions, things did slowly begin to change at Faulk, although most of us were unaware of the change at first. The "little wheels" of change occurred as individual teachers began to pilot-test innovative practices in their own classrooms, with the hope of schoolwide implementation in the future. One of these projects was the use of whole-language units, abandoning textbooks for process writing; hands-on discovery learning; and whole-class art projects. Another innovation was the development of multicultural units that concentrated on the predominant race in the school, African American.

One program that helped students to become aware of children with special needs was developed by myself and the special education teacher Bridget Borne. What began as a way for her children to become more socially aligned with the regular population by joining them for lunch quickly evolved into Bridget's class joining mine for reading instruction. This interaction allowed her students to reach beyond their expected capabilities and allowed my class special assistance with reading instruction.

Minigrants from the local arts council allowed the children in the third-grade wing to create and paint murals on the walls of our building. To provide for the needs of the older children in the school—the students who had all but given up on traditional classroom instruction after so many years of failure—Lisa Ewing, a fifth-grade teacher, developed and implemented an alternative program reflective of what we hope our Accelerated Schools program will become. Students in her

classroom packed away textbooks and concentrated on the local newspaper as their basal reader, the checkbook and newspaper advertise-
ments as their math text, and a vegetable garden as their science lesson.
She was successful not only in helping students remain in school for the
year but in reigniting their pride in themselves and the belief that failure
in life is not their destiny.

Next Steps

The inquiry cadres have developed whole-language and multicultural projects for the coming school year. Projects are also under way
for family and community involvement. But so far the greatest change
has come not from the physical products produced by these ideas, but
from the ideas themselves. For in a few short months in the process,
although battle scarred and sometimes frustrated, the teachers at Faulk
have a changed concept of what education is and what their role in it
can be. This concept has been fundamentally altered and can never be
reversed. The notion of teacher empowerment and the realities of working together for collaborative change with a common vision for what
we want our students to know and be able to do when they leave our
school have created new understandings of school and schooling. We
have begun to feel the results of building on our strengths as well as on
those of the families and students. We will no longer be able to go into
our classrooms and close our doors as the rest of the school goes on
without us. Now, all the children in the school are "our" students. The
challenges of each teacher are "our" challenges. And the needs of each
family impact all of us.

As for the children of Faulk, who already feel that change is in the
air, I believe that they will eventually be empowered enough in Faulk
and in their own lives to have hope for their future. As Jonathan Kozol
(1991) writes in *Savage Inequalities*, "These urban schools were, by and
large, extraordinarily unhappy places. . . . It occurred to me that we had
not been listening much to the children in recent years" (p. 5). With
Hollibrook as our model and the Accelerated Schools process as our
guide, Faulk can become a place where children can be happy—and
their voices can be heard.

℘12

Full Inclusion in Accelerated Schools

Equal Access to Powerful Learning

HENRY M. LEVIN
JANE McCARTHY

A debate is raging across the United States about the degree to which all children should be given a common set of opportunities within our nation's schools. This controversy swirls around such practices as tracking by ability group, pulling students from classrooms for special services such as remediation or special education, and the separation of special education students into their own classrooms or schools. The purpose of this chapter is to provide some thoughts on the issue of inclusion for a particular movement of school reform, the Accelerated Schools Project.

The terms *inclusion, full inclusion,* and more recently, *inclusive education,* are popular in the current educational literature. Commonly, these terms refer to the belief that all children should be educated to the greatest degree possible in the regular classroom. Full inclusion usually refers to the delivery of special services in the regular classroom with special assistance provided to the regular classroom teacher (Rogers,

AUTHORS' NOTE: An earlier version of this chapter was presented by Dr. Henry M. Levin as a paper at the Wingspread Conference in Racine, Wisconsin, of the National Center on Educational Restructuring and Inclusion of the Graduate School and University Center, The City University of New York, April 28 through May 1, 1994. Other portions of this chapter were presented by Dr. Jane McCarthy as a paper at the Association of Teacher Educators-Europe, Annual Conference, Prague, the Czech Republic, September 6, 1994.

1993). Inclusion also means celebrating the diversity of all students and educating them in a learning environment that creates a sense of community in which the needs of all are met (Sapon-Shevin, 1994-1995). In the context of this chapter, the term *inclusion* will refer to the philosophy of providing a common experience for all children in a common setting. Obviously, the real world is characterized by degrees of inclusion, so the options go beyond "full inclusion" or "full exclusion" of particular types of students in all situations. We attempt to show that even with nuances of practice, a single philosophy embracing inclusion and access must be central to all school activities if it is to take equity and community as the bedrock to which it is anchored.

The specific purpose of this chapter is to present the connection between the Accelerated Schools process and full inclusion of all students in the mainstream of school instructional activities and experiences. The overriding theme will be that inclusion should not be viewed as an add-on to a conventional school. It must be viewed as intrinsic to the mission, philosophy, values, practices, and activities of the school— the accelerated school is a place where full inclusion of all students into the lifestream of the school is foundational in every respect. In contrast, a conventional school with tracking of students by ability grouping and special needs might be coerced to create heterogeneous grouping and inclusion of all students in "regular" classrooms, but the compliance response is likely to be mechanical and pay obeisance only to the letter of the obligations. Historical analysis has shown that educational impacts are determined largely by the substance of the response rather than procedural compliance (Cuban, 1984). For this reason, we believe that full inclusion must be embedded deeply in the very foundation of the school, in its mission, its belief system, and its daily activities rather than serve as an appendage to a conventional school.

In this chapter, we provide a picture of how inclusion is not only compatible with but absolutely integral to the Accelerated Schools process—it is "doing what comes naturally." We divide the chapter into four major parts. First, we present a brief picture of the Accelerated Schools Project. Second, we demonstrate why full inclusion is integral to the Accelerated Schools model. Next, we present four snapshots of schools in which inclusion has been planned and provided for, and finally, we provide a more in-depth case study of a school as it uses the Accelerated Schools process to provide equity of opportunity for all of its students in an inclusive school community.

The Accelerated Schools Project

The Accelerated Schools Project (ASP) is described in more detail earlier in this book. We provide some brief highlights of the project here to inform the discussion and narrative that follow. Established in 1986-1987 with the launching of two pilot elementary schools serving high concentrations of at-risk students, the project began with the goal of eliminating remediation by using all of a school's resources to accelerate the growth and development of all students and bring them into the academic mainstream by the end of elementary school (Levin, 1987c). The focus of the Accelerated Schools model is to advance the growth and development of all children by using teaching and learning approaches usually reserved for gifted and talented students.

The Accelerated Schools Project has been focused especially on schools with high concentrations of at-risk students, large numbers of whom had previously been relegated to remedial and special education programs. The project grew out of earlier research examining the demography of at-risk students and their educational prospects in conventional schools (Levin, 1986, 1987b, 1988d). The researchers found that the predominant policy of tracking these students into remedial instruction characterized by drill and practice and associative learning had extremely deleterious consequences. At-risk students fell farther and farther behind the educational mainstream the longer they were in school, and many began to view school as arduous and punishing, even in the early elementary years.

Out of this research came a quest for a different kind of school that would accelerate rather than remediate. Acceleration necessitates the radical transformation of the school to advance the academic development of children in at-risk situations, not slow it down. This meant creating a school in which all children were viewed as capable of benefiting from a rich instructional experience, where at-riskness was a situation that occurred when there was a mismatch between the experiences and strengths children brought with them to school and those expected by the school. It meant a school that creates powerful learning situations for all children that integrate curriculum, learning strategies, and context (climate and organization) rather than piecemeal changes through new textbooks or instructional packages. It meant a school whose culture is transformed internally to encompass the needs of all students through creating a stimulating educational experience that builds on their identities and experiences.

Such transformation is neither simple nor swift. Training in the model requires the participation of the entire school community. The process used to facilitate this transformation is detailed in *The Accelerated Schools Resource Guide* (Hopfenberg et al., 1993) and in the *Accelerated Schools Newsletter* (1994). The training uses constructivist activities designed to lead to school change and the transformation of school culture (Finnan, 1994). Through a particular governance structure and an inquiry approach to decision making, the school addresses its major challenge areas in a way that will create powerful learning throughout the school.

The Accelerated Schools Project now encompasses over 700 schools across the nation. Evaluations of accelerated schools have shown substantial gains in student achievement, attendance, full inclusion of special needs students into the mainstream, parental participation, and numbers of students meeting traditional gifted and talented criteria. They have also shown reductions in the numbers of students repeating grades, student suspensions, and school vandalism (see, e.g., English, 1992; Knight & Stallings, 1994; Levin & Chasin, 1994; McCarthy & Still, 1993).

Accelerated Principles, Values, and Inclusion

The accelerated school is not just a collection of programs or an attempt to put a school through a piecemeal accumulation of different policies and practices. It is a set of practices based upon a coherent philosophy and principles. In this respect, inclusion is not an optional feature for an accelerated school, but is embedded in the very structure and belief system of the school. The goal of the Accelerated Schools Project is to bring all students into a meaningful educational mainstream, to create for all children the dream school all of us want for our own children. This is the guiding sentiment for the transformation of an accelerated school, one that embodies the three central principles: unity of purpose, empowerment with responsibility, and building on strengths.

Unity of Purpose. Unity of purpose refers to the common purpose and practices of the school on behalf of all its children. Traditional schools separate children according to abilities, learning challenges, and other distinctions; staff are divided according to their narrow teaching, support, or administrative functions; and parents are usually relegated to marginal roles in the education of their children. The

Accelerated Schools model requires that the school forge a unity of purpose around the education of all students and all of the members of the school community, a living vision and culture working together in behalf of all children. Strict separation of either teaching or learning roles works against this unity and results in different expectations for different groups of children. Accelerated school communities formulate and work toward high expectations for all children, and children internalize these expectations for themselves. Thus, unity of purpose also means inclusion.

Empowerment With Responsibility. Empowerment with responsibility refers to those who make educational decisions and take responsibility for their consequences. Traditional schools rely on higher authorities at school district and state levels as well as on the content of textbooks and instructional packages formulated by publishers who are far removed from schools. Staff at the school site have little discretionary power over most of the major curriculum and instructional practices of the school and students and parents have almost no meaningful input into school decisions. In this respect, the powerlessness leads to a feeling of exclusion in terms of the ability to influence the major dimensions of school life.

In an accelerated school, school staff, parents, and students take responsibility for the major decisions that determine educational outcomes. All constituents participate in an all-encompassing principle of *inclusion* in daily school life. The school community is no longer a place in which roles, responsibilities, practices, and curriculum content are determined by forces beyond the control of its members. Teacher isolation and segregated teaching assignments are broken down and replaced by a collaborative effort that embraces the entire school community. In its daily operations, the school community hones its unity of purpose through making and implementing decisions that determine its destiny. At the same time, the school takes responsibility for the consequences of its decisions through continuous assessment and accountability, holding as its ultimate purpose its vision of what the school will become. This is accomplished through a parsimonious, but highly effective, system of governance and problem solving that ensures inclusion of students, staff, and parents in the daily life of the school.

Building on Strengths. Traditionally, schools have been far more assiduous about identifying the weaknesses of their students than in looking for their strengths. A focus on weakness and deficiencies leads naturally to organizational and instructional practices in which children are tracked according to common deficiencies. The logic is that "lower" groups cannot keep up with a curricular pace that is appropriate for "higher" groups. But an accelerated school begins by identifying strengths of the members of the school community and building on these strengths to overcome areas of weakness or challenge.

In this respect, all students are treated as gifted and talented students, because the gifts and talents of each child are sought out and recognized. Such strengths are used as a basis for providing enrichment and acceleration. As soon as one realizes that all students have strengths and weaknesses, a simple stratification of students no longer makes sense. Strengths include not only the various areas of intelligence identified by Gardner (1983), but also areas of interest, curiosity, motivation, and knowledge that grow out of the culture, personalities, and experiences of all children. In classrooms such as these, flexible and cooperative grouping patterns emerge. Classroom themes can be those in which children show interest and curiosity and in which reciprocal teaching, cooperative learning, peer and cross-age tutoring, and individual and group projects can highlight the unique talents of each child in classroom and school activities. These group processes and the use of specialized staff enable the recognition of and building on the particular strengths and contributions of each child while providing assistance in areas of need within the context of meaningful academic work.

The Accelerated Schools model requires that all children are fully included in the activities of the school. Thus, all children's strengths are validated and areas of special need addressed. This can be done in regular classrooms employing classroom and schoolwide curricular approaches based on the inclusion of every child in the central life of the school. It can be done not only with multi-ability and multi-age grouping, but by recognizing that all children have different profiles of strengths that can be used to complement each other and create strong teams that provide internal reinforcement among students. By teaching to many modalities and by providing multilevel curricula in the heterogeneous classroom, the learning needs of all students can be met.

It should also be noted that the process of building on strengths is not limited to students. Accelerated schools also build on the strengths of parents, teachers, and other school staff. Parents can be powerful allies if they are placed in productive roles and provided with the skills to work with their own children. Teachers bring gifts of insight, intuition, and organizational acumen to the instructional process, gifts that often go untapped with the mechanical curricula that are so typical of remedial programs. By developing new teams for instructional delivery through collaborative-consultative models, the strengths of all teachers and specialists can be brought to bear on the learning of all children. Through acknowledging the strengths found among all members of the school community, all of the participants are expected to contribute to the success of all children.

Accelerated Schools Values. Accelerated schools operate by a set of values that permeate relationships and activities. These include the school as a center of expertise, equity, risk taking, experimentation, reflection, participation, trust, and communication. Virtually all of these are the values of inclusion, as the focus is on the inner power, vision, capabilities, and solidarity of the school community. But especially important are such values as equity, the view that the school has an obligation to all children to create for them the dream school that we all want for our own children. Such a school must treat children equitably and give them equal access to participation in enriched and accelerated learning environments that facilitate their success. Giftedness may never be identified or nurtured, for example, in a learning environment that does not encourage higher-level thinking skills and creative problem solving.

The school is viewed as an overall community rather than as a building with many separate communities represented, although the cultures and experiences of different students are acknowledged and incorporated into the school experience. Addressing the needs of all children requires experimentation, risk taking, reflection, trust, and communication. Above all, the concept of unity of purpose is present in all of the values and practices of the school, a necessary approach to the inclusion of all students in a common school dream.

Powerful Learning. The three principles and nine values of the Accelerated Schools model are used to create what are called powerful learning situations (Hopfenberg et al., 1993, chaps. 6-10). A powerful learning situation is one that incorporates changes in school organization, climate, curriculum, and instructional strategies to build on the strengths of students, staff, and community to create an optimal learning situation. What is unique about this approach is that change is not piecemeal, but integrated around all aspects of the learning situation. This contrasts sharply with the usual attempts to transform schools through idiosyncratic reforms involving the ad hoc adoption of curriculum packages, instructional practices, and organizational changes to address each perceived problem that the school faces. Over time, some of these are pruned and others are added, without any attempt to integrate them into an overall philosophy and vision of the school. Powerful learning builds on the strengths of all community members and empowers them to be proactive learners by developing skills through intrinsically challenging activities that require both group work and individual endeavor.

Accelerated schools also emphasize the connections between "big wheels" of the school and the "little wheels." The big wheels are the overall school philosophy and change process that are shared by all members of the school community. The little wheels are informal innovations that grow out of participation by individuals or groups in embracing the school's philosophy and change process. These little wheels result from the internalization of the school philosophy and change process in the belief system of school community members, resulting in their individual decisions, commitments, and innovations in classrooms and in individual and group interaction.

Four Illustrations

Thus far, we have attempted to show that the entire framework of the Accelerated Schools concept and practices is based upon inclusion of all members of the community. The three guiding principles of the Accelerated Schools model, the underlying values, the focus on powerful learning, and the links between the big wheels and little wheels provide an integrative setting in which inclusion is foundational. In this section, we provide a brief picture of four schools and how they were transformed from schools characterized by tracking, pulling out students for special services, and special day classes for handicapped students to schools in which full inclusion is embraced. These vignettes were developed from observations by Accelerated Schools coaches; interviews with faculty, administrators, students, and families in the accelerated schools; information gathered in the taking stock process at each school; and minutes kept of cadre meetings.

Thomas Edison Elementary School
(Sacramento, California)

Thomas Edison Elementary School in Sacramento, California, is a prototype of a school in a rapidly transforming neighborhood (Chasin

& Levin, 1994), a phenomenon that is quite common in California with its rapid influx of immigrants and rise in child poverty. In the fall of 1989, Edison had a total of 360 students, of whom 36% received public assistance under Aid to Families With Dependent Children (AFDC). Only English was spoken at the school. Just 3 years later (1992-1993), the school's enrollment had grown by one third to 494 students who spoke 13 different languages. Eighty percent of these students were on AFDC.

In the earlier time period, there was one self-contained classroom for children with severe learning disabilities, and other children with learning challenges were pulled out of their regular classrooms for services. As children from new language backgrounds were drawn into the school, they were provided with bilingual instruction in separate settings. With the introduction of the Accelerated Schools process, the Edison community began to work to bring specialists into regular classrooms to provide services to children within the context of their classroom projects and activities. Special needs teachers and regular classroom teachers planned together to meet the needs of each child, a practice that was embraced by the big wheels of school organization and inquiry. However, the special day class was still separated, although teachers began to introduce powerful learning approaches through the little wheels of the Accelerated Schools process.

By the beginning of the third year of the Accelerated Schools Project, the school began to focus on the full integration of the special day class into the life of the school. Using the inquiry process, the staff and parent representatives developed a collaborative approach in which all of the students in the self-contained class would be mainstreamed into regular classrooms. By January 1994, the new approach was implemented and regular classroom teachers and specialists are now working together. Early results have been very positive, although requiring continuous collaboration and inquiry to address the challenges that have arisen. By the beginning of the third year of the Accelerated Schools process, Edison had used the philosophy and practices to make the transition from traditional pull-out programs and isolation of severely handicapped children to full inclusion of all children in the lifestream of the school.

Despite a larger, more diverse student body with much higher concentrations of at-risk students, suspensions have fallen; school vandalism has vanished; and attendance, parent participation, and test scores have risen. Classrooms are buzzing with student projects, research, writing, discussions, and problem-solving activities for all students.

Samuel Mason Elementary School
(Boston, Massachusetts)

Samuel Mason Elementary School ("Mason Elementary School," 1993) is located in Roxbury, one of the most infamous inner-city neighborhoods of Boston, an area known for gangs, poverty, and crime. In 1990, Mason enrolled only 130 students and was scheduled to be closed because it was unable to attract more students under Boston's system of controlled choice. In 1990-1991, Mason launched its Accelerated Schools program, and by 1993-1994, enrollment had reached 300 students, 11% above capacity. In addition, there were as many as 60 students on waiting lists in some grades. Grade retentions had been reduced from 25% of students to zero, and attendance rates increased by 10 percentage points. Test scores had also risen.

Early in its adoption of the Accelerated Schools program, the Mason community began to experiment with ways of providing a better school environment and improved learning opportunities for all children. Using cadres and the inquiry method to create powerful learning situations, Chapter 1, special education, and regular classroom teachers began to plan shared curricular and instructional innovations for the first time. This resulted in special needs teachers working with children directly in the classroom and collaborating with other teachers on a common set of educational experiences and expectations for all children. Beginning with the early childhood program, the Mason community set up collaborative teams including the regular classroom teacher, a classroom aide, and special needs teachers who took responsibility for particular classes.

Even with an expanded range of abilities in the classroom, the class was so successful that outsiders were unable to identify students with special needs from observing class activities and participation. In subsequent years, other classes have been combined using this inclusion model. Not only students, but their teachers participate in combined classrooms. This model has significantly reduced class size in all grades, providing the benefits of individual attention for all students, and served as a powerful incentive for teacher collaboration. The entire school community has benefited from full inclusion at Mason. As the principal, Mary Russo, stated, "Becoming an accelerated school has helped us become a multi-age, multi-ability, multi-neighborhood, multirace, multiclass, multicultural school."

Oakridge Elementary School
(Granite School District, Salt Lake City, Utah)

Oakridge Elementary is located in an upper-middle-class neighborhood in Salt Lake City. The setting is one of beauty. Nestled in the foothills of a mountain, the school enjoys panoramic views of the entire valley. Vegetation and trees are abundant. Students who attend the school are the children of professionals, many of whom teach at the local universities or work in the medical center. They come to school well dressed, well fed, well behaved, and equipped with home resources such as computers, private lessons, travel experiences, and cultural and sports activities. Standardized test scores at the school are among the highest in the district at each grade level and are close to the top of all scores statewide. Such advantages and achievements would make it seem unlikely that the school would want to join the Accelerated Schools Project, which is designed primarily for students in at-risk situations. And yet in the spring of 1993, the school community applied for admission to the project.

When interviewed as to the reasons for their application, the faculty and principal stated that they had read some materials about the Accelerated Schools model and talked to teachers in an accelerated school in their district and that the philosophy and principles matched their own very closely. Their students all scored well on standardized tests, but they did not exhibit a joy for learning or an enthusiasm for coming to school. They did just enough to get their As and then stopped. The district, meanwhile, had a special program for gifted children, but each school was allowed to identify only a small percentage of students as eligible for the program. These students were then pulled out of class and provided with an enriched program of academics. Oakridge parents and staff believed that all children could benefit from these enriched, accelerated instructional experiences. They wanted their students to become lifelong learners and to achieve to the maximum of their potential, not the minimum. The Accelerated Schools process seemed to provide the tools necessary to make their vision come alive. The beliefs of the school community with regard to pull-out programs for gifted students are supported by others in the literature. Sapon-Shevin (1994-1995) states that no children should be forced to endure "inflexibility, boring curriculums, lack of creativity, . . . and limited conceptions of teaching and learning" (p. 67).

The engagement of the school community in the taking stock process enabled its members to identify their strengths and challenges.
They looked at curriculum materials and test scores. They disaggregated test scores. They interviewed students and parents. They had
students fill out questionnaires about what they would most like to
learn about in school. The analysis of the data led to the formation of
cadres to address specific areas of concern. It was decided to focus on
the math curriculum as a schoolwide project. Meanwhile, all teachers
enrolled in the district certification program for gifted and talented
teachers, and by the end of the first year as an accelerated school, all but
two teachers had attained their gifted and talented endorsement and
were implementing strategies schoolwide in every classroom. Oakridge
received a waiver from the district to do away with the pull-out gifted
and talented program and to meet the needs of all students in the regular classroom. Test scores at the end of the year showed that scores had
not fallen. Interviews with students, teachers, and parents indicated
great satisfaction with the new project.

Rather than a small percentage of children receiving services for
enriched and stimulating instruction, the faculty at Oakridge provide
these services for all children attending the school. Expectations are
accordingly high for all students. Problem-solving skills are taught to
all children and opportunities for discovery and inquiry are made available to all children, not just the privileged few. An outdoor classroom
has been developed by one of the teachers and a curriculum has been
evolving that allows all students to explore ecology, botany, forestry,
and conservation right in their own backyard. Other exciting projects
are also under way to provide motivating experiences for all students.
Teachers at the school report that their enthusiasm for teaching has
increased as well. Parents are also involved in a number of different
ways as their expertise is used by the school. Inclusion at Oakridge has
resulted in high expectations for all students and an equity of access to
rich, stimulating educational experiences. By respecting the diversity of
all students and providing for ways to meet their needs, Oakridge Elementary School is creating an environment that truly creates a community of learners.

North Middle School
(Aurora, Colorado)

North Middle School in Aurora, Colorado (adjoining Denver), has
a population of 700 students, more than half of whom are educationally

at risk (*Together Inclusion Works,* 1993). These numbers include 100 students identified with mild to moderate disabilities. Prior to launching the Accelerated Schools program in the fall of 1992, North was facing a widening learning gap among its students, a rising teenage pregnancy rate, and other symptoms of a school that was becoming increasingly impacted with at-risk students. During the 2 years North has been implementing the Accelerated Schools process, discipline problems have diminished, test scores have risen, student and parent participation have increased, and the entire school has taken on a new life. Thematic teaching across subjects and collaborative teaching and learning teams have created an environment in which students eagerly participate in challenging learning activities.

Prior to the advent of the Accelerated Schools Project at North, pull-out programs existed for students with learning disabilities and problem behavior. The school now began to address the possibility of full integration of all students in the regular classroom and the elimination of pull-out programs. Through the inquiry process, strategies were developed to help move the school toward its agreed-upon goals. One long-term solution was to hire teachers with dual certification in the regular classroom and in special services any time an opening occurred at the school. One immediate strategy that was employed was the placement of regular classroom teachers and special education teachers in teams to work with fully integrated groups of students. The two- or three-member teams plan together during a common planning period at each grade level. This allows the needs of specific students to be met by collaborative problem solving and instructional delivery.

The result of these strategies has been higher academic performance of special education and "regular" students as all classes now pursue activities previously reserved for gifted and talented students. Another result has been the difficulty teachers have in identifying the "special education" students in the regular classroom. The inclusive curriculum has blurred the boundaries and given all students access to an enriched and powerful learning environment.

A Case Study of Inclusion:
Rolling Meadows Accelerated Elementary School
(Granite School District, Salt Lake City, Utah)

In the previous section, we presented vignettes of four schools using the Accelerated Schools process and developing programs for inclusion. In this section, we present a more detailed description of a school in which the process was used to develop and implement a pilot program of inclusion that now has been expanded to five grade levels. The story of Rolling Meadows underscores the importance of careful planning and assessment as inclusion begins and the importance of providing all teachers with the tools necessary to be successful in the inclusive classroom. This case study was developed from field notes of the Accelerated Schools coach; classroom observations; interviews with resource and regular classroom teachers; observations of cadre, steering committee, and school as a whole meetings; standardized and teacher-developed test and assessment data; and interviews with the school principal.

The school community of Rolling Meadows entered the Accelerated Schools Project in 1992 with the dream that all children can learn when building on their strengths and provided with the support they need to perform in the academic mainstream. The school, with a population of 658 students, is located in an area where the demographics are changing from uniformly White, middle-class families to a mix of ethnic groups and incomes. The school serves children from several day care centers. These children live outside the school zone but are accommodated because of the day care center locations. With changing demographics came the problem of transiency. This formerly stable school population was now beginning to experience the challenges of other urban schools as families in rental units moved in and out. As part of the taking stock process, the Community Cadre obtained district maps and piled into a van to drive the school zone perimeters. They noted several apartment buildings and trailer parks that they had not even realized were within their zone.

The school was running an entrenched resource program for identified learning disabled, behaviorally disabled, and intellectually disabled students. The progress of these students was slow in the resource room and they never caught up to their peers. In addition, they bore the label of resource room student, which the teachers believed affected self-esteem and motivation. The school community wanted to make a radical change in this practice.

By engaging in the process of taking stock, the school community identified and described its challenges carefully. First-grade teachers expressed frustration with several low-achieving students in their classes. Because of the large class sizes, the teachers felt they could not devote adequate time to giving these students the one-on-one help they needed. Resource teachers also expressed frustration with their program. In spite of the fact that they often had only eight students in a class, the students were not motivated to attempt academic work. Their self-esteem was low and they knew they had been labeled as "resource kids." Teachers of the upper grades expressed concern that resource kids were pulled from their classrooms for extended periods of time and missed out on the activities other students were engaged in. The taking stock data were carefully compared to the vision the school community had crafted. The discrepancies were listed and prioritized and cadres were developed. As might be expected from the previous discussion, curriculum and instruction were the highest priorities and teachers and parents self-selected themselves into this cadre.

Through the inquiry process, the Curriculum and Instruction Cadre carefully defined the challenges and the reasons they existed. Cadre members then planned a pilot intervention program for first-grade resource children, children who had been identified as being at risk of failure when they entered first grade. First-grade teachers helped develop criteria based on what they thought children should know and be able to do when they entered first grade. They then screened kindergarten children at the end of the year on skills such as number and letter identification, sounds, and recognition of short words. Teachers also screened children on social and academic developmental levels. Fifteen children were selected for the pilot classroom. Four of these children were formally identified as meeting the criteria for resource on the basis of disabilities.

Two teachers volunteered to work with these children in an intensive program of acceleration to give them a strong foundation for second grade. Other first-grade teachers volunteered to take larger numbers of students in their classrooms and to give up the use of a teacher aide so that the experimental first grade could proceed with the program with a smaller class size. Parents and other volunteers were recruited to work with the class as well.

Teachers in the pilot first-grade program provided an enriched, stimulating, intensive instructional program for all students. Parents and aides worked with small groups of students. Reading and math skills were emphasized, but students were taught in developmentally appropriate ways that involved a number of learning modalities. Resource teachers provided help within the regular classroom and helped the regular classroom teachers with planning for instruction.

The results of the intervention have been dramatic. The Key Math Diagnostic Arithmetic Test was given at the beginning and end of the first grade, 1992-1993. Students in the pilot program experienced growth rates ranging from 85% to 250%. Grade-level equivalents ranged from 1.0 (this student had started at 0.4) to 2.8 (this student had started at 1.4). All students had progressed at more than one grade level of growth in math for the year. The reading test administered (Woodcock, Form A) was inadequate in that it did not test below first-grade level at the beginning of the school year. Five students tested below the first-grade level in the fall, but the test gave no precise measurement. Grade-level at the end of the year ranged from 1.1 to 2.0. Thirty-one percent of the students tested at 1.8 grade level and above. Seventy-five percent scored at 1.5 grade level and above. There was an average 70% increase in scores in reading from fall to spring.

The results of this initial pilot study were so encouraging that the school community agreed to expand the program to the second grade for the 1993-1994 school year. Another class of at-risk first graders was identified and the program continued in the first grade. The faculty voted to redistribute teaching positions so that the second graders received the services of a 15-hour-per-week aide. The resource teachers once again worked in the regular classrooms with all children. The students in the pilot program were all included in regular second-grade classrooms and received special assistance within the classroom. Pre- and post-Woodcock Reading Mastery Tests were administered to the students, and all have experienced tremendous growth on the measures tested. The gains far outdistanced the gains made by the regular second-grade students and an identified control group of second-grade students. The average resource student gain was 327% and the average second-grade gain was 28%. These findings are consonant with the Accelerated Schools goal of accelerating the progress of at-risk students rather than slowing it down through remediation. The reading rate of included resource students showed steady growth throughout the year. One student had attained a 1,400% gain; others showed gains of 300% to 500%. Students who did not show such large gains were those who had transferred midyear or later from other schools and thus did not reap the benefits of a full year of inclusion.

Gains for the second group of first graders to participate in the program were once again impressive, with an average math gain of 118% and a reading gain of 318%. Other data were obtained on the growth of students who had been in a pull-out program in 1992-1993 and an inclusion program in 1993-1994. These students doubled or tripled their growth in the regular classroom versus a pull-out program.

The end-of-second-grade evaluations provided data to the school community that convinced the members the plan was working beyond their wildest dreams. The meeting at which the data were presented was emotional, with lots of cheers and tears as the graphic illustration of the successes of individual students was shared with the school community. It was decided to continue the program on up through fourth grade for the 1994-1995 school year and to expand into the upper grades the next year. Teachers and parents expressed satisfaction with the results and were encouraged to continue with the project. A summer reading program was established with parent volunteers. In June, the students reviewed vocabulary and stories and in August they previewed material for the coming school year. In January 1994, a reading club was established for third-grade students. Twenty-five students voluntarily come to school early to read with parent and teacher volunteers. Teachers, parents, and students are eagerly participating in the inclusion process.

The Effects of Inclusion

Test score data for the project present compelling evidence that it works. Anecdotal data collected by means of informal interviews with classroom and resource teachers indicate that they have seen dramatic evidence of behavioral changes on the part of resource students in the inclusive classroom. Confidence and self-esteem are higher for these students. Teachers report that students are willing to take risks and try things they have never tried before. Their participation rates have increased as their academic skills have increased. Resource teachers observed that when they pulled children out for work in the resource room in the past, students knew that they had been labeled and often would not even attempt the work. Now, they observed these same students in the regular classroom and were amazed at the levels of participation and the enthusiasm they brought to the learning situation.

Teachers reflected that they had undergone a paradigm shift and began to view resource students differently. Their teaching styles changed as they began to work together to meet the needs of diverse students in the classroom. Teachers stated that inclusion was hard work, as they had to learn about individual education plans (IEPs) in more depth. They felt ownership of these plans now, however, because they were included in the decision-making process: They took responsibility for the learning of *all* the students in their classrooms. Teachers have learned to work collaboratively with the specialist teachers and as a result have learned techniques that work with non-resource-identified students as well.

The included resource students are not all at grade level yet, but their progress is much greater than it was in the resource room and the movement is in a positive direction. The goal of the teachers and parents is to continue the effort to meet the needs of all students in the classroom and to retain the extra resources that are enabling them to do this.

Summary

The cases presented in this chapter illustrate and confirm the consonance between the Accelerated Schools principles and inclusion. Four vignettes, examples of reflective practice, provide illustrations of schools in which the Accelerated Schools inquiry process has been used to design and implement programs of inclusion that meet the needs of the individual school community. The case of Rolling Meadows adds dramatic evidence to the body of research on the effectiveness of the inclusion policy with regard to student growth and achievement and answers the criticism that there is little evidence in the literature to this effect (Scruggs & Mastropieri, 1994, p. 807). All schools developed programs of inclusion as they worked to make their unified school community visions become reality.

The thrust of this work has been to argue for first establishing schools that embrace a profound philosophical commitment to a rich and empowering education for all students. Clearly, this must move beyond the slogans of the day that wind up on pencils and bulletin boards. It requires a deep transformational process that engages all members of the school community and creates new beliefs and practices that mirror the philosophy on a daily basis. Given this philosophical commitment and the demonstrated capacity to pursue it, schools will create their own unique solutions to equality and inclusion that are informed by their strengths, research, and the experiences of other schools. This is what we have learned from accelerated schools and their natural inclination to seek full inclusion as such schools develop and grow.

✐13

Teaching All Children to Read

Hoover Elementary School

VICKY GONZALEZ
CAROLYN TUCHER

It hardly seems possible that one could be a failure at six or seven years old, but that is exactly what happens to some first graders. They experience confusion, frustration, and anxiety over something that is fairly natural for most children: learning how to read. In a few short but critical months, educational life passes them by, and they begin a pattern of thinking that tells them they can't do things in school very well. This pattern may last for years.

Reading Recovery:
Executive Summary (1992)

Teachers at Hoover Elementary School in Redwood City, California, are determined that their young students will all learn to read. Because they believe that reading skills are critical for success in school, they want each of their students to have the help needed to become fluent readers in the primary grades. The purpose of this chapter is to look at how Hoover, as an accelerated school, responded to the challenge of teaching every student to read.

Staff members accepted the Accelerated Schools philosophy and used the Accelerated Schools process to define the problem Hoover students were having with reading, consider alternative solutions, develop an action plan, implement it with the help of foundation funding, and evaluate their results. Teachers found that nearly all children in the program made substantial gains in reading in spite of earlier school failures and that some students gained the equivalent of 2 or 3 years' growth in a single school year. Student, staff, and parent attitudes changed as the students learned to read. Students gained in other areas of the curriculum as well and in their ability to work successfully in the classroom environment.

Students like those at Hoover do not always get such a good start. More than 90% of Hoover's almost 800 children are Hispanic. Three quarters of the kindergartners speak little or no English. Many families come to Redwood City from rural Mexico; some older children who enroll have had no formal education. Many parents have had very few educational opportunities themselves. Some are illiterate or semiliterate. Student mobility is high. Records indicate that half of Redwood City's Hispanic population drop out of high school. At Hoover, 80% of the students qualify for free or reduced-price meals.

Hoover Becomes a Pilot School
of the Accelerated Schools Project

In 1987, Hoover became one of the first two pilot schools in the Accelerated Schools Project at Stanford University, headed by Professor Henry M. Levin. As a pilot school, Hoover worked with a Stanford team in the early development of the project. The training and the process used at Hoover differ in significant ways from the training currently offered schools entering the project. For example, Hoover did not go through a formal taking stock process, although the individual cadres have gathered data necessary to make informed decisions. Parents have not yet actively participated as members of the cadres. Lessons learned from Hoover's early days in the project have informed recent training efforts around the nation.

The Hoover staff worked with the project team to consider how to realize their common goal of bringing every child into the academic mainstream. The staff embraced the Accelerated Schools principles of building on strengths, unity of purpose, and empowerment with responsibility. Over the years, these principles have become not only catalysts for change but also part of the school culture. Teachers are committed to the central premise of the Accelerated Schools Project that every child can learn.

Hoover Sets Up Cadres

To translate the premise that every child can learn into tangible results, Hoover school community members worked with the Accelerated Schools process. They began by developing a vision for the school. They identified four challenge areas: language arts, math, parent involvement, and student and staff self-esteem. Then they formed cadres to address these challenges.

From the time of the school's entry into the Accelerated Schools Project, each of the cadres has contributed to finding solutions adapted to the school's needs and resources. The Language Arts Cadre recommended several steps that the school as a whole adopted to improve instruction. In this chapter, we focus on the Language Arts Cadre's efforts, initiated in 1991, to ensure that every child would become a successful reader. We trace the evolution of the program as it was implemented, reviewed, and revised. We include indications of student progress and changes in teachers' and parents' perceptions, and conclude with some general observations on the school's success in achieving this goal.

Meeting the Challenge
of Teaching Every Child to Read

During the 1990-1991 school year and at the beginning of the following year, many teachers reported that four or five children in each classroom were having serious problems with reading. Not only were they falling farther behind as the year progressed, but their inability to read also affected their work in other areas of the curriculum. Language Arts Cadre members, using the Accelerated Schools inquiry process, identified and defined the challenge areas that they believed had an impact on the reading of Hoover students and began by trying to understand the underlying causes for the substantial number of children experiencing difficulty. Surveys confirmed that many teachers were nearly overwhelmed by the needs of their students and unable to give the time and attention they felt individual pupils required. There was widespread agreement that class sizes were too large. Through informal teacher assessments, the cadre learned that about a third of the children with reading difficulties came from homes where alcoholism or physical and emotional abuse appeared to be chronic. School records indicated that a disproportionate number of children who had transferred to Hoover were lacking skills. Funds for supplementary programs diminished annually. Most discouraging of all, young children seemed caught in a spiral of failure.

A successful solution would need to address the causes identified by the cadre. If class sizes were too large, smaller instructional settings were needed. If children's homes were unstable, the classroom must provide stability and a strong sense of belonging. If parent involvement was a challenge throughout the school, the right solution would engage parents as part of the team helping their children. If young children were already caught in a spiral of failure, they needed to experience success. Early intervention would prevent children from falling farther behind each year. The inquiry process gave the cadre the tools to identify the challenges, find out why they existed, brainstorm potential solutions, devise a pilot program, implement the program, and then evaluate the program. Once the action plan was formulated, it needed to go to the steering committee and then to the school as a whole for approval.

The Language Arts Cadre's
Proposed Action Plan

The cadre's main goal was clear-cut—all children at Hoover must learn to read. Subgoals identified were as follows:

- Children needing help should enter the program as early as possible.
- Children should experience success.
- Class size should be small to allow for individual instruction and attention to each child.
- Students should feel a sense of belonging.
- Parents should become partners in the school's efforts to help their children.
- The reading program should strengthen students' participation in the regular classroom instructional program until they could

work successfully in the class setting, no longer requiring additional help.

The cadre decided on an after-school reading program for students more than a year below grade level. They recommended intensive daily instruction—in Spanish or in English—from trained teachers for second and third graders identified as falling behind or already failing. Classes would be small—five to eight children in a group. Teachers would use high-interest, well-illustrated storybooks purchased especially for the program. Poetry and plays as well as materials written by the children themselves would be part of the curriculum. Each child would read each day. Writing would be integrated into instruction, which would follow the district scope and standards for language arts. Classes would meet for 50 minutes a day, 4 days a week. Teachers would receive stipends for their extra time from Hoover's existing categorical funds.

The Role of Parents

From the outset, Hoover had had a Parent Involvement Cadre. Early data collection showed that few parents actively participated in school activities or supported their children's learning at home. Through research into class records, the cadre established a high correlation between student achievement and family participation in school activities. This discovery, along with their other findings, supported the need for efforts to promote family involvement.

The cadre used the inquiry process to identify and define what all members thought family involvement was and then to identify the challenges with regard to family involvement at Hoover. The cadre next hypothesized why these challenges existed. For example, some hypotheses were that parents have often had unpleasant experiences at school themselves, so they hesitated to become involved at school; that many children lived with grandparents or in single parent homes; and that school schedules conflicted with the work schedules of parents. These hypotheses and many others were then tested for accuracy.

Once challenges were accurately identified, the cadre piloted potentially effective solutions. Under the cadre's leadership, the school provided parenting classes, developed phone trees, recruited volunteers, installed a special hot line for school events with messages in

English and Spanish, and greatly increased home-school communication. As a result, parent attendance rose dramatically at open houses, parent conferences, and other school activities. The work of the Family Involvement Cadre convinced the members of the Language Arts Cadre of the importance of parent support for their efforts.

The Language Arts Cadre used the same inquiry process to identify its challenge areas and to propose potentially effective solutions. Members used information from the Family Involvement Cadre to help develop the pilot program. Parents would be asked to sign a letter from the school outlining their responsibilities before their children could be accepted into the program. The letter would emphasize that the children must attend all class sessions. The school would urge parents to participate in a series of evening classes for families at which teachers would explain the program and show parents how to help at home. By demonstrating teaching methods used in the children's classes, teachers would illustrate that learning can be fun, and perhaps in many cases, quite different from the schooling the parents had had as children. Family members with limited reading ability would be shown how they could also help their children. Classes would be offered in Spanish and in English. The school would provide child care to encourage attendance.

Plan for Evaluation

Assessment was an integral part of the action plan from the outset. The cadre felt that both student evaluation and program evaluation were important. The proposal for student evaluation included student interviews, parent questionnaires, and surveys of both classroom and reading-class teachers. In addition, teachers would give oral pre and posttests to assess students' reading levels. They would collect samples of students' writing throughout the year and determine students' reading levels according to publishers' guidelines in the basal reading series. Cadre members believed that these means of evaluation would give more useful data than standardized test scores—Comprehensive Test of Basic Skills (CTBS) or the Spanish Assessment (SABE)—which seldom showed significant results for Hoover students as a group. Multiple-choice questions and time limits for reading a passage seemed to them to distort results, rather than accurately reflect what students had achieved.

The School as a Whole Adopts and Implements the Cadre's Proposal

The school as a whole adopted the cadre's proposal. In the winter of 1992, it was implemented on a pilot basis. One of the teachers agreed to head up the program, taking responsibility for coordination, purchasing, and evaluation of the overall results at the end of the year. The principal, who had participated from the outset as a member of the Language Arts Cadre, gave the proposal his full support.

Classroom teachers identified 42 second and third graders who were either nonreaders or reading at a first-grade level. The group constituted approximately 20% of the second and third-grade en rollment. All but five of the students had scored below the 10th percentile for their grade level in reading comprehension on the CTBS or the SABE. Unable to participate successfully in class work, many were exhibiting behavioral problems as well.

The children were divided into six English classes and three Spanish classes. Given the population of the school, many students in the English-language reading groups spoke Spanish as their first language. These included children who came to Hoover from schools without bilingual programs, from families requesting that their children be taught in English, and from families that spoke English at home. Tongan, African American, and Anglo children also participated. Approximately one third of the children had transferred to Hoover within the preceding year.

Results of the Pilot Program

Six months later, in June 1992, using the planned methods for evaluation and assessment, teachers observed what they considered to be substantial growth in both the reading and writing skills of those children participating in the program. Students' self-confidence improved noticeably, a result teachers attributed in part to the attention they received in the reading program and in part to their improved skills. Many were more willing to take risks, to try something new, and to participate actively in classroom activities.

Each student's progress was evaluated based on written assessments from the reading teacher and the classroom teacher as well as from the parents. Audiotaped samples of students' reading at the beginning and end of the program and folders of student work backed up teacher observations. The reading teachers also interviewed all of their students. In addition, they assessed students' reading abilities according to guidelines in the district basal reading texts in order to track progress from the start of the reading classes to the end of the school year. Results were most encouraging. In quantitative data, teachers found that almost every student had progressed measurably. In June, 18 of 42 children in the program were reading at grade level. Seventeen more had reached early fluency, according to the method devised to track growth in reading ability.

Teachers' Perceptions of the Progress Made by Students

Each teacher filled out a questionnaire at the end of the school year, noting changes not only in students' ability to read and write, but also in their classroom behavior and self-esteem. One second-grade teacher wrote about a student of hers who had participated in the program:

> She has gone from knowing no letter-sound correspondence to being a confident reader. She is as able as the other children who have been reading for over a year and does very well on spelling tests. She is constantly writing minibooks and has developed her own series of books about a girl named Rosie. She confidently signs all her work Conejita Lupe [Bunny Lupe].

Another classroom teacher reported that two of her students had previously been recommended for special education. Of the two, one had progressed from a nonreader to grade-level reading. The other student qualified for special education but did not receive services from the resource specialist. As a result, she continued in the reading program, progressing from a nonreader to the top student in a group designated emergent readers. The program also proved helpful in distinguishing between students needing help in reading and students needing special education services. In instances where a single child in a group did not make progress commensurate with the others, the child was referred to the Student Study Team.

Teachers also noted that as the students became better readers, they were more cooperative in the classroom and more successful in other areas of the curriculum. A third-grade teacher wrote,

All of [my students in the reading program] have gained in esteem that can only come from an inner sense of true accomplishment. As a teacher, I do activities to heighten the students' sense of self, but nothing beats a real improvement of their skills. Learning to read opens many doors for them.

Students participated enthusiastically in the reading classes. As one teacher wrote, "The kids in my class felt it was an *honor* to be in the after-school reading group." Attendance was excellent. Students particularly responded to the attention possible because of the small number in each group. Their feelings were reflected by their friends begging to be included in the classes as well.

Teachers benefited from the program also. Their reactions were characterized by the comments of a second-grade teacher who wrote,

It has been a great relief to me to have these students receive extra help and instruction. They are able to improve and progress in a small group in a way that would never be possible in the larger group. That relieves me of the pressure of trying to meet the needs of these students in impossibly large classes.

Parental Response to the Pilot

Because some parents walked to Hoover to pick up their children at the end of the school day, teachers had a chance to visit informally with them. Their support for the program was clear from the outset. The principal had been concerned that absenteeism would hamper the program because many families rely on primary-school-aged children to assist with child care. Attendance was excellent, however. Parents took seriously the principal's admonition that only children with good attendance would be allowed to remain in the program. Participants were enthusiastic about the evening classes for parents. A parent questionnaire at the end of the school year indicated that parents were reading with their children at home more than before.

Hoover Reviews and Revises the Action Plan

In addition to looking at student achievement, the Hoover staff reviewed the program itself, comparing results with the original objective. Based on the information the staff had collected regarding student progress, the program was considered very successful with regard to the primary goal of teaching all children to read. Pupils were receiving help early and experiencing success. Groups of five or six children were small enough for students to have the attention, encouragement, and practice that they needed. Parental support at home and at school was growing. The evening classes for families were lively, informative, and well attended.

The Language Arts Cadre, after reviewing the program, did recommend some changes, however. For staffing reasons, half of the classes during the pilot period had been held after school, half during school. Cadre members felt that the students would progress as intended only if they remained in their classes during the entire school day. They did not want children to miss other important parts of the curriculum in order to have special help in reading. The school as a whole decided all reading classes would meet after school and strongly endorsed the original goal and objectives of the program.

1992-1993 After-School Reading Program

Students Succeed, Funding Fails

In spite of the documented success, state and district budget cuts made it impossible for Hoover to fund the program for the 1992-1993 school year. The school staff members, accustomed to responding flexibly to budget cutbacks and too committed to their reading program to let it drop, met to consider possible funding sources. They decided to approach foundations to ask for help. Their responses were immediate and most generous. With the help of the Peninsula Community Foundation, the David and Lucille Packard Foundation, and the Walter S. Johnson Foundation, the program was fully funded and expanded to include first and fourth-grade students as well as second and third graders. Foundation funding enabled the payment of stipends to teachers participating in the after-school reading program as well as purchase of books for classroom use and classes for parents. The budget also allowed teachers to provide snacks for the children before the after-school program began. Total funding for Hoover's after-school reading program for the 1992-1993 school year was $47,600, approximately $500 per child.

Implementing the Action Plan in 1992-1993

In October 1992, classroom teachers selected 66 second, third, and fourth graders—approximately 20% of the students—to participate in the after-school reading classes. The lead teacher and the principal selected 12 teachers for the reading program based on the teachers' willingness to take on an additional assignment and their skill in teaching reading. Six Spanish-speaking and six English-speaking classes were set up. Of the 34 children in the English speaking classes, 26 had limited English proficiency.

The teachers decided to reduce the size of the reading classes to a maximum of six children to allow for more individual instruction and attention. They also agreed not to place first graders in the program until midyear in order to give children time to demonstrate how much they could do and give teachers time to determine which reading problems were severe and which could be worked out in the classroom setting. Teachers also felt the children would have greater stamina after they had become accustomed to the first-grade schedule.

The outside funding made it possible for each reading teacher to have a "minilibrary" of children's books for the students to take home. They would be encouraged to read a book to a family member and return it the next day with a parent's signature. The "homework packets" would further strengthen home-school cooperation.

Teachers used the methods of teaching reading that they found most satisfactory in their regular classrooms or that they individually judged most effective in meeting the needs of the children in their reading groups. No set curriculum was adopted by the staff.

Midyear Review

In January, the reading teachers met to review all aspects of the program. They shared informal assessments of student progress both in the reading program and in the regular classroom. Based on their observations, they were convinced that the students were making substantial progress. In a telling example, a teacher reported that prior to starting in the after-school reading program, one boy in his class had been fighting frequently and lying. He participated in the reading program faithfully, however. As his reading skills dramatically increased, his personality seemed to change as well. The fighting and lying decreased. He evidenced an ability to get along with other students. He participated in classroom activities. His classroom teacher reported that not only had his attitude changed completely, but he also had become a constant reader, with a book never far from his hand.

The homework books had several benefits. One teacher wrote,

[The library] not only allows students to read at home, hopefully involving a parent, it also gives students responsibility
and respect for books. Students show genuine excitement over
choosing a book, taking it home, bringing it back, and sharing
the story with the group.

On the basis of the midyear assessment, classes for 28 first graders
were added to the program. Teachers agreed to maintain a limit of six
students per group in spite of considerable interest in allowing other
children to participate. The staff moved several students from one reading group to another because of changes in students' reading levels.

Evaluation of the 1992-1993
After-School Reading Program

As the school year came to an end, the reading teachers and classroom teachers met together to share their perceptions of the after-school
reading program. Ninety-eight children had participated; 79 continued
in the program until the end of the school year. Four were taken out of
the program at midyear to make room for others because they were
reading at or near grade level. Six were dropped for poor attendance;
one, for unruly behavior. Eight children moved away.

The teachers were eager to find out if their students had made substantial improvement over the course of the year. They had agreed on
a variety of evaluation measures at the start of the school year. The lead
teacher took responsibility for collecting information and for developing questionnaires. She requested the following information about the
students:

- Interviews of each of the students by their reading teachers
- Reading levels as determined by both the reading teachers and
  the language arts teachers based on descriptions in the basal readers
- Comments on each student's progress by the reading teacher using not only the teacher's observations and records but also tapes
  of students reading and samples of their writing to get "before"
  and "after" snapshots of their skill levels
- Reports on each student's progress from the regular classroom
  teacher

The teachers also sought out ways to include parents in the evaluation of the program. They reviewed attendance at classes for families and information about parents who were reading with their children at home. Questionnaires went to the parents of all children in the program. Teachers also took note of informal conversations with parents on the playground and at school functions.

Individual Students Make Substantial Progress

The after-school reading program transformed the school experience for many, but not all, of the participants (see data below). Teachers reported many remarkable successes. A first grader in an English-speaking class was unable to focus on her work at the beginning of the school year. She seemed to be in her own world, far away from the task at hand. The family was in crisis. The mother was serving a prison sentence on a drug charge. Her teacher selected her for the program in January. Her father became a regular at the classes for parents. He maintained that the change in his daughter's attitude toward school was like the difference between night and day. She became eager and joyful. Laughing, she would point to her head and say, "My computer is turned on now." She began to participate actively with her classmates during the school day. Her reading ability increased $1\frac{1}{2}$ years in 6 months from nonreader to Grade 1.5, within $1\frac{1}{2}$ year of grade level. These results occurred in spite of the fact that the family situation did not change.

A boy who was such a discipline problem in kindergarten and first grade that his mother had to come to school repeatedly to pick him up and take him home started second grade as a nonreader. He did not participate in class activities. His teacher chose him for the reading program. In 1 year, the boy gained 2 years in reading ability. He finished second grade at the 2.0 level. Although his teachers had a high regard for the reading program from the beginning, even they were amazed at the change in his behavior and in the work he did in class by the end of the year. His mother never missed a parent class. She said she understood that she needed to be directly involved in his education and that she had learned how to help him at home.

A fourth-grade boy entered school reading at the preprimer level. He was lost in all his classes, isolated from the other children, and always on the margin of class activities and assignments because he could not read. He gained 2 years in reading ability in 1 year and in June was reading at the 3.0 level. Although still 2 years behind grade level, he was well on his way. His attitude was positive. He became an active participant in class work and was integrated into the group of children. By the end of the year, he was able to complete written assignments in social studies and science along with his classmates.

Student Reading Levels

The language arts teachers assessed all of the children's reading levels at the time they placed them in the program. They used the Scott Foresman series *Collections* and the Macmillan series *Campanitas de Oro*. At the end of the year, both the language arts teachers and the reading teachers checked the pupils' reading level by the same benchmarks. Correlation between the two assessments was high. In instances where teachers differed by more than half a year, the lead teacher retested the students.

Of the 79 children assessed at the end of the school year, 69 made gains at least equal to the norms spelled out in reading textbooks—a year's growth for a year in school or half a year's growth for half a year in school. Two thirds progressed twice as quickly as the norms applied by the teachers—or even more. All but 7 of the 39 children assessed who had participated a full year in the program showed from 1 to 3 years' growth according to benchmarks in the basal readers as determined by the children's teachers. Of the 40 in the program for the second half of the year, all but 3 showed from ½ to 2 years' growth. Nineteen participants were no longer in the program at the end of the school year—having moved from Hoover, been "graduated" from the program, or dropped for poor attendance—and were not assessed.

Teachers' Observations on the Effectiveness of the After-School Reading Program

Teachers were consistently enthusiastic about their students' progress. The following is typical of comments from the after-school reading teachers:

Academically, the children have made tremendous progress. Almost all the children started as nonreaders and have shown more than a year's growth during this school year. Naturally, they are quite proud of themselves, and their self-esteem has improved. Prior to the program, the children had not learned to read and consequently felt bad about themselves. To cope with feeling bad about themselves, they would act out. As they acted out, they would fall further and further behind in their schoolwork. It was a vicious cycle, spiraling downward. This reading program has allowed them to do a complete about-face in a very positive direction.

One of the most noticeable themes in responses from the classroom teachers was the relief they felt from knowing that the neediest students were getting help in the after-school program. Several commented that these children were improving as they never would be able to in regular classes of 30 and more pupils. Teachers also felt that the other students benefited indirectly.

Knowing that my emerging readers were in the after-school program was a great relief. I was able to develop a program to meet the Redwood City language arts standards, knowing that my struggling readers were getting the support they needed. We were able to spend the majority of class time enjoying and analyzing literature, and everyone was able to participate to their level of ability. No one who wanted to participate was lost.

Parental Perceptions

Children were so eager to participate in the program that they urged their parents to attend evening classes, read with them at home, and support their being in the program. Parents who saw the benefits of the program came to the school to ask that their other children be included. Those who picked their children up at school waited on the playground with siblings without complaint in order that their children could participate in the after-school classes. One poignant moment came when a father arrived early to get his son from class. "Why don't you read your book to your dad?" the teacher suggested. The father, illiterate himself, was deeply moved and very proud that his son had learned to read.

Approximately 25% of the parents returned questionnaires about their children's progress in the program. All were very supportive of the program. One responded:

I have seen [my son] change in his reading ability. He was not able to read when he started. Now he reads all the time. His sentences and spelling have improved.

Another parent noted a change in her son's attitude:

His attitude in the beginning was one of frustration. The other was he refused to read. Now when we are out or at home, he is so proud that he is able to read.

Results of Classes for Parents

Initially, teachers had hoped that at least 50% of the families would attend the evening classes with their students. Because a child could only come if a family member came and the children were eager to come, parents did attend who had not participated in school events previously. On average, about one third of the families attended.

The primary purpose of the sessions for parents was to engage them as active players in their children's education in general, and to demonstrate their essential role in reading to and with their children in particular. At the classes, parents and children worked together on reading activities and games. Parents beamed with pride as they watched their children dramatize well-known stories. Classes were conducted in English and in Spanish. The school provided child care as well. Each family went home with a gift—a book for the child to keep and a packet of ideas for activities to do at home. Three hundred books were given to families in the course of the year.

A teacher of the parent classes summed up her observations as follows:

In retrospect, what was most impressive to me was the bridge of trust which *slowly* developed between the parents and the staff at Hoover. At the beginning of each session, parents were shy to participate and ask questions. However, with each class, trust and confidence slowly developed, accelerating parents' participation in their children's education and in the school.

At the final class for families, parents presented certificates to their children, recognizing the students' accomplishments in the after-school reading program. More than one parent cried. One mother, with tears in her eyes, gave her son his certificate and told him how proud she was of him. He had started second grade unable to read and become such an enthusiastic reader that he begged her to turn off the television in order to read with him. Many parents spoke of the changes in their children.

Reading at Home

When children finished a book in the after-school reading class, they were given the book to take home to read to a family member. Each child had a book envelope with a form for the parent to sign, testifying that the child had read the book at home. Each class also had a minilibrary, made possible by foundation funds, from which children could take home books. Some children took home books every day and returned them promptly. A few had difficulty getting their forms signed, and a few books were not returned. Generally, the families supported the school and helped their children at home.

Making a Good Program Better

At the end of the 1992-1993 school year, the Language Arts Cadre reviewed the after-school reading program. Members felt that their efforts had paid off even beyond their expectations. They definitely wanted to continue the program, but they also had some ideas about fine-tuning it. The cadre proposed adding an orientation meeting for parents before the start of classes in the fall to make sure the parents understood the program and the importance of their role in it. They also decided to strengthen the reading-at-home aspect of the program by devising incentives for students who read a certain number of books and by keeping records of overall student participation.

In other additions, intended to strengthen assessment of student progress, the cadre selected a Houghton Mifflin reading test, An Informal Reading Inventory, to use as a pre and posttest to supplement teacher assessments of students' reading levels. In addition, a doctoral candidate from Stanford was engaged to collect and analyze data. There was also discussion of methods of following up with students who had participated in the program during the 1992-1993 school year to get some indication of longer-term effects. The cadre recommended these changes, and the school as a whole adopted them for the 1993-1994 school year.

Conclusions

Observations that emerge from looking back over Hoover's accomplishments can help the school continue to build on the strengths of the after-school reading program.

- The program appears to be accomplishing its purpose. The spiral of failure seems to have been reversed for the pupils at Hoover most in need of help. By all the measures the staff used, the students' results have been remarkable. Children who were unable to read or far behind their classmates are now reading and writing with enthusiasm. Because of their improved skills and their growing self-confidence, they are also succeeding in other areas of the curriculum as well. Changes in students' attitudes and behavior have been pronounced. Many families are seeing themselves as part of the team helping their children. Classroom teachers feel supported in their efforts to meet the wide variety of needs in their large classrooms.
- The Accelerated Schools Project enabled the Hoover staff to address these challenges and find solutions to them. The Language Arts Cadre implemented several important improvements to the reading curriculum, but as the work continued, members became more and more focused in their efforts. Finally, they determined that their principal challenge was making sure that every child learned to read, and that in particular, children in the primary grades who were nonreaders or substantially behind grade level should have the help they needed to succeed. The cadre used the inquiry process, discussed in more detail earlier in this chapter, to find solutions and proposed small classes after school taught by Hoover teachers using high-quality children's literature. Building on the work of the Parent Involvement Cadre to gain help and support from parents, the cadre included plans for evaluating the program as well as individual student's progress, as the Accelerated Schools process required. The cadre gained schoolwide support for its action plan. The three principles of the Accelerated Schools model—building on strengths, empowerment with responsibility, and unity of purpose—were clearly evident both in the planning and in the implementation. The staff's "can do" attitude exemplified the Accelerated Schools approach.
- Since entering the Accelerated Schools Project in 1987, teachers have worked closely together. Staff members support one an other and value the collegial climate of the school. They have also developed a strong sense of ownership of the school and its programs.
- Hoover recognizes that parents are essential partners in their children's education. For their part, parents are also coming to understand the importance of their role. They are feeling more and more part of the school community.

- The lack of standardized data to support other assessment information collected by the teachers limits the conclusions Hoover staff members can draw from their work. As encouraging as the teacher and parent comments are, they will be stronger when backed up by uniformly collected data from which generalizations can be drawn.
- Hoover does not yet have comparable results from individual classrooms to use to test the approach of letting each teacher use whatever method of instruction he or she may choose. We anticipate the staff will want to know whether all approaches are equally effective with the children in the program.
- At an average cost of approximately $500 per student, the program is low-cost by comparison with other programs intended to help the same population. Expenditures are targeted directly to the children identified as especially in need of help. To the extent that the program reduces special education placements and student retention, as staff members believe it does, it will generate substantial savings. Although these savings do not accrue directly to the school itself, they benefit the district. If the school was able to keep the savings, they might be able to pay for the program directly from those funds. With less than $50,000 in 1992-1993, Hoover provided 100 hours of instruction in small groups of 5 to 6 children; 500 books for the minilibraries in individual classrooms; six evening classes for parents and families, which included child care and packets with books and materials to use at home; and snacks for the children to eat before reading classes began.
- Most important of all, children are discovering that they can succeed in school. Small classes provide the direct instruction that helps them take big steps forward in both reading and writing. Not only do they gain proficiency in the skills essential to schooling, but they also learn to love reading. What a difference the after-school program makes in the possibilities open to the students who have participated!

Can Hoover's Success Be Replicated in Other Schools?

There are talented teachers in every school, Hoover staff members are quick to point out. They add, however, that the philosophy and process of the Accelerated Schools Project have provided a setting at Hoover that does not exist in all schools. The staff is close-knit, and morale has been high in spite of many challenges, including repeated cuts in the school budget. Hoover teachers are accustomed to taking the initiative, to working collaboratively to solve problems, and to involving families in children's education. The principal expects the cadres to propose solutions to challenges facing the school, and he supports their efforts.

Hoover staff members would like to think that their experience will be instructive to any accelerated school and to other schools with similar characteristics. They would not expect other accelerated schools to imitate their after-school reading program, but rather to use the Accelerated Schools philosophy and process in a similar manner to devise their own solutions to the challenges they face.

14

The Influence of the Accelerated Schools Philosophy and Process on Classroom Practices

BETH M. KELLER

PILAR SOLER

Accelerated schools are designed to bring all students into the mainstream of U.S. education in the richest sense of those terms. The Accelerated Schools process represents both a philosophy and a process for reaching those goals. These practices are based upon three principles—unity of purpose, empowerment coupled with responsibility, and building on strengths—a set of values and beliefs, and powerful learning tenets. Through the Accelerated Schools philosophy, principles, and practices, the school community works together to redefine its roles, goals, responsibilities, methods of decision making, and pedagogy. This process results in changes in school-based practices that reach throughout the school community. The three principles, the powerful learning philosophy, and accelerated practices are discussed in greater detail earlier in this book.

The purpose of this chapter is to initiate a preliminary exploration of the impact of these school-based practices on classroom practices of individual teachers. All of the components of the Accelerated Schools philosophy and process contribute to systemic change in the school—referred to as "big wheels." From these big wheels, "little wheels" spin off that work together with the big wheels to change the very culture of the school (Brunner & Hopfenberg, 1992). For example, a staff member working in cadres using the inquiry process may begin to use that same process with the students in the classroom. In our study, we hoped to begin to find out how much the philosophy and process permeate teacher practices with students in the classroom. To explore this issue, we conducted a study of a single school that could then feed into a larger, longer-term study.

The central focus of this exploratory research is on two questions:

1. Does participation in the Accelerated Schools philosophy and process change teachers' attitudes, practices, and behaviors in their own classrooms beyond those changes that are identified with the implementation of schoolwide Accelerated Schools practices?

2. Does the specific problem-solving process embodied by the decision-making groups in accelerated schools carry over into individual classrooms?

Although these are the specific questions that we address, we are mindful that they are part of a more general dilemma in education, that of affecting significant changes in teachers and schools (Cuban, 1984; Fullan & Stiegelbauer, 1991; Sarason, 1982; Schlecty, 1990). The literature suggests that deep changes in school culture and teacher behavior are rare events, and when they occur, are a result of long-term internalization of beliefs and practices that influence many dimensions of the school culture. That larger issue is taken up in specific studies of the Accelerated Schools process and outcomes (Finnan & Levin, 1994), but this study is devoted to the impact of that process on teacher practices.

This chapter is organized in the following way: First, we give a brief description of the school we studied. Second, we provide a brief description of the research and some of our insights. Then, we discuss the implications of these insights for a preliminary understanding of the issues, as well as the next steps for a full-scale research project. In the chapter appendix, we provide a conceptual rationale for asking the research questions and a method for undertaking exploratory work to answer these questions.

School Background

The school used for this exploratory study was chosen for several reasons: (a) It is located in a large district that includes constituents from both rural and urban areas, (b) it had been using the Accelerated Schools philosophy and process as developed at the National Center for the Accelerated Schools Project for more than 2 years, and (c) the school community willingly agreed to take part in the study.

The school's own history is interesting, as the school has gone from a large, suburban neighborhood school in the early 1980s to one that faced a rapidly declining student population and was being considered for closure by the district. In the fall of 1989, the school had a total of 360 students, of whom 36% received public assistance under Aid to Families With Dependent Children (AFDC) and the free and reduced-price lunch program. The mobility rate was approximately 30%, and English was the only language spoken. Behavior was a problem that year with a total of 103 days of suspension, primarily for fighting.

Just 3 years later, in 1992-1993, the school's enrollment had grown by one third to 494 students. Eighty percent of the students were receiving AFDC or free or reduced-price lunches. Thirteen different languages were now spoken at the school. But contrary to what might have been expected given these demographics, the mobility rate had dropped to 23%, student behavior had improved with only 34 days of suspension that year, and sixth-grade test scores on the Comprehensive Test of Basic Skills (CTBS) had risen in all three areas tested. In schoolwide surveys, students and staff reported higher levels of self-esteem and enjoyment from school than ever before.

Prior to the introduction of the Accelerated Schools Project, the school followed very "traditional" practices in school management and decision making as well as classroom teaching. At that time, most decisions were made at the state and district level with the school being held accountable for the implementation of those decisions. The principal and the school staff did not have a method for addressing specific school needs and concerns. The school community felt little ownership of the school. Traditional teaching methods were used in self-contained classrooms with a heavy reliance on textbooks and state-mandated curriculum. There was little active student involvement and input in the classroom. Teachers worked in isolation in their classrooms with little knowledge of what was being taught in the room next door (Levin & Chasin, 1994).

The school's involvement in the Accelerated Schools Project began in the spring of 1992 after a lengthy exploration and buy-in process on the part of the school community. All of the training and follow-up activities incorporated the full staff as well as parent and student representatives in a constructivist set of activities focused on the Accelerated Schools philosophy and process. During the spring of 1992, the school community took stock of its situation, created a shared vision that reflected the input of all the different stakeholders of the school, set priority areas (after comparing the differences between the vision and taking stock data), set up its Accelerated Schools governance structure, and was trained in both the inquiry process and group dynamics. The school also received continuous training in constructing powerful learning situations—the establishment of an integrated approach to curriculum, instructional strategies, and school climate and organization that builds on strengths and accelerates learning.

Throughout the 1992-1993 school year, cadres met regularly to work through the inquiry process in their area of concern. During this first full year of cadre work, many changes took place in the school that derived from the early work of the cadres and the overall practice of the Accelerated Schools philosophy and process. For example, the move to active learning was pronounced, as was a far more supportive emotional climate for students and staff. Parent participation expanded along with schoolwide multicultural events and multicultural awareness across the curriculum. Cadres explored the establishment of a very active learning approach to science and a new reinforcement system for good attendance and student behavior (Levin & Chasin, 1994).

Description of the Research and Initial Findings

All of the five teachers we interviewed (see chapter appendix), described changes that had occurred since the implementation of the Accelerated Schools model, but their comments ranged greatly in the level of specificity about how these changes played out in their classroom. Three teachers gave us examples that clearly illustrated changes in attitudes, behaviors, and practices in their classroom. The other two teachers provided more general comments to illustrate the changes to which they referred. To help inform our understanding of the kind of changes in teaching and learning that had actually taken place, we also drew upon the observations of the principal and the Accelerated Schools trainer as well as other school community members (see chapter appendix).

Prior to the Accelerated Schools Project, three of these five teachers—who had been teaching 6 to 17 years, with at least 4 of their most recent years at the school—were fairly traditional in their teaching approach, relying primarily on textbooks and teacher-directed activities. The other two teachers used a greater variety of instructional strategies, but these were still based heavily on the teacher directing the lesson. For the most part, all five teachers followed the district-mandated curriculum and they did not feel free or qualified to modify or adapt it. The teachers admitted their primary focus was trying to cover the required material and they did not give much attention to why they were teaching the lesson or its relevance to students. One teacher described himself as an "out of the book boy" who was just "jamming and cramming it down the throats [of students]." He described his teacher training experience as more traditional in its approach:

> [It was], you know, cover the material, do that Madeline Hunter anticipatory set . . . get through your lesson that way and have some kind of quiz or test for checking for understanding. Make sure you cover the material because you know you are worthless, you really aren't much of a teacher if you aren't covering the material. . . . I was going nuts trying to cover all the material, trying to correct everything and so forth.

Three of the teachers described a classroom environment that was focused on maintaining student behavior and staying on task. Learning was very much teacher directed with few opportunities for discovery that went beyond the teachers' initial lesson plan. One teacher described how she taught writing using a five-step approach: "I would be up there and I would be teaching in more of a directed teaching atmosphere where I showed them specific examples, checked for understanding, and that kind of environment."

Although all the teachers felt that they had tried to find ways to build on the strengths of their students prior to the Accelerated Schools process being adopted, they acknowledged that they had had different expectations for the students and that the learning pace and materials were different depending upon the students' ability level. One of the teachers described the remedial approach she used to pull a number of students out of class, explaining, "We were trying to help children, if you want to use the older word we were trying to help *remediate* the skills that they have, that they were having problems with, or problems that were indicated because they took the test and didn't get whatever the criteria score was." Another teacher said that although the pull-out program had always bothered her, "I felt very pressured to follow the regular way of doing things."

One of the most noticeable issues we discovered from our data was that prior to the Accelerated Schools Project teachers worked very much in isolation with few opportunities for sharing teaching strategies and ideas. As Fullan and Stiegelbauer (1991) assert, when teachers do not have an environment for sharing, observing, and discussing their practices with each other, then there is little opportunity for the school to develop a shared understanding of teaching practices. This was a recurring theme that surfaced regularly in all of the interviews and surveys— that prior to the Accelerated Schools Project, teachers felt there were no clearly articulated goals or objectives for teaching and learning schoolwide, resulting in confusion and ambiguity about what they *should* be doing.

Through the compilation of the five teacher interviews and the other data collected during the course of our exploratory study, a number of issues surfaced that helped to inform our initial questions as summarized below.

Question 1:   Does participation in the Accelerated Schools philosophy and process change teachers' attitudes, practices, and behaviors in their own classrooms beyond those changes that are identified with the implementation of schoolwide Accelerated Schools practices?

Through our interviews, we found that the teachers talked about the three principles, the values, and the philosophy of powerful learning not in isolation but as being interdependent and closely embedded into their curriculum and teaching practices. This was an important discovery for us, as we saw how the teachers had internalized the philosophy in a much more comprehensive way than we had originally assumed from the data gathered from the surveys.

As a result, it was difficult for the teachers to pinpoint which element of the Accelerated Schools model had contributed to the changes they described. What the teachers often described to us was that the participation and collaboration in Accelerated Schools practices by themselves and other members of the school community had been instrumental in improving schoolwide environment, providing more unity and direction as a school, placing greater focus on the children, and establishing greater respect and support from their peers. As their own commitment to and belief in the Accelerated Schools philosophy and process grew, they began to reexamine their own teaching practices.

Because it was hard to separate the different components of the Accelerated Schools model that contributed to change based upon our feedback from the teachers, we organized the data in the context of interrelated themes that began to emerge. These key themes—instructional style, curriculum, and classroom and schoolwide environment— are the cornerstones of the Accelerated Schools powerful learning philosophy and provide a glimpse of the kinds of changes that a number of teachers were beginning to experience in their classrooms as a result of the Accelerated Schools Project.

Instructional Style

Throughout our data, teachers commented that the Accelerated Schools Project had created a more open and accepting schoolwide environment, giving them more freedom within the classroom to try new things and take risks they might not have otherwise. One teacher in particular mentioned that the Accelerated Schools Project helped "validate" many ideas he had about what constitutes "good" teaching, but in the past had felt too intimidated to try. His participation in developing an accelerated school resulted in his becoming a true instructional leader as acknowledged by a number of his peers, particularly in using a constructivist approach. Another teacher described how the supportive environment had given her more confidence as a teacher:

> I'm not as afraid of falling on my face any more. I'm more willing to take some risks and try something new and different to help the student learn better. Not everything will work, but I know it's okay and I can learn from each experience.

The data we collected from teachers show that their participation and collaboration in the Accelerated Schools Project has led to a growing belief in establishing higher expectations and greater equity among students. Several teachers mentioned that although they thought they had tried to build on students' strengths in the past, the focus and practice of seeking out the strengths and talents in every child as part of the Accelerated Schools approach had been instrumental in their growing realization that they could use the same curriculum and instructional approach for *all* students despite the differing ability levels of the students. One of the biggest schoolwide indicators of this change has been the school's commitment to eliminating pull-out programs and bringing special education teachers into the regular classroom. One of the teachers we interviewed talked at length about how her approach in the classroom had changed from a remedial one to one that focuses and builds upon what students do well. She said,

> So, we're building on the strengths that they have. I now see that it's okay to let some of the other students become more of the teachers, because that's building on their strengths. It doesn't mean that I'm not doing my job as a teacher, it means that I'm finally relying on the strengths that they have to help other students. . . . So, I guess it's [Accelerated Schools] taught me to be comfortable with where they're at and know that's a strength for them and to try also to give more to the students who are ready to go on, and not to slow the pace down. But we also don't pull students out to remediate anymore. We work with them in the classroom and we've tried to use collaborative teaching groups [a group of special education teachers who work with the classroom teacher] and we've also tried to use cooperative groups within the classroom.

This teacher now believes that all children can learn if the curriculum is presented in a manner that allows all styles of learners to succeed. She described how her teaching style has become much more flexible and includes a variety of ways for students to exhibit their knowledge; she uses much more cooperative grouping so that each child learns to work and learn by sharing ideas and contributing to the solution of a problem. All of her students are encouraged to think, process, and challenge ideas and concepts. She focuses more now on students trying their best at a task and understanding the overall process rather than getting the "right" answer. Actual content is not as important as the ability to process and use information. Another teacher described how his use of the constructivist approach within the classroom includes modeling himself as a learner for the students. When he doesn't know the answer to something he admits it and challenges the students to find the answer. "Sometimes I have kids who take that challenge and they will actually teach me at the same time they are teaching the kids." When students work with adults who themselves reflect, ask questions, and are open to different avenues of approaching learning, they are more likely to emulate these attitudes, practices, and behaviors (Brooks & Brooks, 1993).

The changing instruction a number of people described has meant that the role of the teacher has evolved from someone directing and presenting knowledge to someone who is "becoming more of a facilitator," as one teacher described it. Teachers described lessons and activities that put more focus on the students constructing and discovering their own learning instead of the teacher always directing the student' learning. The principal's observations showed how one of the most traditional teachers in the school—who had previously used textbooks and worksheets as his only source of instruction—was experimenting with several self-discovery activities and a variety of instructional approaches for the first time. These kinds of activities in turn provide greater opportunities for student creativity, reflection, and participation. As testimonial to these changes, students in the focus group said that "more people are involved now in our classes" and that classrooms (after adoption of the Accelerated Schools model) are more "creative," and "fun," with more opportunities for "hands-on activities" and projects. Said one student, "Before, you always felt like you heard about how students should be seen and not heard. Now, you really do hear that students should be seen *and* heard."

Curriculum

In both surveys and interviews, a number of teachers mentioned that they felt that the adoption of the Accelerated Schools process had allowed for greater flexibility to adapt the curriculum to meet the needs of all children. One teacher explained that the growing conversation among her colleagues about what and how students should be learning had resulted in her changing her curriculum to focus on providing more hands-on and meaningful activities, as well as more opportunities for student input. She described how providing more open-ended activities instead of narrowly defined information and instructions gave students the opportunity to come up with different ideas and see different ways others might approach a problem. Said another teacher,

All the teachers are trying to reach higher and higher and present more and more rich curriculum for the students and really looking at "What is it I am trying to teach?" Before they looked at "What page am I on and where am I in the manual and what skills do I need?" Now they look at "What am I trying to teach and how am I going to get there?" and "Will this work?" If it doesn't, let's do something else so we can get there.

Another teacher attributed this new sense of freedom to "try something different" and the support he felt from a number of his colleagues and the principal as the catalyst for him to expand his curriculum into a much more constructivist approach, giving the children more opportunities to create and discover their own learning. Prior to the adoption of the Accelerated Schools process, he thought that there had to be another way of covering the material, but he felt stifled to explore alternatives because of his teacher training, the educational system, and the lack of support within the school culture. His internalization of the Accelerated Schools philosophy and process through his participation on cadres and the resulting collaboration with his colleagues has influenced his development as a teacher and helped him change his focus in the classroom. He now feels, "I teach a little bit less, but do a better job of it, you know, I get them into it and they get more out of it." He has adapted his curriculum so that it has become more understandable for his students. "I think we have opened our math books twice this entire school year because I pull everything out of the book in an order that I think works better for the kids." He also feels that learning is integrated and doesn't fall under any particular schedule:

> I know they say that it is really important for kids to say that math is coming up from 9:00 a.m. to 9:30 a.m. type schedule and what have you, but in my opinion, how can you do that if you are truly going to go by the kids' strengths, you know, by reflecting on how well they are doing, and so forth, how can you put a time schedule on that? You might finish 15 minutes ahead of time or you may go 2 hours beyond. . . . The kids want to know more. If they want to know more, I am going to tell them.

This flexibility in what he teaches has also made him more aware of focusing on what the children want to learn and whether it is relevant to their lives. One of the first things he does is put himself in the place of the student, asking, "What do I care what you are teaching unless you can tell me what value it is to me?" An example of how he adapted his curriculum to be more meaningful for his students is a unit he developed called "video language." Building upon the enjoyment and learning students had demonstrated from this activity, he expanded it into a 5-month-long activity that drew more fully upon students' ideas and creativity and made them more active participants in the project's development. During this activity, students learned how to make videos, culminating in a final video that they researched, wrote, and produced themselves. In addition, the students also helped the teacher select the criteria on which the videos would be graded.

Environment: In the Classroom and Schoolwide

Several teachers expressed in their interviews a belief that the collaborative practices that come about as the result of the Accelerated Schools model have led to their individual professional growth and increased communication and sharing among colleagues. A by-product of this collaboration and sharing of philosophy has been a greater feeling of peer pressure, camaraderie, and accountability among the staff to provide a better education for all of the students. One of the teachers explained that the Accelerated Schools process had been a real "kick in the pants" for him because as he saw others experiment with new instructional strategies it forced him to confront what he was doing and whether it was really working. As a result of this self-examination, he found that although he had a strong language arts and social studies program, his science program was not as effective. This realization— and the growing climate of support he felt from his colleagues—caused him to ask others if he could observe what they were doing in their classrooms to get some ideas. This teacher admitted that he was not comfortable asking other colleagues for help prior to the Accelerated Schools Project because he was afraid of how he might be perceived.

This changing schoolwide climate that supports and encourages risk taking and experimentation also has changed the individual classroom environment of the teachers we interviewed. One teacher described how she tries to promote a safe environment for students to share ideas and try something new by showing them that she is not afraid to make mistakes:

I have a student who came in to me in the beginning of the year and would just have a fit if she made the most minor, little mistake and now she laughs at my mistakes and she is beginning to laugh at hers and it is like "Good, great—we are getting there! We can take some risks."

This teacher acknowledged that this openness with her students would not have existed without the principal's strong belief in the values and beliefs underlying the Accelerated Schools process:

> He strongly believes that we are all learners and that it is okay to try things and not have them work out. If we didn't have that support from the principal, we wouldn't feel like we had the freedom to try things in our classroom, and if we didn't get out there and try new things in our classrooms, our kids would still not be risk takers.

As a result of a classroom climate that includes higher expectations and greater opportunities for self-expression and a range of ideas, students have begun to believe in themselves more. Says one teacher,

> I think they [the students] perceive themselves differently because of the high expectations we all have. . . . They know they can't get away with just sloughing, you know, they have to try their best. They don't have to be right, they don't have to not make any mistakes, but they have to try their best.

In addition to the supportive and nurturing environment that has evolved throughout the school, a number of teachers as well as the principal and school counselor talked about how much more student centered the school had become. They explained that the focus on powerful learning and developing a shared philosophy about what the school community wants for its students was instrumental in the school's transformation into a place where there is real respect for children, and students' ideas are valued and used. The school counselor said,

> Bit by bit, the individual child-orientation has really taken over from within the school. Staff are really asking the students what they think instead of assuming they [the staff] know the answers. And kids have amazed us with their insights.

This focus on students was not only a result of the school establishing a unified focus and direction but also a reflection of the Accelerated Schools process, which encourages participation and collaboration. In the surveys, interviews, and focus groups, school community members consistently referred to the strength of having a structure in place that allows for all of the members of the school community to provide input and be a part of the decision-making process. Throughout our study, we found that there was evidence of a great deal of ownership from both students and staff members in the activities and practices taking place throughout the school.

Question 2:   ***Does the specific problem-solving process embodied by the decision-making groups in accelerated schools carry over into individual classrooms?***

In the Accelerated Schools model, the inquiry process is a vehicle for reflecting on the different dimensions that make up the school and using a systematic process to address the challenges. For many, this is the first time the whole school has begun to work collaboratively to understand challenges and identify solutions to these challenges. In talking with the teachers in this study, we found that the process of bringing inquiry into the classroom was hard for teachers to identify easily. Although a number of teachers remarked that their classroom had more opportunities for student reflection and participation, they could not answer whether or not inquiry had actually filtered into the classroom. Only two of the teachers interviewed talked specifically about how inquiry had become a tool for student collaboration and problem solving and a means for students to construct and discover their own knowledge in their classroom.

One of these two teachers talked about how she had begun to use the inquiry process with her students to solve problems that arose. For example, her students tackled the dilemma of how to plan the annual winter holiday program so that it would best represent the diverse student body. Because the student population had changed so drastically, the previous program format would not adequately represent the different cultures within the school. Instead of deciding how to solve this problem herself—something she said she would have done in the past—she decided to ask her students. The students talked extensively about the problem and brainstormed possible solutions. Out of this discussion the children discovered that there were many different cultures and ways to celebrate the holidays and they decided to have a celebration where this multiculturalism could be expressed through poetry reading, art projects, music, and dancing. She and her students plan to conduct an assessment of the program, including what worked as well as what didn't, so that next year's class can feed the results back into the inquiry process. This teacher also described how the inquiry process influenced her own way of thinking of classroom instruction as well as how she communicates to her students:

> I guess I'm learning to verbalize and ask the right question. You know, when you do inquiry, the one thing I have learned is that you do need to learn how to define the problem or you need to learn how to define the question, and I wasn't doing a very good job of that. . . . It taught me that even though I thought I was doing a fairly good job in the classroom, I still wasn't defining things and presenting them clearly. I knew what I wanted, but I began to see that I wasn't articulating that to my students. . . . So that's what I've learned to do through using the inquiry process.

Both teachers said that using inquiry in the classroom has helped them develop higher-order thinking skills in their children as well as provide more opportunities for student participation in the learning process. Said one of the teachers,

> I see a comfort there now that they can come up with their own ideas and it will be okay. It allows them to sort of expand on concepts and maybe look at things a different way, because we all know learners have different modalities that you use within the classroom, and while I think I try to provide all that, I found that children can still come up with different ways to pursue something. And so I see it too as promoting their critical thinking skills. They're not just relying on me to spoon-feed them the answer. They're starting to take ownership, you know, that it's theirs and that it's okay to think about it maybe in their own way.

The other teacher described how he encourages students' inquiry about their own learning, asking them to reflect on their prior knowledge and what they want to learn. In planning a social studies unit on ancient civilizations, he asked the students to brainstorm everything that came to mind on the subject and what they wanted to learn. He found that when they had finished, the students had discussed 90% of everything he was going to cover that year. He used this as a foundation to decide what the focus of the unit would be as well as to teach to their strengths and interests. Because he felt this process was so effective in giving students more ownership and input into their own learning, he has made this a regular part of his instructional approach. Both teachers explained that their internalization of the inquiry process had led them to reflect on the purpose of what they were teaching as well as what the students were learning.

In addition, one of the teachers acknowledged that the inquiry process had caused her not only to expand her thinking but also become a more reflective person. As a result, she understands the importance of helping students to become reflective questioners in all that they undertake. She explained one way that she tries to do this in her classroom:

> I'm asking the students to reflect more, too. I have two different journals now. I have a work journal where they can put down ideas about what I consider more content area things. Then I have a feelings and idea journal and . . . I give them a chance to reflect on anything they want to. . . . In their work journal, it really gives them a time to reflect on things that they've done . . . how they feel about it, how they would change it, how would they do something differently.

Summary of Exploratory Findings

The two central questions that we attempted to answer were whether the participation in the Accelerated Schools philosophy and process changed the way teachers organize the learning process in their own classrooms, and whether the inquiry process used in the decision-making groups of accelerated schools carries over into individual classrooms.

In attempting to answer these questions, we analyzed a range of data for a single school, including teacher surveys, follow-up interviews, focus groups, a trainer's observations made during 2 years of working with the school, and the principal's observations and evaluation notes. The compilation of these different data helps provide a reasonable picture of the school both before and after the implementation of the Accelerated Schools model and further substantiate the teacher interviews upon which we focused.

Through our analysis, we found that the practices and behaviors in the classroom clearly changed for a number of teachers as a result of the internalization of the Accelerated Schools philosophy and process although it was less clear as to how much the inquiry process had filtered into the classroom. Teachers described classroom changes in teaching style, expectations, accountability, collaboration, reflection, and participation. These changes have been observed not only in the teachers interviewed but also in other teachers surveyed, including several who came to the school after the implementation of the Accelerated Schools model. According to the principal's and trainer's observations, these teachers were able to adapt to the Accelerated Schools practices because of the hiring guidelines developed at the school that supported the philosophy and process.

Teachers identified these kinds of changes as taking place because of their internalization of the philosophy and process as well as a system that is now in place at the school that encourages and supports these types of behaviors and practices. Clearly, accelerated schools led the school community to work more collaboratively than ever before, to address what they were currently doing and identify schoolwide goals and practices, and to establish a structure for decision making and systematic problem solving to take place. As found by Finnan (1992), participation in this transformation process alters school culture by transforming school norms, relationships, expectations, and practices. As we found at this school, this changing culture brought about a more trusting, collegial, and open environment in which change could take place. As individuals began to internalize the Accelerated Schools philosophy and process into their own belief systems, they began to bring it into their classroom practices. From our data analysis, we conclude that the individual changes that resulted could not happen in isolation; the changes influence each other and contribute to the overall transformation of the school. As Fullan and Stiegelbauer (1991) suggest, "The meaning of change for the future does not simply involve implementing single innovations effectively. [Rather] it means a radical change in the culture of schools and the conception of teaching as a profession" (p. 142).

Finally, we want to mention that throughout our data collection, teachers mentioned that the principal had been instrumental in supporting and encouraging the internalization of the philosophy and process by building on strengths and consistently following the process. We believe that this style of leadership—among administrative and other school community members—is crucial in building a new culture and warrants further study as to the level of impact it has on a school's success.

Future Research

We believe that this exploratory study has provided us with enough information to assist us in the next stage of research as we attempt to study more fully the changes in classroom attitudes, behaviors, and practices that result from the internalization of the Accelerated Schools philosophy and process. The findings in the initial stage of our exploratory study have produced several challenges that we will have to address in the second phase of this study:

- Teachers did not remember specific teaching examples that occurred prior to adoption of the Accelerated Schools process. Because of this, we feel that it is important that we regularly observe classrooms and interview teachers in a school that is about to embark on the Accelerated Schools model so that we will have accurate baseline data with which to compare the changes that occur as the school develops as an accelerated school.
- Although our surveys did not elicit specific examples, the questions were very helpful in providing a general understanding of people's perceptions as well as preparing us for the follow-up interviews. In the future, we would undertake more extensive interviews, both before and after the implementation of the Accelerated Schools model, and maintain a portfolio with specific lesson plans and activities.
- Because of the nature of the Accelerated Schools model, everyone in the school community has the opportunity to influence classroom practices, especially nonteaching staff members who work directly in the classroom. In our next study, we plan to focus on the influence of other school members on classroom practices and their internalization of the process and philosophy. We also plan to spend more time interviewing children about classroom changes and their understanding of the Accelerated Schools philosophy and process.
- Finally, the issue of causality for the kinds of change this exploratory study focused on continues to be a challenge. Although we

can clearly identify certain factors that contributed to individual and schoolwide change, there are many other elements that muddy this area. Even in the course of this exploratory study, one of the teachers expressed concern over how to distinguish between change that resulted from her professional growth as a teacher and from her participation in the Accelerated Schools Project. We see this as an ongoing issue for any study of accelerated schools, as the model is so firmly embedded in school culture and practice.

Appendix

Research Methods

To answer our two central research questions, we designed an exploratory study that proceeded in two stages. First, we designed and administered a survey to teachers, asking them to describe changes in their practices that had occurred over the 2 years since the Accelerated Schools model had been introduced into the school. We constructed our survey and refined it after input from colleagues who had strong knowledge of the Accelerated Schools philosophy and process as well as others who had conducted similar types of school research. The rationale behind the design of the survey was to compare what we could find out about classroom teachers' practices, attitudes, and beliefs prior to the school's adoption of the Accelerated Schools process with practices, attitudes, and beliefs 2 years after that initial launch of the school. We chose two Accelerated Schools principles (building on strengths and empowerment coupled with responsibility) and five values (equity, reflection, participation, risk taking, and high expectations) because they were more easily observable at this stage of our exploration and because they are very important components for creating and sustaining powerful learning. We hope to address the principle of unity of purpose and the other Accelerated Schools values in the course of further study. We included questions about powerful learning in our survey because we wanted to see how classroom practices and teaching philosophy had changed over the past 2 years in the views of the teachers. The last section of the survey focused on how the use of the inquiry process had influenced the classroom environment.

The surveys were distributed to all 15 teachers in the school. We chose to distribute the surveys only to teachers because we wanted to focus primarily on the changes in teacher attitudes and practices. However, the principal also gave the survey to the school counselor because he felt that she had made significant changes in her practices with students and could add some insight to our study. We realize that there are many other members of the school community who influence classroom practices and we hope to study them in the next stage of our research.

In the second stage of our exploration, we conducted follow-up interviews of a select number of teachers who had completed the survey. By interviewing these teachers one on one, we felt we could draw out more specific examples representing the changes in classroom practices due to the Accelerated Schools philosophy and process. We selected teachers to interview based on two criteria: (a) They had completed our initial survey; and (b) they had been at the school *prior* to the launch of the Accelerated Schools Project, and thus would be able to provide more insight into the changes the school community had experienced. The principal also suggested that we include the school counselor as well as a resource teacher in our interviews because he felt that their attitudes and practices had significantly changed. This meant that we had a mix of interviews that included five classroom teachers, one resource teacher, and the school counselor. All interviews were recorded and transcribed by an outside party.

In the process of conducting our interviews to see if and how classroom practices had changed, we found that it was difficult for teachers to recall specific examples of what they had done in the classroom prior to adoption of the Accelerated Schools process. In examining survey responses, we found that although teachers consistently referred to changes that had occurred at the school, their comments were much more general in content and lacked specific examples. Based upon our observation and Hook and Rosenshine's (1979) findings on the inaccuracy of teacher reports, we further substantiated the initial information we gathered by (a) conducting follow-up interviews lasting from 40 to 90 minutes in which we asked for specific examples of classroom practices rather than general perceptions, (b) drawing on the observations of the Accelerated Schools trainer who had facilitated the school's initial launch and had observed teachers' classrooms prior to the implementation of the Accelerated Schools model, (c) drawing on the principal's classroom observations of teachers as well as the changing school culture, and (d) eliciting feedback from two focus groups—one with eight sixth-grade students and one with five teachers (two who had participated in follow-up interviews)—for further insight into the kinds of changes that had infiltrated the classroom since the implementation of the project.

Reflection

Making Learning Come Alive
in Accelerated Schools

JANE McCARTHY

The four chapters in this part provide illustrations of the impact that the Accelerated Schools philosophy and principles can have on the way schools facilitate teaching and learning. All of the chapters describe how the Accelerated Schools Project provides a structure and process that allows change to occur in a school. The transformation of a traditional school to an accelerated school takes time—approximately 6 years. However, the process also facilitates immediate changes, some as a result of the participants simply looking at the realities of life in their school community for the first time and identifying the strengths and challenges.

School communities are usually fairly united in the belief that all children should have equitable access to powerful learning experiences that allow them to accelerate their learning. The practices selected and pilot-tested for achieving this goal vary according to the dynamics of the specific school community. Some schools are unsure what powerful learning should or could look like. A visit to another accelerated school sometimes makes the vision become reality, as evidenced by the visit of the J. W. Faulk faculty to Hollibrook School in Houston. As Olivier describes in Chapter 11, seeing the principles and practices being lived in the classrooms and seeing children successfully engaged in academic endeavors while remaining focused and on task provided the Faulk teachers with the belief that they too could do this!

My own years of experience with accelerated schools as the national director of the Satellite Center Project and now as the director of the University of Nevada-Las Vegas Satellite Center have enabled me to experience the growth of schools all over the country as they engage in the process of acceleration. As the school communities formulate their visions of an ideal school, almost without exception, they state that they want to keep all children in the regular classroom. They do not like pull-out programs, whether for learning-disabled students or for gifted and talented students. Teachers are clear in their desire to keep all children with them throughout the day. In Chapter 12, Levin and I detail the stories of five schools as they developed unique solutions to the issue of full inclusion. Shared vision enabled them to make sacrifices in time and energy to plan carefully for programs in which children and teachers are supported in the regular classroom. The enthusiasm and dedication of these efforts stand in stark contrast to schools in which inclusion is mandated by the state or district, and teachers and the school community are not allowed to plan carefully for its implementation, support, and evaluation. I think the success of these five programs should send a strong message to policymakers trying to bring about inclusion at the school or district level. Vision and belief must come first. Otherwise, compliance may be superficial and short lived.

A common theme runs through all four chapters in this part—the theme of the enthusiasm and passion that are generated in students, teachers, parents, and administrators as powerful learning practices are implemented in classrooms. School becomes a place where people want to be. Absences decrease. Transiency decreases. Teacher turnover drops. People in the school community become empowered, and in particular, students become empowered as learners who help to direct and take responsibility for their own learning. In Chapter 14, Keller and Soler report from interviews with students that they recognize clearly the profound changes in the way that teaching and learning took place in their classrooms after the advent of the Accelerated Schools Project. In Chapter 13, Gonzalez and Tucher found dramatic changes in the level of participation of families in the education of their children. Parents began to share in the responsibility for the education of their children. They, too, became actively involved in powerful learning experiences that built on their strengths. Olivier found that teachers who were burned out and overwhelmed by the hopelessness of their situations came alive with a renewed sense of direction and the possibilities of success for themselves and their students.

Each chapter also describes the risk taking in classrooms that brings the Accelerated Schools philosophy and practices to life in small stages as well as in schoolwide stages. The notion of the big wheels, little wheels change is dramatically described in Chapter 12 (Levin & McCarthy) and Chapter 14 (Keller & Soler). Small risks often lead to schoolwide implementation. The use of inquiry by individuals in the school community parallels the schoolwide change efforts that take time to design and implement. The little wheels are what help keep the vision and dream alive during the schoolwide change efforts. As Olivier stated, consensus comes hard and is a practice many schools must spend time developing and perfecting. The old top-down practice of decision making dies hard. "But we've always done it that way" is commonly heard as school communities struggle to break out of old ways of teaching and learning. Although what we have always done may not be working, we at least know how to do it. When we break out of the familiar role of classroom teacher, we are leaving our comfort zone behind.

The courageous pioneers who break the old molds and blaze new trails in the classroom enable others to follow and take their own risks with new ways of providing curriculum and instruction. The first-grade teachers in Salt Lake City who piloted full inclusion paved the way for the second grade to follow the next year and the rest of the school the following year. Through the inquiry process, they were able to pilot-test and evaluate new ways of inclusion and to provide powerful data describing the success of their efforts. Few can argue with the kinds of successes they produced in the growth rates of their children in reading. High expectations for all students resulted in dramatic growth.

Hoover's success with their after-school reading program is another example of pioneering efforts. By taking the "yes, buts" out of their vocabulary, they created a shared vision of what they wanted their students to know and be able to do and then set out to get the resources to initiate the powerful learning necessary for success.

The message of these chapters is clear. Research, evaluation, and documentation of the powerful learning and curricular practices implemented in accelerated schools are critical to inform future efforts. School communities can take strength from the successes of other projects and draw caution from the challenges faced in implementation. We cannot aspire to what we cannot envision. The stories presented in these chapters show the possibilities of dreams enacted as diverse school communities create and implement powerful learning strategies designed to enable all students to achieve to the maximum of their ability.

The change process can be painful, as all of the stories attest. However, the struggle with beliefs leads to changes in practice that irrevocably affect the lives of students, teachers, administrators, and parents in accelerated schools. As Olivier asserts at the end of Chapter 11, the teachers at her school now "have a changed concept of what education is and what their role in it can be. This concept has been fundamentally altered and can never be reversed." The results of this change can only lead to improved educational experiences and equitable access to powerful learning for all children. We are creating children who are empowered learners who take responsibility for creating their own knowledge. We are building the capacity of these children to become lifelong learners and inquirers by building on their strengths and giving them the tools necessary to be successful in the classroom and in life. We are also adding to the body of knowledge about effective teaching and learning.

Curriculum and instruction in accelerated schools are challenging and dynamic. The implementation of powerful learning, which builds on the philosophy and principles of the Accelerated Schools model, leads to amazing success stories. As more school communities develop their own plans for change geared to their own particular strengths and challenges, the successful results cannot help but be multiplied. The Accelerated Schools process provides the tools necessary for radical changes to take place in the way schools approach learning. These schools are exciting, happy places for teachers, students, administrators, and parents.

Resources

Accelerated Schools Philosophy and Process Defined

Accelerated Schools Philosophy

The Accelerated Schools philosophy draws heavily on the work of the educator and philosopher John Dewey. Dewey was concerned that society treated schools in poor neighborhoods unfairly and that schools were stifling the creativity and inquisitiveness of children by not allowing them to be actively involved in their own learning. He chided educators who felt that schools for the poor and underprivileged were adequate, because he knew that they would be considered inadequate for more privileged children (Dewey, 1984). This principle of doing for all students what any of us would want to do for our own children is at the heart of the Accelerated Schools Project. The Accelerated Schools Project carries this principle one step further—do for all students what we do for our brightest students, accelerate their learning. The Accelerated Schools Project also builds on Dewey's belief that a democratic education implies faith in the potential of children and adults to understand and shape the world around them (Dewey, 1984). He also believed that individuals begin to realize this potential when they take active roles in exploring and understanding shared problems (Dewey, 1984). This belief is evident in the Accelerated Schools principles and in the collaborative governance structure established at each school.

The Three Accelerated Schools Principles

The Accelerated Schools Project is built upon three principles; a set of values; and a commitment to powerful learning through integration of curriculum, instruction, and organization that reflect Dewey's philosophy of education. Three principles lie at the foundation of the project—unity of purpose, school-site empowerment through decision making, and responsibility for results at the school site—together with an instructional approach that builds on the strengths of the school community (students, teachers, administrators, other staff, and parents) rather than on their weaknesses. The Accelerated Schools Project is based on the notion that lasting change cannot occur in schools without a change in thinking similar to that reflected in these principles.

Unity of Purpose

Unity of purpose refers to the striving among parents, teachers, students, and administrators toward a common set of goals for the school that is the focal point of everyone's efforts. A central element of the unity agreement must be to transform the school into an accelerated one that will make students academically able at an early date so that they can fully benefit from their further schooling experiences and adult opportunities. The Accelerated Schools Project is built on the belief that the all-inclusive process of defining a common purpose is extremely important in and of itself. Only by including from the start all of the parties involved in the planning and design of educational programs, the implementation of those programs, and the evaluation of those programs can one ensure more cohesive educational efforts and a greater commitment to those efforts. Unity of purpose stands in contrast to disjointed planning, implementation, and evaluation of educational programs.

Empowerment Coupled With Responsibility

Empowerment with responsibility means the key participants in a school community (a) make important educational decisions, (b) take responsibility for implementing those decisions, and (c) take responsibility for the outcomes for those decisions. In the Accelerated Schools Project, it is seen as necessary to break the present stalemate among administrators, teachers, parents, and students in which the participants tend to blame each other as well as other factors "beyond their control" for the poor educational outcomes of students. Unless all of the major actors can be empowered to seek a common set of goals and influence the educational and social processes to realize those goals, it is unlikely that the desired improvements will take place or be sustained.

Building on Strengths

Building on strengths means using all of the learning resources that students, parents, school staff, and communities bring to the educational endeavor. According to the Accelerated Schools Project, in the quest to place blame for the lack of efficacy of schools in improving the education for students at risk, it is easy to exaggerate weaknesses of the various participants and ignore their strengths. Parents, students, teachers, and administrators all have strengths no matter what their educational, economic, cultural, or linguistic background. The Accelerated Schools Project is based on the belief that parents can be powerful allies in the educational process because they have a deep love for their children and a desire for them to succeed. The key is making parents feel comfortable at and important to the school, and guiding them in activities that assist their children educationally.

The Accelerated Schools Values

Underlying the principles of Accelerated Schools are a set of values, beliefs, and attitudes that are necessary to create the culture for accelerated school change. The following values, attitudes, and beliefs are interrelated:

Equity: All students can learn and have an equal right to a high-quality education.

Participation: Students participate in learning; all school staff participate in school decision making; parents participate in the school and have decision-making responsibilities and opportunities.

Communication/community: Students engage in active and group learning. School staff and community work toward a shared purpose by meeting, talking, and learning from each others' experiences.

Reflection: Students engage in problem-solving exercises and interpretive approaches to curricula. Teachers and other adults constantly scrutinize the world of the school and address challenges to school improvement.

Experimentation: Students are involved in discovery exercises. All school staff and parents launch, implement, and evaluate experimental programs as a result of communicating about and reflecting upon the school's problems.

Trust: Teachers, parents, administrators, and students must believe in each other and focus on each other's strengths.

Risk taking: All parties must be more entrepreneurial in their efforts. Although some new programs fail, the ones that succeed are the keys to lasting school improvement.

Professionalization: The entire school community has the ability to understand and respond to school challenges, and because of the wealth of talent and experience within the school, can acquire additional expertise.

Powerful Learning Through Integration of Curriculum, Instruction, and Organization

The Accelerated Schools Project does not set forth a recipe for creating powerful learning experiences. There is no checklist of features that make up an accelerated school. Rather, the model builds the capacity of each school to assess its needs and develop integrated plans that will lead to the school's unique vision. Although each accelerated school will choose a different path according to its unique needs, every accelerated school should aim to bring all children into the educational mainstream by a set deadline and should adhere to a common core of powerful learning tenets.

In the Accelerated Schools Project, one of the most important aspects of powerful learning philosophy is the fact that the education we use with "gifted" children works well for *all* children. The Accelerated Schools model encourages school communities to create situations in which every school day encompasses the best things we know about curriculum, instruction, and organization. The Accelerated Schools philosophy creates learning situations in which each student has an interest in learning, sees a meaning in the lesson, perceives connections between this school activity and his or her real life, is able to learn actively, and can learn in ways that build on his or her own strengths. Accelerated school communities should work together to create powerful learning experiences in which each child is treated as gifted; higher-order and complex activities are stressed; content is relevant; and children actively discover the curriculum objectives in a safe environment, rather than passively going through textbooks and filling out worksheets. The safe environment for learning extends far beyond the classroom into every aspect of the school, home, and community. The Accelerated Schools Project encourages participants to think about their own powerful learning experiences and what made those experiences so powerful.

The second part of the Accelerated Schools learning philosophy is seeing every powerful learning experience as having three dimensions.

The first dimension is *what* is taught—the content or curriculum. The second dimension is *how* the content is taught—instruction. The third dimension is the context, or organization in which one galvanizes all available resources to *achieve* the what and how. Context, or organization, includes the use of time, flexibility of the schedule, deployment of staffing, funding, and so forth. Part IV further examines powerful learning in accelerated schools.

Accelerated Schools Project Process

Taking Stock

Taking stock, one of the first steps in becoming an accelerated school, is designed to encourage the school community to look extensively and intensively for pertinent information about the present situation at the school. The focus is on finding the strengths as well as the challenges currently present at the school. Information is gathered on areas the school deems important. Areas can include the history of the school and information on students, staff, school facilities, curriculum, instruction, the organization of the school, the existing governance structure, and the community of the families.

The process of collecting, reporting, and discussing the baseline information usually takes several months of research, compilation, analysis, and discussion. Schools are encouraged to collect data through document review, surveys, interviews, and observations. The process provides important baseline information on which the more extensive inquiry process rests and to which participants can later compare progress. The Accelerated Schools Project encourages the entire school community to actively participate in gathering the baseline data so that participants will begin to develop a sense of ownership over the process.

Developing and Celebrating a Vision

All accelerated schools establish a vision for the school during the early phases of the project. The vision is a shared product of the dreams of all participants (teachers, administration, other staff, parents, district administrators, the community, and students). Everyone is asked to contribute attributes of the ideal school. These attributes are synthesized into a statement of shared hopes. The process of defining a vision results in ownership of a common goal and long-term commitment to jointly achieving that goal.

Setting Priorities

After completing the above phases, accelerated schools compare their baseline (which they systematically examined through taking stock) with their vision to determine how to move toward the vision. School community members examine the baseline information to determine how and where it falls short of the vision. They generate a set of priorities that, if addressed, will move the school toward the vision. The Accelerated Schools Project encourages schools to limit themselves to three or four priorities, saving some for future work. This is a crucial activity because the cadres set up to address the priorities form the core of the Accelerated Schools governance structure.

Creating a New Governance Structure

The new governance structure of an accelerated school brings the three guiding principles to life. The vision gives the governance groups clear goals toward which to organize their work. The principle of building on strengths acknowledges the contributions all members of the school community (both individually and collectively) can make as they become more active in the governance of the school. The principle of empowerment coupled with responsibility is the essence of school-based management. The Accelerated Schools Project researchers have found that three levels of participation are necessary to encompass the range of issues that must be addressed in a democratic and productive way: cadres, a steering committee, and the school as a whole. To function democratically, all of these governance vehicles should have members drawn from the school staff, parents and community, and the student body.

Cadres are the small groups organized around the school's challenge areas (as determined during the setting priorities stage). Cadres can be formed for continuing inquiry into areas such as curriculum or family involvement or for episodic challenges, such as planning for new facilities or finding time for other cadres to work. The cadres analyze and solve problems using the inquiry process. They systematically examine the underlying causes of the specific problems that the school faces and search for, implement, and evaluate solutions. Cadres comprise a self-selected membership set during the setting priorities stage.

The roles in the cadres are clearly defined so that all of the work does not fall to one person. Each cadre should have a facilitator, recorder, visionary, timekeeper, and closure person.

The steering committee consists of the principal and representative teachers, aides, other school staff, students, and parents. The steering committee serves at least five purposes: First, it serves to ensure that cadres continually move in the direction of the school vision. Second, it serves as a clearinghouse of information so that cadres communicate and do not operate in isolation. Third, the steering committee ensures that cadres stay on track with the inquiry process. Fourth, the steering committee monitors the progress of the cadres and helps develop a set of recommendations for consideration by the school as a whole. Finally, it deals with incoming information to the school as a whole.

School as a whole refers to the principal, teachers, teachers' aides, other instructional and noninstructional staff, and parent representatives as well as student representatives. The school as a whole is required to approve all major decisions on curriculum, instruction, and resource allocation that have implications for the entire school. The school as a whole must approve decisions before cadres begin implementation of experimental programs.

Inquiry

Inquiry is a process of identifying and solving problems. It is an ongoing process that does not stop after a few meetings or once initial challenges are met. Inquiry and the Accelerated Schools governance structure perpetuate restructuring and keep a school accelerating. The inquiry process is focused on asking the right questions—questions whose answers truly address a school's original concerns stemming from the comparison of the school's present situation with its vision. Decision making in accelerated schools is very systematic and is accomplished in five phases: focus on the problem, brainstorm solutions, synthesize solutions, implement or pilot-test, and evaluate and reassess. Chapter 2 provides a more complete description of the process.

References

Accelerated Schools Newsletter. (1994, Winter). Stanford, CA: National Center for the Accelerated Schools Project.

Accelerated Schools Project Team. (1991). *Accelerated Schools Project: Resource guide.* Stanford University, Accelerated Schools Project.

Argyris, C. (1993). *Actionable knowledge.* San Francisco: Jossey-Bass.

Argyris, C., Putnam, R. W., & Smith, D. M. (1985). *Action science.* San Francisco: Jossey-Bass.

Argyris, C., & Schön, D. A. (1973). *Theory in practice: Increasing professional effectiveness.* San Francisco: Jossey-Bass.

Ascher, C. (1993). *Changing schools for urban students: The school development program, accelerated schools, and success for all* (Trends and Issues No. 18). New York: Educational Resources Information Center Clearinghouse on Urban Education.

Ascher, C., & Burnett, G. (1993). *Current trends and issues in urban education, 1993* (Trends and Issues No. 19). New York: Educational Resources Information Center Clearinghouse on Urban Education.

Austin, G. R. (1979). Exemplary schools and the search for effectiveness. *Educational Leadership, 37*(1), 10-14.

Bardach, E. (1980). *The implementation game: What happens after a bill becomes a law.* Cambridge: MIT Press.

Barrett, P. A. (1991). *Doubts and certainties: Working together to restructure schools* (NEA School Restructuring Series). Washington, DC: National Education Association.

Barth, R. (1990). *Improving schools from within: Teachers, parents, and principals can make the difference.* San Francisco: Jossey-Bass.

Bass, B. M. (1987). *Leadership and performance beyond expectations.* New York: Free Press.

Beck, L., & Murphy, J. (1993). *Understanding the principalship: Metaphorical themes, 1920s-1990s.* New York: Teachers College Press.

Berman, B., & McLaughlin, M. W. (1976). Implementation of educational innovation. *Educational Forum, 40*(3), 345-370.

Berman, B., & McLaughlin, M. W. (1977). *Federal programs supporting educational change: Vol. 7. Factors affecting implementation and continuation.* Santa Monica, CA: Rand.

Bogue, G. (1985). *The enemies of leadership: Lessons for leaders in education.* Bloomington, IN: Phi Delta Kappan.

Bolman, L. G., Johnson, S. M., Murphy, J. T., & Weiss, C. H. (1991). Rethinking school leadership: An agenda for research and reform. In P. W. Thurston & P. P. Zodhiates (Eds.), *Advances in educational administration: An annual series of analytical essays and critical reviews: School leadership* (Vol. 2, pp. 21-50). Greenwich, CT: JAI.

Bonstingl, J. J. (1992). *Schools of quality. An introduction to total quality management in education.* Alexandria, VA: Association for Supervision and Curriculum.

Bowles, S., & Gintis, H. (1976). *Schooling in capitalist America.* New York: Basic Books.

Bowles, S., & Levin, H. M. (1968a, Winter). The determinants of scholastic achievement— An appraisal of some recent evidence. *Journal of Human Resources,* pp. 1-24.

Bowles, S., & Levin, H. M. (1968b, Summer). More on multicollinearity and the effectiveness of schools. *Journal of Human Resources,* pp. 393-400.

Boyd, W. L. (1989, October). *What makes ghetto schools work or not work?* Invited paper prepared for the conference The Truly Disadvantaged, sponsored by the Social Science Research Council, Committee for Research on the Urban Underclass, and the Center for Urban Affairs and Policy Research, Northwestern University, Evanston, IL.

Bradley, A. (1989, November). School-restructuring efforts forcing principals to redefine their roles. *Education Week.*

Bradley, A. (1990, May). Study notes lack of policy activity on principalship. *Education Week.*

Brandt, R. (1992a, February). On rethinking leadership: A conversation with Tom Sergiovanni. *Educational Leadership, 49*(5), 46-49.

Brandt, R. (1992b, September). On building learning communities: A conversation with Hank Levin. *Educational Leadership, 50*(1), 19-23.

Bridges, E. M. (1992). *Problem based learning for administrators.* Eugene: University of Oregon, ERIC Clearinghouse on Educational Management.

Brooks, J., & Brooks, M. (1993). *In search of understanding: The case for constructivist classrooms.* Alexandria, VA: Association for Supervision and Curriculum Development.

Brown v. Board of Education, 347 U.S. 483 (1954).

Brunner, I., & Hopfenberg, W. (1992, April). *The interactive production of knowledge in accelerated schools: Big wheels and little wheels interacting.* Paper presented at the Annual Meeting of the American Educational Research Association, San Francisco.

Burns, J. M. (1978). *Leadership.* New York: Harper & Row.

Carnoy, M., & Levin, H. M. (1976). *The limits of educational reform.* New York: Longman.

Carnoy, M., & Levin, H. M. (1985). *Schooling and work in the democratic state.* Stanford, CA: Stanford University Press.

Chasin, G., & Levin, H. (1994). Thomas Edison accelerated elementary school. In J. Oakes & K. H. Quartz (Eds.), *Creating new educational communities, schools, and classrooms where all children can be smart* (pp. 130-146). Chicago: University of Chicago Press.

Chenoweth, T. (1992, July). Emerging national models of schooling for at-risk students. *International Journal of Educational Reform, 1*(3), 255-269.

Christensen, G. (1992, April). *The changing role of the administrator in an accelerated school.* Paper presented at the Annual Meeting of the American Educational Research Association, San Francisco.

Christensen, G. (1994). *The role of the principal in transforming accelerated schools: A study using the critical incident technique to identify behaviors of principals.* Doctoral dissertation, Stanford University.

Coleman, J. S., Campbell, E. Q., Hobson, C. J., McPartland, J., Mood, A. M., Weinfeld, F. D., & York, R. L. (1966). *Equity of equal education opportunity.* Washington, DC: Government Printing Office.

Conley, D. T. (1992). *Some emerging trends in school restructuring.* Eugene, OR: ERIC Clearinghouse on Educational Management.

Coons, J., Clune, W., & Sugarman, S. (1970). *Private wealth and public education.* Cambridge, MA: Belknap Press of Harvard University.

Crow, G. (1994). The principalship: In search of an identity. *Educational Leadership, 23*(1), 33-34.

Cuban, L. (1984). *How teachers taught: Consistency and change in American classrooms, 1890-1980.* White Plains, NY: Longman.

Cuban, L. (1992). What happens to reforms that last? The case of the junior high school. *American Educational Research Journal, 29*(2), 227-252.

Davidson, B. M. (1992). *Building school capacity to accelerate learning: A study of school restructuring processes in four elementary schools.* Doctoral dissertation, University of New Orleans.

Dewey, J. (1929). *The sources of a science education.* New York: Liveright.

Dewey, J. (1984a). Creative democracy: The task before us. In J. A. Boydston (Ed.), *John Dewey: The later works, 1925-1953. Vol. 2: 1925-1927.* Carbondale: Southern Illinois University Press.

Dewey, J. (1984b). The public and its problems. In J. A. Boydston (Ed.), *John Dewey: The later works, 1925-1953. Vol. 2: 1925-1927.* Carbondale: Southern Illinois University Press.

Dunlap, D. M., & Goldman, P. (1991). Rethinking power in schools. *Educational Administration Quarterly, 27*(1), 5-29.

Elmore, R. F. (1990). *Restructuring schools.* San Francisco: Jossey-Bass.

English, F. W., & Hill, J. C. (1990). *Restructuring: The principal and curriculum change. A report of the NASSP curriculum council.* Reston, VA: National Association of the Secondary School Principals.

English, R. A. (1992). *Accelerated schools report.* Columbia: University of Missouri, Department of Educational and Counseling Psychology.

Epstein, J. L. (1988). Effective schools or effective students: Dealing with diversity. In R. Haskins & D. Macrae (Eds.), *Policies for America's public schools* (pp. 89-126). Norwood, NJ: Ablex.

Finnan, C. (1992). *Becoming an accelerated middle school: Initiating school culture change* (Report prepared for the National Center for the Accelerated Schools Project).

Finnan, C. (1994). Studying an accelerated school: Schoolwide cultural therapy. In G. Spindler & L. Spindler (Eds.), *Pathways to cultural awareness: Cultural therapy with teachers and students* (pp. 93-129). Thousand Oaks, CA: Corwin.

Finnan, C., & Levin, H. (1994, April). *Using school organization and culture to raise school effectiveness.* Paper presented at the Annual Meeting of the American Educational Research Association, San Francisco.

Flanagan, J. C. (1954). The critical incidental technique. *Psychological Bulletin, 51*(4), 327-358.

Fullan, M. G. (1982). *The meaning of educational change.* New York: Teachers College Press.

Fullan, M. G. (1992, February). Visions that blind. *Educational Leadership, 49*(5), 19-20.

Fullan, M. G. (1993). *Change forces: Probing the depths of the educational reform.* London: Falmer.

Fullan, M. G., Bennett, B., & Rolheiser-Bennett, C. (1989). *Linking classroom and school improvement.* Invited address, American Educational Research Association, San Francisco.

Fullan, M. G., & Stiegelbauer, S. (1991). *The new meaning of educational change.* New York: Teachers College Press.

Gardner, H. (1983). *Frames of mind.* New York: Basic Books.

Gideonse, H. D. (1990). Organizing school to encourage teacher inquiry. In R. F. Elmore & Associates (Eds.), *Restructuring schools: The next generation of educational reform* (pp. 92-124). San Francisco: Jossey-Bass.

Giroux, H. (1992). Educational leadership and the crisis of democratic government. *Educational Researcher, 21*(4), 4-11.

Goodlad, J. I. (1984). *A place called school: Prospects for the future.* New York: McGraw-Hill.

Gorton, R., & Schneider, G. (1991). *School-based leadership: Challenges and opportunities* (3rd ed.). Dubuque, IA: William C. Brown.

Griffiths, D. E. (1989, April). *Where are the administrators in the reform movement?* Paper presented at Portland State University, Portland, OR.

Guthrie, J., Kleindorfer, B., Levin, H. M., & Stout, R. (1971). *Schools and inequality.* Cambridge: MIT Press.

Guthrie, L. F., & van Heusden Hale, S. (1990, September). *Improvement efforts for low-performing schools.* San Francisco: Far West Laboratory for Educational Research and Development.

Halcomb, E. (1993). The rule for change: Show, don't tell. *Educational Leadership, 51*(2), 17-18.

Hall, G. E., & Hord, S. M. (1987). *Change in schools.* New York: State University of New York Press.

Hallinger, P. (1992). The evolving role of American principals: From managerial to instructional to transformational leaders. *Journal of Research and Development in Education, 30*(3), 35-48.

Hallinger, P., Murphy, J., & Hausman, C. (1991). Restructuring schools: Principals' perceptions of fundamental educational reform. *Educational Administration Quarterly* (Special edition).

Holly, P. (1989). Action research: Cul-de-sac or turnpike? *Peabody Journal of Education, 64*(3), 71-108.

Hook, C., & Rosenshine, B. (1979). Accuracy of teacher reports of their classroom behavior. *Review of Educational Research, 49*(1), 1-12.

Hopfenberg, W. S., Levin, H. M., Brunner, I., Chase, C., Christensen, S. G., Keller, B., Moore, M., Rodriguez, G., & Soler, P. (1993). *The accelerated schools resource guide.* San Francisco: Jossey-Bass.

Hopfenberg, W., Levin, H., Meister, G., & Rogers, J. (1990, February). *Accelerated schools for at-risk youth* (Accelerated Schools Project, CERAS 402S). Stanford, CA: Stanford University, School of Education.

House Subcommittee on Elementary, Secondary, and Vocational Education. (1992, August). *Hearing on innovative approaches for teaching disadvantaged students.* Washington, DC: U.S. Congress.

Jackall, R., & Levin, H. M. (Eds.). (1984). *Worker cooperatives in America.* Berkeley & Los Angeles: University of California Press.

Jacullo-Noto, J. (1992). *Action research and school restructuring: The lessons learned.* Paper presented at the Annual Meeting of the American Educational Research Association, San Francisco.

Joyce, B., Hersh, R. H., & McKibbin, M. (1983). *The structure of school improvement.* New York: Longman.

Joyce, B., Wolf, J., & Calhoun, E. (1993). *The self-renewing school.* Alexandria, VA: Association for Supervision and Curriculum Development.

Keedy, J. L. (1990). Traditional norms of school and the issue of organization change. *Planning & Changing, 21*(3), 140-145.

Knight, S., & Stallings, J. (1994). The implementation of the accelerated schools model in an urban elementary school. In R. Allington & S. Walmsley (Eds.), *No quick fix: Rethinking literacy programs in American elementary schools* (pp. 236-252). New York: Teachers College Press.

Kozol, J. (1991). *Savage inequalities.* New York: Crown.

Leithwood, K. A. (1992, February). The move toward transformational leadership. *Educational Leadership, 49*(5), 8-12.

Leithwood, K. A. (1993). *Contributions of transformational leadership to school restructuring.* Invited address to the 1993 Convention of the University Council for Educational Administration, Houston, TX.

LeTendre, B. G. (1991). *Implementing accelerated schools: Leadership roles of principals.* Paper presented at the Annual Meeting of the American Educational Research Association, Chicago.

LeTendre, B. G. (1993a). *Examples of activities during on-site visits to guide the self-renewal cycle.* Unpublished manuscript.

LeTendre, B. G. (1993b). *The self-renewal cycle of Missouri accelerated schools.* Unpublished manuscript.

Levin, H. M. (1968a, June). The failure of the public schools and the free market remedy. *Urban Review, 2,* 32-37.

Levin, H. M. (1968b). *Recruiting teachers for large-city schools* [memo]. Washington, DC: Brookings Institution.

Levin, H. M. (1970a). *Community control of schools.* Washington, DC: Brookings Institution.

Levin, H. M. (1970b, Winter). A cost-effectiveness analysis of teacher selection. *Journal of Human Resources,* pp. 24-33.

Levin, H. M. (1970c). A new model of school effectiveness. In A. Mood (Ed.), *Do teachers make a difference?* (pp. 55-78) (U.S. Office of Education). Washington, DC: Government Printing Office.

Levin, H. M. (1974). Educational reform and social change. *Journal of Applied Behavioral Science, 10*(3), 304-320.

Levin, H. M. (1976). A taxonomy of educational reforms for changes in the nature of work. In M. Carnoy & H. M. Levin (Eds.), *The limits of educational reform* (pp. 83-114). New York: Longman.

Levin, H. M. (1985). *The educationally disadvantaged: A national crisis.* Philadelphia: Public/Private Ventures.

Levin, H. M. (1986). *Educational reform for disadvantaged students: An emerging crisis.* Washington, DC: National Education Association.

Levin, H. M. (1987a). *Accelerated schools for at-risk students* (CPRE Research Report RR-110). Paper commissioned by the Center for Policy Research in Education, Rutgers University.

Levin, H. M. (1987b). Accelerated schools for the disadvantaged. *Educational Leadership, 44*(6), 19-21.

Levin, H. M. (1987c). New schools for the disadvantaged. *Teacher Education Quarterly, 14*(4), 60-83.

Levin, H. M. (1988a, September). *Accelerated schools for at-risk students* (Research Report Series RR-010). New Brunswick, NJ: Rutgers University, Center for Policy Research in Education, Consortium for Policy Research in Education.

Levin, H. M. (1988b). Accelerating elementary education for disadvantaged students. In Council of Chief State School Officers, *School success for students at risk* (pp. 209-226). Orlando, FL: Harcourt Brace Jovanovich.

Levin, H. M. (1988c, November). *Don't remediate: Accelerate.* Paper presented at the Accelerating the Education of At-Risk Students, an invitational conference sponsored by the Stanford University School of Education with support from the Rockefeller Foundation, Center for Educational Research at Stanford, 402 SCERAS, Stanford University, Standard, CA.

Levin, H. M. (1988d). *Towards accelerated schools.* New Brunswick, NJ: Rutgers University, Center for Policy Research in Education.

Levin, H. M. (1989a, May). Accelerated schools: A new strategy for at-risk students. *Policy Bulletin* (Bloomington, IN), 6.

Levin, H. M. (1989b). Financing the education of at-risk students. *Educational Evaluation and Policy Analysis, 11*(1), 47-60.

Levin, H. M. (1989c, November). *Interview conducted with author at Stanford University* [Transcribed audiocassette].

Levin, H. M. (1993a, January). *Accelerated schools after six years.* Paper presented at Learning Research and Development Center, University of Pittsburgh, Pittsburgh, PA.

Levin, H. M. (1993b). Learning from accelerated schools. In J. H. Block, S. T. Everson, & T. R. Guskey (Eds.), *Selecting and integrating school improvement programs.* New York: Scholastic Books.

Levin, H. M., & Chasin, G. (1994). Thomas Valley School accelerated elementary school. In *Creating new educational communities, schools and classrooms where all children can be smart.* Chicago: University of Chicago Press.

Lieberman, A., Zuckerman, D., Wilkie, A., Smith, E., Barinas, N., Hergert, L., & Harrington, D. (1991, August). *Early lessons in restructuring schools: Case studies of schools of tomorrow . . . today.* New York: Teachers College Press.

Lipham, J. M., & Daresh, J. C. (1970). *Administration and staff relationships in education: Research and practice in IGE schools.* Madison: Wisconsin Research and Development Center for Individualized Schooling.

Lipham, J. M., & Rankin, R. E. (1981). *Administration and operation of selected secondary schools.* Madison: Wisconsin Research and Development Center for Individualized Schooling.

Little, J. W. (1993). Professional development in a climate of educational reform. *Educational Evaluation and Policy Analysis, 15*(2), 129-152.

Lofland, J., & Lofland, L. H. (1984). *Analyzing social settings: A guide to qualitative observation and analysis.* Belmont, CA: Wadsworth.

Lortie, D. C. (1975). *Schoolteacher: A sociological study.* Chicago: University of Chicago Press.

Lugg, C., & Boyd, W. (1993). Leadership for collaboration: Reducing risk and fostering resilience. *Phi Delta Kappan, 75*(3), 253-258.

Lunenburg, F. (1992). The current educational reform movement—History, progress to date, and the future. *Education and Urban Society, 25*(1), 3-17.

Mason Elementary School: Helping children beat the odds. (1993). *Accelerated Schools, 3*(1), 4-9.

McCarthy, J., & Still, S. (1993). Hollibrook Accelerated Elementary School. In J. Murphy & P. Hallinger (Eds.), *Restructuring schooling: Learning from ongoing efforts* (pp. 63-83). Newbury Park, CA: Corwin.

McKernan, J. (1989). Action research and curriculum development. *Peabody Journal of Education, 64*(2), 6-19.

McLaren, P. (1989). *Life in schools.* New York: Longman.

Meza, J., St. John, E. P., Davidson, B., & Allen-Haynes, L. (1993/1994). Discovering the meaning of empowerment. *Louisiana Educational Research Journal, 19*(2), 11-22.

Miles, M. B., & Huberman, A. M. (1984). *Qualitative data analysis.* Beverly Hills, CA: Sage.

Miron, L. F., & Elliott, R. J. (1991). The moral exercise of power: A post-structural analysis of school administration. *Review Journal of Philosophy and Social Science, 16*(1), 32-42.

Miron, L. F., & St. John, E. P. (1994). *The urban context and the meaning of school reform* (Working Paper No. 21). University of New Orleans, Division of Urban Research and Public Policy.

Mitchell, D. E., & Tucker, S. (1992, February). Leadership as a way of thinking. *Educational Leadership, 49*(5), 30-35.

Mitchell, R. (1992). Measuring up: Student assessment and systemic change. *Educational Technology, 32*(11), 37-41.

Murphy, J. (1990). *Restructuring schools: Looking at the teaching-learning process.* Paper presented at the Annual Convention of the University Council for Educational Administration, Pittsburgh, PA.

Murphy, J. (1991). *Restructuring schools: Capturing and assessing the phenomena.* New York: Teachers College Press.

Murphy, J., & Hallinger, P. (1992). The principalship in an era of transformation. *Journal of Educational Administration, 30*(3), 77-88.

Nadler, D. A., & Tushman, M. L. (1989). Leadership for organizational change. In A. M. Mohraman, Jr. & Associates (Eds.), *Large-scale organizational change* (pp. 100-119). San Francisco: Jossey-Bass.

National Commission on Excellence in Education. (1983). *A nation at risk: The imperative for educational reform.* Washington, DC: Government Printing Office.

Norris, C. A., & Reigeluth, C. M. (1991). *A national survey of systemic school restructuring.* In Proceedings of Selected Research Presentations at the Annual Convention of the Association for Educational Communications and Technology.

Patterson, J. (1993). *Leadership for tomorrow's schools.* Alexandria, VA: Association for Supervision and Curriculum Development.

Prager, K. (1992). *Bibliography on school restructuring, 1992.* Madison, WI: Center for Research on the Context of Secondary School Teaching.

Reading recovery: Executive summary. (1992). Columbus: Ohio State University.

Reitzug, U. (1994). A case study of empowering principal behavior. *American Educational Research Journal, 31*(2), 283-307.

Roberts, N. (1985). Transforming leadership: A process of collective action. *Human Relations, 38*(11), 1023-1046.

Rogers, J. (1993, May). The inclusion revolution. *Research bulletin 11.* Bloomington, IN: *Phi Delta Kappan,* Center for Evaluation, Development, and Research.

Rogers, J. S., & Polkinghorn, R. J. (1990). *The inquiry process in accelerated schools: A Deweyan approach to school renewal.* ERIC Document Reproduction Services, No. 3231636.

Rosenblum, S., & Louis, K. S. (1981). *Stability and change.* New York: Plenum.

Rosenholtz, S. J. (1989). *Teachers' workplace: The social organization of schools* (Research on Teaching Monograph Series). New York: Longman.

Sagor, R. D. (1991, October). *Operational transformational leadership: The behavior of principals in fostering teacher centered school development.* Paper presented at the Annual Meeting of the University Council for Educational Administration, Baltimore, MD.

Sailor, W. (1991, November/December). Special education in the restructured school. *Remedial and Special Education, 12*(6), 8-22.

Sailor, W., Kelly, D., & Karasoff, P. (1992, December). *Restructuring education in the 90s.* San Francisco: San Francisco State University, California Research Institute.

Sapon-Shevin, M. (1994-1995). Why gifted students belong in inclusive schools. *Educational Leadership, 52*(4), 64-70.

Sarason, S. B. (1971). *The culture of the school and the problem of change.* Boston: Allyn & Bacon.

Sarason, S. B. (1982). *The culture of the school and the problem of change* (2nd ed.). Boston: Allyn & Bacon.

Sarason, S. B. (1990). *The predictable failure of educational reform.* San Francisco: Jossey-Bass.

Sashkin, M. (1988, May). The visionary principal: School leadership for the next century. *Education and Urban Society, 20*(3), 239-249.

Sashkin, M., et al. (1992, April). *School change models and processes: A review of research and practice.* Paper presented at the Annual Meeting of the American Educational Research Association, San Francisco.

Schlecty, P. (1990). *Schools for the twenty first century: Leadership imperatives for educational reform.* San Francisco: Jossey-Bass.

Schön, D. A. (1983). *The reflective practitioner.* New York: Basic Books.

Schön, D. A. (1987). *Educating the reflective practitioner.* San Francisco: Jossey-Bass.

Schön, D. A. (Ed.). (1991). *The reflective turn: Case studies in and on educational practice.* New York: Teachers College Press.

Scruggs, T. E., & Mastropieri, M. A. (1994). Successful mainstreaming in elementary science classes: A qualitative study of three reputational cases. *American Educational Research Journal, 31*(4), 785-811.

Seeley, D. (1991). *Needed: A new kind of educational leadership.* Paper prepared for the National Center for School Leadership, Shanghai, China.

Senge, P. M. (1990). *The fifth discipline: The art and practice of the learning organization.* Garden City, NY: Doubleday/Currency.

Sergiovanni, T. (1990). *Value-added leadership: How to get extraordinary performance in schools.* San Diego, CA: Harcourt Brace Jovanovich.

Sergiovanni, T. (1992, February). Why we should seek substitutes for leadership. *Educational Leadership, 49*(5), 41-45.

Smey-Richman, B. (1991). *School climate and restructuring for low-achieving students.* Philadelphia: Research for Better Schools.

Smith, G. R., Tourgee, B., Turner, M., Lashley, C., & Lashley, L. (1992). *Restructuring public schools: Theorists versus practitioners.* Research report, Indiana University.

Smith, M. S., et al. (1992). State policy and systemic school reform. *Educational Technology, 32*(11), 31-36.

Smylie, M. (1994). Understanding school restructuring and improvement. *Educational Researcher, 23*(3), 39-40.

St. John, E. P. (1995). Parents and school reform: Unwelcome guests, instruments of school initiatives, or partners in restructuring? *Journal for a Just and Caring Education, 1*(1), 80-97.

St. John, E. P., Allen-Haynes, L., Davidson, B., & Meza, J. (1992). *The Louisiana Accelerated Schools Project: First year evaluation report.* New Orleans: University of New Orleans, Louisiana Accelerated Schools Project.

St. John, E. P., Miron, L. F., & Davidson, B. (1992). Inquiry and school transformation. *Louisiana Social Studies Journal, 24*(1), 9-16.

St. John, E. P., Miron, L. F. & Meza, J. (1991). *Using research to support accelerated schools: Toward an action research agenda for the UNO satellite center.* New Orleans: University of New Orleans, Urban Education Laboratory.

Stefkovich, J. A. (1993, May). *Sourcebook of restructuring initiatives.* Philadelphia: Research for Better Schools.

Strike, K. (1993). Professionalism, democracy, and discursive communities: Normative reflections on restructuring. *American Educational Research Journal, 30*(2), 255-275.

Thurston, P., Clift, R., & Schacht, M. (1993). Preparing leaders for change-oriented schools. *Phi Delta Kappan, 75*(3), 259-265.

Together inclusion works. (1993, December). *1*(20, 1-2). (Newsletter of the Association for Retarded Citizens/Texas)

Tyack, D., & Tobin, W. (1994). The "grammar" of schooling: Why has it been so hard to change? *American Educational Research Journal, 31*(3), 453-479.

Villa, R., et al. (1992). *Restructuring for a caring and effective education: An administrative guide to creating heterogeneous schools.* Baltimore, MD: Brooks.

Vroom, V., & Jago, A. (1988). *The new leadership: Managing participation in organizations.* Englewood Cliffs, NJ: Prentice Hall.

Wax, M. (1993). How culture misdirects multiculturalism. *Anthropology and Education Quarterly, 24*(2), 99-115.

Webster's new collegiate dictionary. (1979). Springfield, MA: Merriam.

Wehlage, G., Smith, G., & Lipman, P. (1992). Restructuring urban schools: The new futures experience. *American Educational Research Journal, 29*(1), 51-96.

Wilkes, D. (1992, April). *Schools for the 21st century: New roles for teachers and principals. Hot topics: Usable research.* Tallahassee, FL: Southeastern Regional Vision for Education.

Wilson-Pessano, S. R. (1988, April). *Defining professional competence: The critical incident technique 40 years later.* Paper presented at the Annual Meeting of the American Educational Research Association, New Orleans.

Wong, P. (1994, December). *Accomplishments of accelerated schools.* Stanford, CA: Stanford University, National Center for the Accelerated Schools Project.

Yin, R. K. (1984). *Case study research: Design and methods.* Beverly Hills, CA: Sage.

Index

CORWIN
PRESS

The Corwin Press logo—a raven striding across an open book—represents the happy union of courage and learning. We are a professional-level publisher of books and journals for K-12 educators, and we are committed to creating and providing resources that embody these qualities. Corwin's motto is "Success for All Learners."